58 DEGREES NORTH

58 DEGREES NORTH

The Mysterious Sinking of the *Arctic Rose*

HUGO KUGIYA

BLOOMSBURY

Published by Bloomsbury Publishing, New York and London
Distributed to the trade by Holtzbrinck Publishers

All papers used by Bloomsbury Publishing are natural, recyclable
products made from wood grown in well-managed forests.
The manufacturing processes conform to the environmental
regulations of the country of origin.

The Library of Congress has cataloged the hardcover edition as follows:

Kugiya, Hugo.
58 degrees north : the mysterious sinking of the Arctic Rose / Hugo Kugiya.—
1st U.S. ed.
p. cm.
ISBN 1-58234-286-5 (hardcover : alk. paper)
1. Arctic Rose (Trawler). 2. Shipwrecks—Bering Sea. I. Title: Fifty-eight degrees
north. II. Title.

G530.A66K85 2005
910'.9164'51—dc22
2004030340

First published in the United States by Bloomsbury Publishing in 2005
This paperback edition published in 2006

ISBN-10: 1-59691-095-X
ISBN-13: 978-1-59691-095-9

1 3 5 7 9 10 8 6 4 2

Typeset by Hewer Text Ltd, Edinburgh
Printed in the United States of America
by Quebecor World Fairfield

Contents

Preface

The night the trawler *Arctic Rose* sank in one of the most remote quadrants of the Bering Sea, the fifteen men aboard must have felt as though they were the only souls on the planet. No other fishing boat was in sight. And the desolate wilderness of two continents lay more than seven hundred miles in either direction, the Alaskan mainland and Russia's Kamchatka Peninsula. From where the *Arctic Rose* recorded her last position just below the Arctic Circle, civilization, if it can be called that, was no closer than the tiny Bering Sea island of St. Paul, two hundred miles away, a lonely rock to cling to for fishermen hearty enough to test the farthest edges of the continental shelf. The crew of the *Arctic Rose* had gone to fish near the rim of the Zhemchug undersea canyon. It was difficult to get to, but reliable. There, they could almost count on a good catch when fishing was poor closer to land. And there, at the Zhemchug, they would all perish.

When the boat sank, and by all signs it sank abruptly and swiftly, the men likely had only seconds to contemplate their places in the world. Most were young men in their twenties, nine of them fathers, one of them a grandfather. More than half the crew had never been to sea before. They were born-again Christians and fallen Mormons, wanderers, thrill seekers, illegal immigrants, a fugitive, and a Vietnam veteran, all united by a rusty boat and its search for fish. They were suddenly surrounded by deadly cold and an absence of light that is hard to imagine, filled with thoughts of random terror and disbelief. Quickly, the water consumed them all.

By claiming fifteen lives, the sinking of the *Arctic Rose* became the most deadly American fishing accident in more than fifty years and began a two-year Coast Guard investigation that would become the most exhaustive and expensive ever for a fishing boat casualty. The death toll was surprising, even given the accepted dangers of the occupation. Fishing boats sink frequently off Alaska, and every year someone dies. But it is a rare instance in which so many die at once. Fishing is thought to have become safer over the years, especially in the past ten after fishing boats were required to carry survival equipment. Few expected such large losses of life to occur again. The *Arctic Rose* may indeed go down in history as the worst single accident involving an American boat.

And seldom does a sinking leave no survivors and so few clues. The loss of the *Arctic Rose* came as a surprise even to those well versed in the perils of fishing in the Bering Sea. The Coast Guard investigators assigned to the case had a true mystery on their hands. The crew reported no problems that night. No one called for help before the sinking. Weather conditions were unremarkable when the ninety-two-foot vessel sank in the early morning hours of April 2, 2001, at about 3:30 a.m. Seas were moderate. Thick clouds obscured the moon and stars. Yet whatever happened to the *Arctic Rose* happened so quickly, only one man, the captain, David Rundall, had time to put on a survival suit, and none were able to get into the vessel's self-inflating life raft. Rundall's body was the only one recovered.

The sinking of the *Arctic Rose* brought some attention to the Bering Sea fishery, which operates out of the Aleutian Islands port of Dutch Harbor, Alaska, in one of the most inhospitable oceans in the world. Humans would have very little reason to go there, if not for the thick schools of fish beneath the freezing waters. The Aleutian landscape resembles no other place. Jagged, treeless, and fog-bound, it is a bracing sight to anyone viewing it for the first time. This was the case for most of the men aboard the *Arctic Rose*, the runt of her fleet of groundfish trawlers.

Fishermen do not belong to unions and are not provided typical benefits like medical insurance and pensions. There are no time clocks. Overtime doesn't exist on a fishing boat because a sixteen-hour day is normal. And when the work is done, comfort is a short, skinny bunk that smells like fish and bounces with the swells. A job interview might be conducted on a dock a few hours before shipping out or in a bar at closing time. Most of the men have little formal education. They are uniformly impervious, with simple needs and limited means. They shrug off close calls, going back out to sea to tempt fate again. These are men who wear their own severed fingers around their necks as lucky charms and joke nervously about their nightmares.

According to the Bureau of Labor Statistics, fishing is the most dangerous job in America. Fishermen are ten to fifteen times more likely to die on the job than police officers or firemen. By far, more fishermen die in the Bering and the Gulf of Alaska than in any other waters. Hurricane-strength storms are commonplace in the Bering winter. The best fishing happens to be in the winter, when weather conditions are most severe. Yet few would call fishermen heroes or their deaths heroic. The risks fishermen are routinely exposed to are taken for granted. Far from a crisis or tragedy, the death rate of fishermen is considered a normal cost of doing business and accepted with relative indifference. When fishermen die, it seems, few people notice. Police and firefighters die in the middle of large cities with newspapers and television cameras to record the whole sad mess. Fishermen die in the middle of the ocean with few witnesses. So as their widows and children weep, the world goes on, oblivious to their losses.

Fishing is virtually recession-proof. The demand will always outweigh the supply. Even as the rest of the country's economy slows, almost nothing slows down the harvest of the waters off Alaska. The market for Alaskan fish is huge, and its products are shipped all over the world. In a relatively short period of time, the Bering and to a lesser extent the Gulf of Alaska have become fish-basket to the world. The end result might be a fillet of flounder or cod. Or it might be fish sticks or a fast-food fish sandwich. But its journey from the deck of a trawler to our mouths has been a costly one.

The open sea is one of the few proving grounds left for ordinary men in love with the myth of conquering the unknown. They are the last hunters, the last cowboys, wage earners walking the tightrope of waves and storms and freezing temperatures.

Before a frozen fillet of fish is thawed, sliced, and served for dinner in Tokyo or Dallas, it is pulled out of an ocean full of secrets by one lonely boat in the middle of nowhere.

1

Departing St. Paul

The last footsteps they took on earth made no discernible imprint on the broken crust of ice that covered their path from the fueling dock to the store, its front painted green, a color alone on the ridge. Their boat, the fishing vessel *Arctic Rose*, was the only one in St. Paul harbor on March 30, 2001, and her crew of fifteen just about the only conscious and complaining fishermen around that unremarkable morning. The crab-processing plant, main employer of the island's seven hundred residents, was closed. It was a quiet morning even by the standards of St. Paul, one of the tiny Pribilof Islands cast off in the middle of the Bering Sea. The winter crab season, responsible for the bulk of fishing activity around St. Paul, was over, the fleet dispersed. In the summer, a modest platoon of halibut boats keeps the harbor occupied. But in late March, time is for the passing and waiting, marked occasionally by the random arrival of a wayward trawler like the *Arctic Rose*. She dragged mostly for sole, a kind of cheap, homely, inconsequential fish, a bottom feeder. And those who fished for it were in turn bottom feeders, men who pulled giant nets across the silt and rock bottom of the ocean in hopes of catching enough tons of sole to make the days of drudgery worth it. Banished to the sea, close to nothing, St. Paul was just a pit stop, on the way to fishing grounds more than a day's journey to the west.

Located just below the Arctic Circle, locked in sea ice for most of the winter, the island of St. Paul itself looks, from certain angles, like a broken ship stuck in the nearly permanent fog, its sudden, volcanic cliffs crudely mimicking the bow of a boat. St. Paul is located about three hundred miles off the western coast of Alaska, shaped roughly like a rectangle about fourteen miles in length, except for two pronounced extensions of land. The town and harbor are located along one of the necks.

Out of Seattle, Washington, the men of the *Arctic Rose* arrived saturated with homesickness, beaten by days of fierce weather, their optimism evaporated to a puddle. They functioned on apathy. Most of the men stayed on the ship or near the dock. A few made the walk to St. Paul's only store, where there was a mail drop and two pay phones.

Most of the crew were from western Washington, while two were from Montana, one from Minnesota, another from Texas, and three from the Mexican state of Veracruz. They came from places far apart, but they were the same kind of men, teamed up by circumstance. Men who didn't easily fit in. Men you could read by their wounds. Men without lives full of options, whose schemes depended too much on luck. They would never be wealthy, but they hoped and dared to be rich, if for just a moment. They went about things the hard way but believed this was the easy way. This was how they went about repairing and replenishing the holes in their lives. They were not much different from everyone else who has come to Alaska, seeking fur, seeking gold, timber, oil, and now seeking flesh from the ocean. None ever truly intend to stay. They are extractors, opportunists, men of last resort and resilient dreams. They are not unintelligent and have, beyond fishing, a respectable number of talents for pursuits best cultivated in solitude.

These fifteen aboard the *Arctic Rose* were relatively fortunate among those who fished for a living. They were Bering Sea fishermen, among the best-paid, most glorified fishermen in the world, even if they were forced to lay over in places like St. Paul. In the hierarchy of Bering Sea fishermen, however, the crew of the *Arctic Rose* ranked low. Their boat was a weak earner and the smallest vessel in its fleet of head-and-gut boats, named so because the crew beheads and eviscerates its catch on board. The name accurately connotes the coarseness of the task. The dozen or so vessels in the head-and-gut fleet are bit players in the Bering industry, dominated by crab boats and the giant factory trawlers that far and away account for most of the seafood, by weight, taken from the Bering. Sole is neither harvested in overwhelming volume nor worth very much. Fishermen in Alaska catch twice as much sole as halibut, by weight, but that smaller total of halibut is worth ten to twenty times more gross dollars at the market.

For all fishermen, the bonanza days of fishing in the Bering had passed, the days of king crab so big a family could feast on a single leg, when there was more halibut for the taking than there were hooks on a ship and twenty-year-olds could come home from two months of fishing and buy a house. In Seattle, decades before the very young became very rich on stock options in software and Internet companies, a kid with little education and ordinary prospects could get rich fishing in Alaska. They are mostly just stories now that tempt only the very desperate and gullible, corn-fed boys who are all dust and calluses and blisters or boys with broken hearts and Kerouac or London in their duffels, who show up at the dock begging for a spot on a crew. Many end up making what they could have made working the summer at McDonald's. Most of the fortune in Alaska is made by a relative few. Fishing is not egalitarian. Entry into its world can be as prohibitive and ruled by elitism as entry into a Park Avenue co-op or a Hollywood nightclub. But the seas here are relatively full, and the fishing, still, is like nowhere in the world. So, unwitting, they continue to come.

The *Arctic Rose* was skippered by Davey Rundall, a great wit with a quick temper. The lure of the sea and lust for Alaska hid themselves cleverly in his DNA. He was the son of a metal fabricator and an elementary school librarian. Yet from them, he somehow inherited this dangerous thirst for the gray days and black nights of ice and storms. He had greater reason to worry about his three foster brothers, Aleut boys, for whom ordinary life on land seemed fraught with more peril. They were literally transfused with it, because of all the alcohol their mother drank before she bore them. Steven died in 1994, in Salt Lake City, hanging himself with worn and dingy bedsheets in a motel room near the drug treatment center he lived in. Norman was on a similarly doomed track, and the rest of the family waited in dread, expecting to hear the worst news any given day. Jimmy seemed to have the best chance of the three brothers, but he too battled drug

addiction and depression. Overall, there was too much accounting for
death in Rundall's family. His paternal grandfather drowned under
mysterious circumstances. Davey's nephew had died as a baby in just
about the safest place anybody can be, his own crib; doctors said it was
sudden infant death syndrome. At least the danger of the sea, Davey
thought, was calculable; at least it made some sense. Anyway, it had
kept him safe enough for more than fifteen years.

He was not naïve about the dangers. When he was a young
deckhand, he had watched a shipmate fall overboard. Davey tossed
a life ring, but the man disappeared into the ocean. His last sight was
of him reaching, trying for the ring. He thought he saw the drowning
man's fingers touch it. Davey wanted to believe he had helped, that he
had at least given his mate a chance. After that incident, Rundall got a
tattoo on his shoulder of the Grim Reaper. On a ship, he had an eye for
seeing, ahead of time, the consequences of inattention. He could size
up a situation and forecast the worst outcome. He yelled at other crew
members for loitering too close to the deck crane.

Rundall grew up in Seattle, where the Bering Sea fishing industry
is based, but now he lived in Hilo, Hawaii, with his wife and three
young sons. It was still his home; he was allowed to call it that, even if
he spent more months of a year away from it and on a boat. While he
worked, the boys went to private school and lacked for nothing except
the time their father spent with them.

The crew and the season had consumed much of Rundall's
patience, which was not one of his strengths to begin with. Loyalty,
drive, consistency, these were his virtues. Charity of mood was not.
Captains can be that way. Captains almost have to be that way. The
boat had just one more trip to make and they could all go home. But
they would have to travel farther out than they had been all season,
about as far out in the Bering as any fishing boat works. The boat
stopped in St. Paul just to fill its tanks. Where they were going to
fish, they would be about as close to Russia as America.

The men were growing indifferent to all aspects of fishing except
the end of it. They were resigned to the fact that they were going to
make far less money than they had hoped for. They had experienced
terrible weather conditions and could not imagine how it could get

worse. Fishing was poor. The ocean bottom tore holes in their net. The crew spent more time mending gear than fishing. Nets came up empty or full of sludge and starfish. Personalities that might have tolerated one another in flush times clashed. Morale expectedly tipped the way of their fortunes.

The island of St. Paul itself felt like a boat, small enough that visitors were intensely aware of its edges and the water that surrounded it, gray, roiling water streaked with the tails of a million whitecaps. Conversely, the boat felt like an island in its workaday sameness, somehow permanent once you have forgotten its state of buoyancy is just temporary. The natural tendency of the sea is to fill all voids it finds and reaches. It is doing that constantly even when it doesn't seem to. From this mission, it never takes a break. And a boat is just one more unfilled, undiscovered void.

Windblasted St. Paul has an unchanging quality. The planes and ships would come now and then with business that was no different from the last. The low, matted tundra is green in summer, covered with snow the rest of the year. But always there are clouds and fog and a monotony that inclined its people to a slowness of speech. Conversations held face-to-face stall for seconds between sentences, as if carried on through satellite relay. The mood of people seems to hang in exactly the same place, too bright to be called melancholy and too belabored to be called cheer.

They are the transplanted residents of this land, brought here two hundred years ago from the Aleutian Islands hundreds of miles to the south by Russian colonialists for the purposes of hunting and skinning fur seal. The hunt consisted of herding the scurrying seals away from the water's edge into a frantic huddle, where they would then be laid upon by clubs, thick at the end like baseball bats but as long as oars. Their hides would be salted in huts called "green rooms" (green because that's what unsalted hides were called), and their carcasses were left to rot on the tundra. The population has changed little over the centuries. The people are descendants of those slaves and bear the surnames of their oppressors, healed scars they have come to live with. So it was that the *Arctic Rose* was greeted by harbormaster Anthony Kochutin and its tanks filled at the dock by fuel handler

Jonas Lestenkof. A handful of surnames dominate the telephone directory on the island: Merculief, Bourdukofsky, Melovidov, Swetzof, Philemonoff. No one is too distantly related.

St. Paul is the largest of the five Pribilof Islands, named after the Russian explorer Gerasim Pribilof, who followed the sounds of barking seal pups through the fog to find St. George, about forty miles south of St. Paul. Pribilof named his first discovery after his ship. One year later, he discovered St. Paul. The seals are now protected. And in the summer, more than a million migrate to St. Paul to give birth. Almost all of the world's northern fur seals breed on the Pribilof Islands. Twice as many seabirds nest there, puffins, rock sandpipers, red-legged kittiwakes, thick-billed murres, fulmars, wrens, auklets, and red-faced cormorants. At one time or another, more than two hundred species of birds have been seen on St. Paul, some from as far away as Argentina. St. Paul is also home of the single largest population of Aleut natives in the world, which says more than enough about how many Aleuts are left on the planet. Only about 3,200 have survived into the twenty-first century. Their continuing survival is still a rickety proposition. The Rundalls can attest to this.

The land of St. Paul appears flat and firm. But the tundra is actually spongy to the footstep, growing in subtle mounds, forming surprisingly deep troughs, deep enough for grown reindeer to crouch in and hide from dumbfounded hunters. Also introduced to the island, the reindeer survive by nibbling at shrubs, grasses, mosses, and berries. The rising and falling lines of tundra mirror the ocean around it, seemingly flat and silent but for the secrets hidden within its creases. Bogoslof Hill, rising to 590 feet, is the highest point on the island. Lukanin Bay along its east coast is home to millions of the now protected seals.

The harbor, on the south shore of the island, can accommodate about half a dozen ships and services several more offshore processing vessels. Facing the harbor is the village of St. Paul. There is a school, the Alaska Commercial Company store, the crab-processing plant, the church, the King Eider Hotel, and the bar next door. The only restaurant is the cafeteria of the Trident Seafoods plant, the island's largest employer.

Streets are tiered, a suspicious mix of gravel and mud and ice. It is an undependable series of roads, laden with chuckholes and best navigated by all-terrain vehicles that are more in favor here than are automobiles. Like all the Bering islands, St. Paul has no trees but for the two sickly pines planted by the Coast Guard outside its radar station. The trees have not died, but neither have they figured out how to grow; they are forever stunted by the unforgiving soil and climate. The pines are facetiously referred to as the St. Paul National Forest.

Outsiders, if they aren't fishermen, come only in the summer. They are usually intrepid bird-watchers who fly in from Anchorage. They bunk in the King Eider, a structure that would surely be condemned by the fire marshal were it not the only public accommodations on St. Paul. The rooms are said to be drunk-proof, as the floors slant away from the doors. If you are overcome by alcohol consumption, you would roll into the rooms, not out of them. Nights spent in the hotel are guaranteed to be noisy because of the bar, except during Lent, when the island's Orthodox Christian residents abstain from alcohol. The church is another legacy of the conquerors. The drink is the inevitable medication of the Bering.

Fishermen on the dock have few places to go, one of them the Alaska Commercial Company store, a miracle of supply, an oasis of fresh lettuce, current issues of *Popular Mechanics*, diapers, sofas, rubber boots, sirloin steaks, light bulbs, and bubblegum, even if twelve sticks might cost you $3. Such is the markup on the tundra. For most fishermen there are two features of concern, the mail drop in the furniture section and the two pay phones near the registers.

One of the men aboard the *Arctic Rose* who used the phone was a deckhand, Jeff Meincke, twenty, the youngest of the crew. He spoke to his mother, Kathy Meincke, in Lacey, Washington, undertaking to address mostly some practical matters at home. He asked his mother if she had remembered to start his Jeep a few times each week and to feed his pet tarantula. He asked about his cat, Spyro, whom he had named after the former vice president, spelling the name differently. He had written away to Washington State University for information on its veterinary program and wondered if the school had responded. Kathy told him some materials had arrived. Then he asked about his

one-year-old niece, Noelle. What did she do this week? Jeff adored
Noelle in a way Kathy found completely charming. His attention
made him seem precocious. Most things about Jeff charmed Kathy.
He was her favorite. His older sisters knew it and did not resent him
for it. She recognized herself in him and reserved a special love for
him. Late in the conversation, Jeff mentioned his girlfriend, Jessica
Hermsen.

"Be nice to this one, Mom; I kind of like her," he said in a way that
suggested understatement.

Kathy told Jeff to expect a package in Dutch Harbor. She had sent
it in time for Easter, filling it with candy, stuffed animals, Oreo
cookies, and extra socks. Jeff always complained about not having
enough clean, dry socks. No matter how he dressed, his socks always
seemed to get wet. You could wear boots and rubber pants, and
somehow water worked its way past cuffs and flaps and reached your
socks. On the deck of a Bering fishing boat, water moved in every
direction, including up.

It is highly unlikely any member of the *Arctic Rose*'s crew knew the
slightest thing about St. Paul or life on it. To them, it was just a gas
station and phone booth in the Bering Sea. That is true about most who
come to Alaska, people oblivious to its culture beyond what is
cartoonish or quaint, igloos and dog sleds and such. For them, Alaska
is defined by what can be gotten out of it, not the culture in it. The
crew of the *Arctic Rose* was large for a boat of ninety-two feet, even after
having lost two crew members by attrition midway through the
season. Rundall, the captain or master, was by far the most accomplished fisherman aboard. He started after graduating from high
school in Seattle, working as a deckhand aboard a large factory trawler.
He met his eventual wife, Kari, on the same ship. She told him she
wanted to marry a rich fisherman. He told her he planned to be a rich
fisherman. They got married in Dutch Harbor. They were both
nineteen. By age twenty-eight, he was a licensed captain. Now
thirty-four, he was not yet rich and had already once tried to get
out of the fishing business, piloting tugboats between the Hawaiian
islands. But the work didn't pay so well and wasn't reliable. So he was
induced to return to fishing.

His first mate was a friend, Kerry Egan, new to the *Arctic Rose* and relatively uninterested in the mechanics and poetry of fishing. If he never learned to mend a net, his world would be no less perfect. He preferred the profession for its scenic and solitary transits across the open ocean. More important, he preferred it over laying telephone cables in Minnesota, as he had done years ago before his divorce. It was mostly a living, and he passed the hours on board calculating ways to invest his salary. He was happy, eager to impart knowledge of mutual funds, annuities, bonds, and retirement funds to anyone who would listen. The center and light of his life was his daughter, Jenna, who attended college in Minneapolis. He had been wrestling with a choice lately, whether to buy Jenna a car without her consultation and surprise her or reveal his intentions so she could pick the car herself.

Perhaps the only man who could say he was still truly glad to be there was the boat's newly promoted assistant engineer, G. W. Kandris, grateful because he figured he would otherwise be in a county jail awaiting trial on three counts of assault. A conviction, he figured, would have been his third in a state that had adopted a three strikes law, and he couldn't bear the thought of a long prison sentence. Kandris had escaped custody of the Puyallup (Washington) Police Department on New Year's morning by sneaking out of a hospital where he was being treated for the beating he received from some of his friends, retaliation for the alleged assaults. His friends were also the alleged victims. After escaping custody, he fashioned a hiding place in his living room out of a convertible sleeper sofa, making a man-size hollow by removing the inner mechanisms. If police showed up, he planned to hide in the sofa. But he did not trust the protection it offered. He had already spent enough of his youth in and out of jails. So when a friend told him about a boat up in Seattle leaving for Alaska for the winter, he thought it was a perfect way to stay clear of the law and immediately took the job. He started the season as a processor cleaning fish but quickly demonstrated an aptitude for the machinery of the boat. He had been employed as a mechanic in Tacoma, Washington, repairing mostly starters and alternators for a chain of garages called Start Mart. Kandris was the kind of man whose mere proximity to an automobile seemed to make it run better. He ran through cars, a Capri, a Marquis, a Metro, and equipped them all with powerful stereos, blasting rap music through the speakers. He had a touch with all things mechanical and electrical. But as a human being, he needed a little work.

He picked fights and enjoyed them. He once pummeled a girlfriend through the window of a drive-through restaurant. He had a big mouth, and it got him into plenty of trouble. He had been punched, stabbed, even knocked to the ground by a car. He possessed an amazing ability to absorb physical punishment.

His co-workers were impressed by his work but often took issue with his personality. Even his best friends thought he could be a jerk. He was a terrible drunk, as the liquor brought out his worst qualities and hid the decent ones he had. But on the boat, he had found an ability to be cooperative and helpful, if for no other reason than because he was forced to stay sober. He willingly and adroitly fixed valves and pumps and couldn't find enough bearings and rings and joints to fuss over. With the departure of the season's original engineer, Kandris became much more valuable in the engine room than in the fish factory. The various minor maladies of the boat became more than a job; they became a concerned obsession. As redemption, it was a small thing. He had done plenty of damage in his life, to himself and to others. His mother, Karla Mae Kandris, more or less gave up on him when he was a teenager. She lived in the same city but never really saw him anymore. He had two sons, one named after him. And he had a daughter due in July, although he did not yet know this.

Although Kandris's circumstances represented an extreme, you could say every man on the boat was there owing to some misfortune or miscalculation in his life, because the *Arctic Rose* was no one's first choice. Experienced fishermen found work on bigger, more profitable boats. Inexperienced fishermen worked on boats like the *Arctic Rose*. If you were on it, chances were you didn't have many choices. But on the boat, some of them found abilities they never knew they had. They were nimble and capable, counted upon in ways that probably surprised them. At sea and on the boat, they were better than themselves, somehow free of whatever plagued them at home.

The one man who should have had better options was the cook,

Ken Kivlin, fifty-five, the oldest man aboard. A decorated medic in the Vietnam War, he spent a respectable career in the navy made even more impressive by the fact that, on his own, he also raised from infancy a son named John, a man most would judge as having been brought up right. Life after the navy and the end of parenthood brought an invigorating freedom for Kivlin, who reinvented himself late in life as a chef. He attended prestigious schools and probably should have been able to find a job in almost any restaurant in almost any city. His obvious fault was his stubbornness, however, which when combined with his meticulousness and the sureness of his opinions made him sometimes difficult to work with. If he disagreed with the boss, he would quit before compromising. He found Alaska somewhat by accident but quickly became smitten with it. He landed a seemingly perfect job on a remote bay on the island of Kodiak as the chef at a hunting and fishing lodge. His employer gave him full control of the menu and kitchen, which solved any potential problems his stubbornness might raise. But the lodge was open only in the summer. So Kivlin occasionally worked on fishing boats, mostly as a productive way to pass the winter and for the unique experience they provided. He relished the chance to dazzle the surprised fishermen who would come off a shift to some gourmet creation that never before graced the galley of a fishing boat. Not all his employers loved him, but none doubted his was the best cooking they had tasted. Taking the job aboard the *Arctic Rose* was a whim, a job he came within seconds of turning down, as he was eagerly toying with the idea of spending the winter with friends in Florida. But in the end, he figured the boat would be an easy $10,000, more than worth the two months of work it would take. And time was something he had plenty of, he thought.

The boat's owner, David Olney, had decided it was not worth replacing the chief engineer and a processor who quit the boat at the end of February. Finding two quick hires would not have been very easy anyway. So the crew was smaller than the one that started the season, when the boat had quartered a fish technician (a quality control expert sent by his Japanese buyers) and a fisheries observer who monitored the types and quantities of fish caught. At the start of the season, Olney was also on the boat himself, taking charge of the trawls during the day. He had returned to Seattle in March. At its fullest, the boat had nineteen aboard. Now it was down to these fifteen. With fishing as poor as it was, fifteen men were more than sufficient. And each would earn a larger share of the catch.

Olney might have preferred a more experienced and studied engineer than his kid brother, Mike Olney, a machinist at a shipyard before he was laid off. By all accounts, Mike was better at taking direction than giving it. He was conscientious as long as he was told what to do. He made a reasonable assistant engineer, a role he had filled on other voyages. As chief engineer, Mike Olney likely could not have handled a serious breakdown on the boat. But since it was relatively new and in good repair, David Olney had no reason to expect anything serious would happen. And if it did, the boat would have to come back to port anyway, where abler hands were available. So for the last few months, Mike would have to do.

The processing crew, the men who did the dirtiest work of heading, gutting, and freezing the catch, were mostly novices to life at sea. The factory foreman was a quiet, winsome man named Aaron Broderick. He did not run the factory with amazing control and efficiency but neither did he take his frustrations out on the men he directed, as factory foremen are inclined to do. He had an agreeable temperament if nothing else, and that was important enough. Two of the processors were last minute hires, boyhood pals from Harlowton, Montana, James Mills and Shawn Bouchard, young men who had survived serious drug addictions and become born-again Christians. They intentionally sought jobs that put them in proximity to men who might be vulnerable to or interested in a promise of answers and eternal salvation. Their mission had not quite shaped up as they expected. For the most part, the crew was uninterested in what Jesus had to offer. It didn't help that three of the men they worked with on the slime line did not understand what the would-be preachers were saying.

They were three immigrants from Mexico, men from the coastal state of Veracruz who paid "coyotes," who act as escorts, to smuggle them across the border. The reasons for their time in the Arctic were purely mercenary. Once in the United States, the men from Veracruz obtained counterfeit green cards and procured Social Security numbers, which they used to get jobs on the *Arctic Rose*. Speaking as much English as would fit on a matchbook cover, they evaded the border patrol and survived unscrupulous coyotes and the desert's deadly heat, their northward momentum carrying them to latitudes they could scarcely imagine. It was nothing like the world they knew and seemed as awful a fit as the obviously fictitious names they chose for themselves, David Whitton, Michael Neureiter, and Robert Foreman. Their real names were Alejandro Ortiz Espino, Austreberto Cortez Opoll, and Justino Opoll Romero, and they had been impelled to fishing through a chain of other Mexicans working illegally in Seattle. They shared an apartment south of the city with Hector Ortiz Espino, Alejandro's older brother. Austreberto and Justino, nephew and uncle, sneaked across the border at Tijuana. Before finding work on the *Arctic Rose*, they cleaned Safeco Field after baseball games. None of their shipmates knew any of this at the time. They were just David, Michael, and Robert.

The most deft man on the slime line was the assistant foreman, Jimmie Conrad, the man they called Fishkiller. He handled his gutting knife with glee and took a theatrical delight in slicing heads and bellies. He was a short, blade-thin man who, once the fisheries observer had left the boat, became the most formally educated person aboard, having put in more than two years of college. He was the type who was almost universally liked, the kind who reordered any circle of friends he entered, charming his way into its center.

He helped recruit for the trip a new friend, an eager and adept kid named Jeff Meincke, for whom the trip represented an experiment in manhood, typical of those who come through these fleets. Meincke had always been a small kid, owing, he thought, to his asthma. He had a little bit of a growth spurt late in high school that left him about five feet seven. Of the first-timers on board, the captain seemed to like him the most. Rundall valued Meincke's eagerness and curiosity. It would have been easy for Rundall to see something of himself in the boy, fourteen years younger. They were of similar build and stature and countenance. Both had been in the Boy Scouts. And

Rundall was about the same age when he, like Meincke, started fishing as a deckhand aboard a processor. Rundall had sometimes given his attention in the form of scoldings, which he figured would do some good in this particular young man. Once, earlier in the trip, he had grabbed Meincke by the collar with both hands and held him high against the ship's gunwales. To some of the crew, it looked as if Rundall were going to throw him to the ocean. One of the deckhands almost intervened but was cautioned against it by another. Rundall eventually released Meincke, who didn't want much to talk about the incident with his mates. He was the only processor who also worked on deck, an endorsement of his ability to handle himself at sea.

The crew on deck, responsible for setting and retrieving the trawler's giant net, was a small one, consisting of Meincke, Eddie Haynes, and the deck boss, Angel Mendez, who had left his mountain village—also, coincidentally, in Veracruz, Mexico—as a teenager twenty years earlier to fish the Gulf of Mexico. To enter the United States, he took the risk of crossing the Rio Grande at night, near Brownsville. His story is that of many, a virtual boy who scraped up menial work as an undocumented immigrant but eventually got his green card. In some ways, he had made it. He owned a home in Texas. He was as much an American as he ever dreamed to be, and so was his wife. They had taken a fancy vacation in Las Vegas. Yet all those years had placed him only ten feet apart from his countrymen from Veracruz, he on deck, they inside the factory, fresh across the border, stunned by where they had come. They and Angel were two ends of the immigrant fairy tale of wishing and striving and success. But for the winter of 2001, they were literally in the same boat, far from what they loved and knew. At least Angel's stomach was stronger. They threw up; he did not.

Eddie Haynes, something of a drifter, had been a welder in the navy but had little to no experience fishing. He was tall and rangy, but the captain deemed him slow to move and he was for most of the trip a source of frustration for Rundall. That easily left Meincke as the captain's favorite. Meincke was also lovesick.

He had left behind on a cold, dark, rain-soaked dock in Seattle the saddest girl he had ever seen. He wanted to marry Jessica. They met only five months earlier at the Eight Ball, a billiards club in Olympia frequented by teenagers. She noticed him right away. He was nineteen. She was eighteen, still a senior in high school. She came with two friends who knew Jeff in high school. He was with Jimmie Conrad and a few other friends. Neither had paper, so he wrote his phone number on her hand. She called the next day, and they met at the Eight Ball. From that moment they held on to each other like lucky charms. Six nights a week, they played pool until midnight. Then they went to Jessica's parents' house to watch movies. As a compromise to their clashing tastes, they watched only comedies, until within a month their selection had been reduced to Disney cartoons. She usually heated ham-and-cheese Hot Pockets in the microwave, and they ate them on the couch while drinking Mountain Dew or Dr Pepper. And at 2:30 a.m., she went to sleep and he left for his job unloading boxes overnight at a United Parcel Service plant in Tumwater, where, coincidentally, Jessica's father also worked. Jeff slept during the day while Jessica went to school and worked as a hostess at the Brewery City Pizza Co. Afterward, Jeff would pick her up at work and the routine would start over again. She disliked nothing about their ritual and was sure this was what growing old together must be like. He opened doors, pulled out chairs, lit her cigarettes, and called her "princess." In the two months and three weeks they spent together before he left on the fishing trip, they were apart no more than two days in a row. In that time, they had fallen in love. Although neither had said so exactly, both knew it. So when he announced that in two weeks he was going to get on a boat and spend the winter fishing off Alaska, she tried to talk him out of it.

"What if I got sick? Would you stay?" she asked him. "What if I broke my arm? Then would you come home?"

"That's so stupid," he said. "I'd send you a card. It's just four months. You're going to be fine. I'm going to be fine. Honey, don't worry about me, it's all going to be okay. I promise. I'll be home before you know it."

Jeff considered Jessica his amulet, thinking their connection would always keep him safe. They said good-bye seven times, twice in person, the other times on the phone. She cried every time. Jeff almost cried once. The second time was the hardest, sitting in the shelter of his Jeep in the middle of a cold January night in the driveway of her house. The Jeep had always represented his arrival. The sound of it delivered him to her. But now it betrayed her, becoming the thing that took him away. Everything about the way it smelled and felt and sounded, once such reassuring sensations, surrounded her as Jeff attempted to say his good-bye. Out of the final prolonged silence between them, Jeff started to tell her, for the first time, that he loved her. Quickly, she stopped him.

"No! Don't tell me that," she said. "You're leaving on this boat. If you tell me that, I want to hear it *every* day, and I want to know it's how you truly feel."

Jeff faithfully wrote letters at sea, mailing a batch every time the boat returned to port to fuel up or unload fish. Because the weather often made fishing impossible, he found an unexpected abundance of time to write. He usually had fifteen to twenty pages to mail each time.

From the phone in the grocery store on St. Paul, Jeff placed another call, this one to Jessica, and he spoke to her for the last time. It was a short conversation. He reminded her how close he was to coming home. He was homesick and irritated but didn't like to talk much about his mood. As a rule, he also didn't talk much about his work. One day was about the same as another. So he asked her about her days, her shift at the pizza parlor, how she did on her last test. They talked about taking a trip to Phoenix, Arizona, to visit his older sister, Jana. He promised her this would be his last fishing trip, that as long as they were together, he would stay close to her.

Within two hours of arriving, the *Arctic Rose* left the harbor. The island grew fainter, a blemish in a corral of fog. The weather was not particularly foreboding. In fact, the opposite seemed true. Seas were calming. The sky was relatively clear. So they sailed off on their final fishing trip of the season to make their sad and inevitable history.

2

Lost on the Zhemchug Flats

She approached the grounds on April 1, 2001, a place on the very edges of the sea charts, included only because of the need to mark some undersea peaks a mariner might have reason to avoid. The charts gave the place no name, but the fishermen have come to call the area the Zhemchug flats. From the surface, the ocean for miles around looked about the same. But below the water, this was a place of sudden change, where the vast continental shelf dropped away to the abyss. The crew of the *Arctic Rose* had traveled far to reach their secret fishing spot.

She was no beauty. A trawler and fish-processing vessel, the *Arctic Rose* was asked to do a lot given her humble dimensions. Boxy and awkward, renovated to ungainly proportions, she did not fit well into her skin. She cut an odd profile, like some forlorn seabird, as she breasted ocean swells, a horizon of cotton all around her. The crew had left Seattle, left Dutch Harbor, left St. Paul harbor, unaware they were part of any great plan or noticeable sequence of events. But on that night, it was as if the eyes of the cosmos were looking straight at the *Arctic Rose*. It found her all alone in the gray.

The curving rim of the Aleutian Islands is the gate to the Bering, around the size of the Gulf of Mexico or the Mediterranean Sea. The Bering is pinched off at the north where the narrow Bering Strait joins it to the Arctic Ocean. At one flank is Siberia, at the other the Alaskan mainland. To the south is the trail of Aleutian Islands, part of the Pacific ring of fire named for the volcanic and associated seismic activity that occurs along its circumference. The ring of fire nearly encircles the Pacific and causes geologic havoc in the coastal regions of Asia and the Americas. The Aleutian archipelago stretches two thousand miles from America to Siberia. By one theory, the Aleutian chain is thought to be what remains of a land bridge that once joined Asia and North America after portions of it sank into the sea. A more popular and accepted theory suggests the chain was never one continuous piece of land, but instead rose in sections as undersea volcanoes erupted. There are about fifty active volcanoes in the Aleutians. Several have given birth to new islands within the last two hundred years, bolstering the latter theory. The youngest is Bogoslof Island, calculated to be about two hundred years old, only a half square mile in total area.

The Bering, a speck of the giant Pacific, is arguably the world's most bountiful body of water. Some biologists estimate 20 percent of the world's edible ocean protein lives in the Bering, where about half of all the seafood caught by American vessels is harvested. The waters of Alaska are among the most heavily managed in the world and the least overfished. While stocks are disappearing in other oceans, they are relatively healthy in the Bering. Conditions are perfect here for all forms of sea life, from the smallest plankton to the biggest whales and everything in between. The native people of the Aleutian Islands lived off this wet feast of fish, bird, and mammal for nearly ten thousand years, unknown to others until Russian explorers found them. In Western history, credit for discovering the Bering Sea was given to Vitus Bering, a Dane and decorated officer in the Russian navy, who led two Russian expeditions into the Bering from 1725 to 1741. On the second voyage, he lost his ship and thirty-two men (almost half his crew) and ultimately his own life to scurvy. But the expedition staked Russia's claim to the new territory and its natural riches, changing forever the landscape and lives of the people who happened already to be there.

The only impediment to human industry the Bering offered was a mighty one. From the north, cold winds blow from the pole. To the south, the islands are bathed by the warm Japan current. The mixing of the two produces a volatile brew of extreme weather, the combination of which is rarely seen on the planet. There is a fog in the summer that rivals any found on earth, fog so thick that men say they could stick a knife in it and hang a coat on the handle. In the winter, when much of the Bering is covered with sea ice, the froth produced by the competing climatic influences turns cyclonic, as winds seem to blow from all directions. The Aleutians are the birthplace of Pacific storms. A surfer in Hawaii has the Aleutian churn to thank for the perfect giant waves that reach Oahu's north shore in the winter.

The weather is highly unpredictable and at times bewildering. Wind socks at both ends of the Dutch Harbor airport have been known to blow in opposite directions. Hurricane-force winds are relatively routine in the Bering winter. What little land there is here is young and raw and vertical, a towering desert of rock and ice for most of the year. In the summer, the ice yields to a green cover of shrubs and mosses. But it is not flat, tillable land. The land is beautiful from a distance, but the experience most have of it is mud and ice, gray and white. The land is not worth the trip. But what can be gotten from the sea is, apparently, worth risking your life, because many have.

In this respect, the men of the *Arctic Rose* were just fifteen in a line of thousands who came before them. Individually, each man aboard the *Arctic Rose* had his own reason to come, some very personal, some practical. But in total, they came for the same reasons every band of men before them came for—to exploit the riches of the sea and take it back home.

After extensive modifications, the *Arctic Rose* resembled a floating box. A fish-processing room or factory was built over the full width of her once open deck. Her pilothouse was on the bow end. She had barely ten feet of deck behind the processing room. Built to tow large nets off its stern, the *Arctic Rose* was a trawler, or "dragger" in the parlance of the industry. She was built in 1988 as a shrimp boat on a sandy lot on the Mississippi bayou, framed with angle iron, an L-shaped beam, and sheathed with welded steel plate. In earlier incarnations, she harvested shrimp from the Gulf of Mexico, scallops from the Atlantic Ocean, and bottom fish from the Indian Ocean. She crossed the Pacific twice before settling into what could charitably be called a marginally successful career as a Bering Sea trawler. Because fish were caught and then headed, gutted, frozen, and stored in thick paper bags aboard the boat, she belonged to a general class of fishing boats called "catcher-processors," although she had little in common with her much larger cousins of the same name. Processors of any kind are typically the largest boats that fish the waters off Alaska, some of them three hundred feet in length. But among her peers, the *Arctic Rose* was tiny, her keel only ninety-two feet long in the Coast Guard books (she was a little more than hundred feet from stern to bow), twenty-six feet wide, just about the smallest processor in the Bering Sea. Undersized and underpowered with a lone 750-horsepower engine, she did not always fill her holds with enough fish to turn enviable profits. But she had proven herself durable and fit for her duty.

Her cramped enclosures were a marvel of function, a seemingly impossible allocation of space for men and their attendant machinery. She could berth and feed up to nineteen people for weeks at a time. She had a full kitchen, a bathroom, a laundry room, and a complex of tanks to hold fuel and fresh water. She had freezers, winches, cranes, and hydraulics to power them all. She generated her own electricity and desalinated seawater. The pilothouse or bridge contained all manner of communications equipment so that the crew was always within word of those on land no matter how far out the men fished. The *Arctic Rose*, by law, also carried dry suits for all the crew, a self-inflating life raft large enough for twenty people, and a water-activated emergency beacon. She was outfitted, wired, and plumbed to support a small society and to deal with almost any consequence or fortune that awaited her on the sea.

The *Arctic Rose* was one of two boats owned by her third owner, David Olney, who called his enterprise Arctic Sole Seafoods. He managed the company out of a narrow and spartan office in Fishermen's Terminal marina in Seattle. His other boat, the *Alaskan Rose*, also a head-and-gut boat, was a larger, more powerful, more naturally configured trawler than the *Arctic Rose*. He was both owner and operator, often acting as skipper of his modest fleet of two. He had spent the first six weeks of the season as master of the *Arctic Rose*. But at the end of February, he returned to Seattle to deal with the administrative demands of his business, handing over command of the boat to Rundall. So on the night of April 1, 2001, Olney was asleep at his small farm in Duvall, Washington, as the *Alaskan Rose* and *Arctic Rose* fished within ten miles of each other in one of the most remote precincts of the Bering Sea, near the lip of the continental shelf.

A little farther to the west and the *Arctic Rose* would have been off the sea charts. The only prominent markings in these waters are the two large underwater peaks, one coming within four fathoms of the surface, the other coming within eight. Four miles away from the two boats, the ocean bottom dropped away to 5,500 feet. And twelve miles away, it dropped to more than 8,000 feet. What fishermen call the Zhemchug flats is a sandy plateau next to a trench called the Zhemchug Canyon, a 9,000-foot, undersea chasm at the edge of the continental shelf responsible for the bounty of sea life in the Bering. Both boats were fishing along the sixty- and seventy-fathom curve, in about four hundred feet of water, for flathead sole, one of a variety of bottom-dwelling fish hunted by the *Arctic Rose* and vessels like her. Flathead season opened on April 1. The boats fished near the Zhemchug because the sole tended to be larger there and they tended to school by species, leading to cleaner catches and fewer fish they were required by law to throw back. And with some luck, both boats could catch some cod with their sole. Although cod was not the primary prey, fishing quotas allowed the head-and-gut crews to keep whatever cod they happened to find in their nets. As far as Olney knew, only his boats bothered with or knew about this place. They had fished the grounds before, sometimes for months at a time without seeing another boat.

They didn't know for sure, but they might have guessed they were just about the only ones in that part of the sea at the time. The Alaskan mainland was about five hundred miles away, as was the Russian wilderness. St. Paul, where they had taken fuel, was about two hundred miles to the southeast. At this latitude, they would normally have been fishing at the edge of the ice pack, a lid of ice that covers the northern part of the Bering Sea for much of the winter. Fish tend to school and feed near the pack's edge, making it a reliable fishing ground. But the winter had been warmer than average, and the ice pack was 120 miles north of the *Arctic Rose* that day. In general, polar ice has decreased over recent years, a trend most scientists associate with global warming. Sea ice both helps regulate the earth's overall temperature and is affected by it. The ice cools the planet by acting as an insulating canopy and reflecting solar energy. But when there is less sea ice, the ocean absorbs more sunlight and heat, interfering with the formation of future sea ice. So a reduction in sea ice compounds the trend. Less ice begets less ice.

Almost half of the Bering Sea's 2.3 million square kilometers of ocean is over the continental shelf. Strong tides and winds churn the seas above the shelf, mixing deep and shallow waters. Sea life is driven primarily by plants at the bottom of the food chain that can survive only as deep as sunlight can penetrate, about five hundred to six hundred feet. But to survive, these plants need elements like phosphorus and nitrogen, which are most plentiful at lower depths. For that reason, sea life is most abundant where upwelling of deep waters brings these elements closer to the surface. This happens in relatively few places in the world's oceans, but with particular efficiency in the Bering Sea. And in the Bering, the upwelling can be spectacular near the edge of the ice pack. Even in the Bering, however, a boat cannot expect to drop its net anywhere and catch fish, at least not anymore and not in the volumes required to survive financially in an increasingly competitive industry. Captains rely on their favorite fishing spots and guard them discreetly.

The winter season had been a poor one for the crew of the *Arctic Rose*, which left Seattle in January for three months of fishing. Problems with the boat's propeller shaft had forced them to return to port, delaying their arrival in Dutch Harbor. The small boat was more prone to the slowing effects of the treacherous Bering Sea weather. Bigger boats could trawl faster and longer, tow larger nets or bags, and haul heavier bags full of fish and could continue to fish in bad weather. The typical perils and setbacks of a fishing season were made worse by the *Arctic Rose*'s novice crew. Of the fifteen men aboard the boat in April, seven had never before been to sea. Several others had only limited experience. The few aboard who could fairly be described as seasoned fishermen and mariners were the captain, Davey

Rundall, first mate Kerry Egan, deck boss Angel Mendez, and to a lesser extent the engineer, Mike Olney, David Olney's kid brother.

David Olney had personally hired everyone aboard his two boats. The more experienced of the men had earned the privilege of working aboard the bigger, higher-earning boat, the *Alaskan Rose*. Newcomers were assigned to the *Arctic Rose*. Inattention by some of them had resulted in a bothersome blunder earlier that day. The crew had allowed fish waste and garbage aboard the boat to clog pumps that remove water from the floor of the processing room. An irritated Rundall informed David Olney of the mishap by e-mail and also recounted the incident to John Nelson, the mate of the *Alaskan Rose*, during a conversation that evening.

Rundall and Nelson, who relieved his captain, Norm Anderson, at 8:00 p.m., spoke by single-sideband radio on a frequency they reserved for each other, catching each other up on their days. Nelson and his crew were having problems of their own, more serious than loose garbage. One of the hazards of trawling is getting the net stuck on the bottom. The *Alaskan Rose* got her net caught on what the crew surmised was a rock and in the process tore the net in half and lost one of her trawl doors, heavy metal flaps that keep the open end of the net deployed. Nelson told Rundall they were done fishing for the night and were going to jog in a northeast direction, into what was then building but moderate weather, while the crew mended the net. To jog means a boat essentially treads water, moving slowly not for the sake of gaining distance, but for the sake of stability and a smoother ride. Nelson drove the *Alaskan Rose*, keeping her speed just below four knots so as not to buck on large waves.

Rundall told Nelson that his crew had picked up the garbage and that the pumps were once again running properly. He also told Nelson that the fishing had been, for a change, relatively good that day. The crew's first haul was a full bag of mostly Alaska plaice or lemon sole, so named because of its yellow underside. The Alaska plaice, usually an incidental catch, had to be thrown back. But the next haul was almost pure flathead. By the end of the first day, the men had plenty of fish to process in the morning and Rundall had decided to stop fishing for the day. Groundfish trawlers generally don't fish at night anyway, because sole and cod leave the bottom at night. Rundall sounded optimistic. This final trip was off to a good start. The seas were subsiding late that night, going from heights of ten feet to five feet. Rundall reported intermittent rain and snow showers. Luckily, it was not cold enough for the spray to freeze on contact. The winds were also calming as they shifted from north-easterly to northerly. The *Arctic Rose* was jogging in a west-northwest direction. When the two last spoke, it was no later than 10:30 p.m. They planned to speak again in the morning and trade information about where they set their nets and what direction they towed them. The boats routinely exchanged this kind of information. At about the same time, first mate Kerry Egan sent an e-mail from the boat's satellite data terminal to his older brother, Doug, and Doug's wife, Trish, in Minnesota:

> *Hi Trish. How are things? We are 425 miles out and on the fish pretty good for a change. We will offload at St. Paul Island so I may not be able to get a hold of you guys . . . Ask Doug to fill out my tax returns and send it in with a check. Everything here is bruise gray and swelling, typical Bering Sea. Talk to you when I can. Thanks. Kerry. P.S. ETA BG's 5/14.*

BG's was a second home of sorts for Egan, a bar owned by his boyhood friend Greg Peterson in Virginia, Minnesota, sixty-five miles north of Duluth, the place where Egan's family would hold his wake just one week later. The short conversation between Rundall and Nelson and the e-mail from Egan would be the last anyone would hear from the *Arctic Rose.*

At about the same time, almost two thousand miles away in Juneau, Alaska's capital city, Chief Quartermaster Paul Webb settled down for what would be at best a fitful nap at the Coast Guard's Rescue Coordination Center (RCC), a sort of emergency command center for sea and mountain rescues in all of Alaska. Those who stand watch do so for twenty-four hours at a time, taking four to five hours of sleep toward the end of their shifts. At least two watch standers are on duty at all times. To stand watch, you must be either an aviator or a navigator and have experience serving aboard a ship or aircraft. Webb was a navigator. He was two weeks away from retirement, after having spent almost his entire Coast Guard career, twenty-one years, in Alaska. He had been billeted in Petersburg, Sitka, and Ketchikan, towns in Alaska's relatively mild, maritime southeast. He had put in ten years of sea duty aboard several buoy tenders and a patrol boat and spent seven years at the Coast Guard air station in Kodiak, assigned to search and rescue. He and his wife raised two children in Alaska, and he intended to grow old here. There are two kinds of Coasties in Alaska: those who wonder aloud which officer or deity they antagonized to get stationed here and those who become permanently intoxicated with Alaska's otherworldliness. Webb was the latter.

Juneau is 160 miles from the Pacific Ocean, although it is joined directly to it by a complex of channels and passes. Built at the foot of two mountains, it is the only state capital that you cannot drive to. It can be reached only by plane and boat, although state politicians have proposed building a highway linking Juneau to Anchorage. Juneau is the largest city on what is called the Inside Passage, a series of waterways from Seattle to Alaska protected from the ocean winds and first charted more than two hundred years ago by the British explorer and naval officer Captain George Vancouver. The Inside Passage is the favored route of cruise ships and recreational boaters and very unlike the Bering. Waters are generally calm. The sight of land is of a lush, towering rain forest.

Juneau began as a gold-mining settlement in 1880 and was named for one of its first prospectors, Joseph Juneau. Its natural resources of gold, lumber, and fish are no longer as relevant economically as the shiploads of tourists brought in every summer by luxury liners so tall that they overtake the city's modest skyline. Tourists come to gawk and imagine a frontier Alaska of storybooks. But mostly they shop. Even in relatively pasteurized Juneau, however, nature is close at hand. Garbage cans in Juneau are bolted to the ground and opened by releasing a latch, a measure taken to thwart the black bears that routinely forage for food in the town, even as swarms of tourists gawk at them with glee. The businesses of Juneau's waterfront downtown are strictly for tourists with its fur salons, galleries, souvenir stores, and restaurants whose fronts are dressed up to evoke the town's now extinct mining days. Most of the real shopping and living is done several miles to the north in what is called "the valley," which resembles many mainland suburbs with its giant Kmart, except that it happens to be located next to Mendenhall Glacier, one of the most visited in the world. Like most Alaskan cities, it imports just about everything it needs: cars, brassières, produce, light bulbs, sheet metal, most of it from Seattle. Juneau is proud of the fact that it brews its own local beer and roasts its own gourmet coffee. In climate, it is more comparable to Seattle than Anchorage. It avoids the extreme weather that hits most of Alaska but pays for the favor by giving up summer. Spring, summer, and fall are all about the same season in Juneau and in much of Alaska's southeast, foggy, chilly, light drizzle. If it were not so, locals say, the population of 30,000 might quickly become 130,000.

The tallest building in Juneau is the federal building, which is headquarters to the Coast Guard District 17 command. In Alaska, almost all of the Coast Guard's manpower is devoted to the enforcement of fishing regulations and the support of fishing vessels. The Coast Guard offices are located on the sixth and seventh floors. The Rescue Coordination Center is in a secure room on the sixth floor. It is relatively small, with the dimensions of an intimate restaurant. Day and night look about the same, as there is only one small window, facing north up Gastineau Channel to Auke Bay. The ceiling feels oddly low because the floor is raised to create ducts for the bundles and strands of wiring for all the computers and communications equipment. The floor feels hollow to the step. The presence of all the electronics requires the room to be kept at a temperature of seventy degrees or cooler. As a result, everyone on duty is in the habit of wearing Coast Guard–issue blue fleece jackets. The Rescue Coordination Center resembles the bridge of a ship, with a twenty-foot-wide console at its center, where the watch standers sit in front of their computers. There are maps and charts, a thirty-six-inch television, and spare workstations with more computers. Through a closed door are a kitchen and bunk room where Paul Webb slept for about four hours before finishing his shift. Having stood watch on ships for years, he had learned to sleep without really being asleep.

He awoke at 1:00 a.m. and retook his place at the watch desk while the officer on duty took his turn in the bunk. Sitting with Webb was First Class Quartermaster Dan Pesnell. The big television was tuned to the FOX cable news channel to which Webb had become addicted. His shift would end at 7:00 a.m.; afterward he would get four days off. The day and the evening had been unusually uneventful, without so much as a flare sighting. Webb used the tranquillity to review folders from older cases.

District 17, responsible for all of Alaska, produces on average eight hundred cases a year in which some form of rescue or assistance is required. The Coast Guard district assigned to New York, by comparison, might log about five thousand such cases in a year. Although fewer in number, Alaska's cases tend to be, on the whole, more grave. And the distances traveled by rescuers in District 17 are easily among the longest in the Coast Guard. The rescue center in Juneau is the only one in the entire district. It is unique among Coast Guard Rescue Coordination Centers in that it must also respond to emergencies on land, like missing hikers, lost hunters, or injured mountain climbers. It also responds to emergencies at sea not just in the Bering, but in the Gulf of Alaska and the Arctic Ocean, answering calls all the way up to the North Pole. The size of the area it must cover is mind-boggling, encompassing millions of square miles. The District 17 Rescue Coordination Center has cooperated on missions with Russia and Finland. At night and on weekends, the rescue center must also take reports of oil spills, fishing incursions by foreign boats, or any other law enforcement issues. Most calls for help come in at night. A recent internal survey of search-and-rescue missions showed a noticeable increase in the number of cases after 4:00 p.m., probably because that's when fatigue and inattention become factors.

One of the oldest pieces of equipment in the rescue center happens to be the most important, a twenty-year-old Citizen model MSP-40 dot-matrix printer. When a boat's emergency beacon is activated, the aging printer is the first sign of it. Because of its vintage—parts for the machine are nearly impossible to buy—the printer is also very noisy, a useful quality given the purpose it serves.

At about 3:30 a.m., somewhere in the middle of the Bering Sea, midway between dusk and dawn, the *Arctic Rose*'s emergency position indicating radio beacon (EPIRB) was activated. The boat's EPIRB was manufactured by ACR Electronics, a company in Fort Lauderdale, Florida, which makes most of the EPIRBs now required aboard all commercial fishing vessels. Most devices cost about $1,000. As it happened, Rundall had bought a new EPIRB the day he left Seattle for the start of the fishing season. His parents, David and Lou Anne, had come to visit their son and take him out to dinner. Short on time, Davey declined but asked his parents if they wanted to accompany him on an errand to a nearby marine supply store. He bought the EPIRB and registered his ship's information at the store. Before entering the car, Davey handed the EPIRB to his father, who sat in the passenger seat. As he held it in his hands, his father got an unsettling feeling, suddenly very conscious of the purpose of the device he was cradling. Rundall had bought an ACR model 2774, Category I EPIRB, about the best the company made. As large as a thermos, weighing $4\frac{1}{2}$ pounds, and sheathed in bright yellow high-impact plastic, the EPIRB was mounted on a bracket outside of the boat's wheelhouse. The bracket was designed to eject the beacon should it be subjected to water pressure equivalent to a depth of thirteen feet.

That night the beacon came free, floated to the surface of the ocean, and began transmitting a coded radio signal at a frequency of 406 MHz. Embedded in the code was a six-digit number registered to the *Arctic Rose*. The signal shot into the polar sky, and within seconds it was received by one of a series of weather satellites 528 miles above the earth. These satellites, fixed in a polar (north-south) orbit, circled the earth every one hundred minutes. The signal was relayed to giant antenna towers at the Mission Control Center in Suitland, Maryland, just outside Washington, D.C. Its geographic origin determined, the signal was automatically routed to the Coast Guard Rescue Coordination Center closest to the signal's origin, in this case Juneau. There, for the first time, the signal was recognized by a human being. About five minutes passed between the time the EPIRB was activated and the time the signal reached the Citizen printer sitting at Paul Webb's elbow.

The printer, whose white plastic cover was yellowed with age, clattered to life at 3:35 a.m., spitting out the name of the boat, the type of boat it was, its length, its radio call number (like a citizens band [CB] radio handle), the name of the owner, the owner's phone number, and a mobile phone number for the vessel. The initial signal did not give the exact position of the beacon. Webb swiveled in his chair, alert but not startled. On average, the Juneau RCC receives three to four EPIRB signals per week. Almost all EPIRB transmissions not preceded or accompanied by a call for help from a human being are false alarms. Vessel operators are not fined for false alarms. If fines were levied, the thinking goes, too many operators would simply turn EPIRBs off, thereby creating a potentially dangerous situation. False alarms are frequent because EPIRB are often activated inadvertently. Sometimes they accidentally fall into the water. False alarms can often be ferreted out within ten minutes, usually with a phone call to the harbormaster, who can verify that the boat in question is actually docked at the harbor. Nonetheless, duty officers are trained to treat every alarm like the real thing. But they have come to expect that most are not. About 98 percent of the time, an EPIRB signal is filed as a false alarm.

Dan Pesnell phoned the vessel's satellite telephone number. Unable to reach anyone, he called the number given for the owner, David Olney, waking him at 3:38 a.m. at his home in Duvall, about twenty miles northeast of Seattle. The timing of the phone call did not alarm Olney, who reached for the phone expecting it to be one of his skippers calling about a mechanical problem. If a breakdown prevented either boat from fishing, Olney wanted to know immediately and at any hour. Putting the phone to his ear, he did not expect to hear the voice of the Coast Guard. Now sufficiently alarmed, Olney told Pesnell the *Arctic Rose* was indeed fishing, working with her sister vessel northwest of St. Paul island. Webb contacted the area's main communications station on Kodiak island and requested that a radio operator attempt to raise the *Arctic Rose* by high-frequency radio. Olney also tried to call his boats, both of which had satellite telephones. Like Pesnell, Olney could not get a connection. He put on his clothes and drove to his office in Seattle. He was by now very anxious and kept telling himself the EPIRB had just fallen out of its bracket.

The Coast Guard's communications station in Kodiak, or Comsta Kodiak, as it is known, is the center for long-range high-frequency (HF) radio communications in the North Pacific, be it ship to ship or ship to shore. Comsta radio operators can take a radio transmission and patch it through to a phone line, allowing someone on a ship to communicate directly with anyone on a telephone. The communications station is a two-story white concrete building with no windows because it is considered a secure facility. It is surrounded by five 350-foot antenna towers and a ring of low mountains. The building is hidden in Bear Valley, named for the black bears that march through the valley in the summer in search of salmon spawning in nearby Buskin Lake.

Very high frequency (VHF) radio is like CB radio and has a range of about twenty-five to fifty miles. All marine-band VHF radios are broadcast on the FM band and used for communications close to shore. If you are boating on Puget Sound or Long Island Sound, you can hear Coast Guard communications on VHF-FM. Channel 16 is the designated channel for emergency communication. HF radio is a single-sideband frequency whose technology is similar to that of ham radio and satellite telephones. Depending on the weather, a high-frequency transmission can travel from Hawaii to Juneau and be heard by anyone in between. At night, such transmissions have been known to skip across the atmosphere like a pebble of light. The Coast Guard reserves two frequencies, 2185 KHz and 4125 KHz, for emergency broadcasts.

As operators tried in vain to raise the *Arctic Rose*, the EPIRB continued to transmit its signal to other passing satellites that recorded and relayed more precise and detailed information with each pass. The *Arctic Rose*'s EPIRB was designed to keep transmitting for forty-eight hours or until someone turned it off manually, whichever happened first. At 3:52 a.m., the printer received another signal, this one indicating the boat's rough position in latitude and longitude. The *Arctic Rose* appeared to be 210 miles northwest of St. Paul island, consistent with the location Olney first reported. Using information Olney provided, Webb was able to send satellite text messages to both vessels at 4:02 a.m. Olney did the same. Neither got any response. The extreme latitude of the Bering and the tempestuous weather make communication by satellite link somewhat unreliable. The satellite telephones on Olney's boats did not tend to work very well in the Bering and sometimes didn't work at all as far out as the two boats were fishing that day. Olney expected as much. Whenever his boats fished west of 175 degrees longitude, he could not reach them by telephone. That morning, his boats were close to that line.

At about 4:00 a.m., still unable to raise the *Arctic Rose*, operators at comsta transmitted an urgent marine information broadcast across the seas: "a 406 MHz EPIRB distress beacon has been received by satellite, in position 58-53 north, 176-11.0 west. The beacon is registered to the *Arctic Rose*, a ninety-two-foot, blue, white, and green fishing vessel. The *Arctic Rose* was last known to be fishing northwest of St. Paul island. All stations having seen or knowing the where-abouts of this vessel are asked to contact the Coast Guard, keep a sharp lookout for signs of distress, and assist if possible." This message was broadcast every fifteen minutes for the first hour and every thirty minutes after that. What the Coast Guard suspected, but did not know at the time, was that the only other boat close enough to be of any help was the one they had been trying and failing to reach, the *Alaskan Rose*.

Although the results were thus far not encouraging, Webb was still optimistic. Only about one out of every four or five EPIRB signals results in a decision to launch a helicopter or rescue plane. And most of those missions end up as false alarms. A boat has been known to steam for hours before realizing its beacon has gone off, unable for various reasons to communicate with rescuers. For that reason, the Coast Guard has sometimes even asked local radio stations to broad-cast announcements of missing vessels: "Hey, Joe, if you're out there fishing, the Coast Guard is looking for you. . . ." Sometimes it works. A captain might not have his marine radio tuned to the right frequency, but he might be listening to Smokey Robinson on his FM radio.

The EPIRB signal from the *Arctic Rose* was unsettling, however, because it did not have the typical earmarks of a false alarm. For one, it did not go off near a fishing port, where the boat might be docked. EPIRBs have been known to go off in garages and even in landfills, where they had been discarded, mistakenly written off as broken. This signal was transmitting from a remote part of the Bering. And the owner had verified that his boat was indeed fishing out there. It was still possible the transmission was a mistake of some kind. Nonetheless, at 4:10 a.m., unable to contact either the *Arctic Rose* or the *Alaskan Rose*, Webb called the Coast Guard air station in Kodiak, several miles from Comsta, to request that it send aircraft to begin a search.

The Kodiak station, a former navy base, is the larger of the two air stations the Coast Guard maintains in Alaska—the other is in Sitka. Kodiak, both the name of the island and its largest town, is in the Gulf of Alaska, about seven hundred miles west of Juneau. Kodiak was Alaska's first fishing boomtown and still lands a substantial amount of seafood each year. Although most of the larger fishing boats now work out of the Aleutian Islands, Kodiak remains home to an impressive small-boat fleet. Driving north into town from the air station, you can smell Kodiak's cannery row from around the bend before you can see it.

The air station has three hangars that house five C-130 search planes, four H-60 Jayhawk helicopters, and five smaller H-65 Dolphin helicopters. The air station is a self-contained community, its population about as large as that of the town of Kodiak. The base has its own restaurants, supermarket, movie theater, beaches, church, and of course housing. Officers with families reside less than a mile from the hangars in concrete, ranch-style homes, arranged in the familiar, reassuring configuration of mid-century American suburbs.

The senior flight officer on duty that night was Lieutenant Commander Todd Schmidt. He and his flight crew also work twenty-four-hour shifts and are encouraged to sleep as much as possible when their duties allow it. The two officers who live on base are allowed to sleep in their homes. The five enlisted men who make up the rest of the crew must bunk in a building next to the hangar, designated as Ready Crew Berthing. Schmidt tends to sleep deeply despite the fact that he knows he may be awakened in the middle of the night. He had been asleep for about four hours when he was paged that morning by someone in the operations center located in one of the hangars. For Schmidt and the other rescue pilots, the transition from sleep to full alertness takes seconds, not minutes. A crew is trained to be up in the air within thirty minutes of being paged. That morning's page was accompanied by a phone call, briefing Schmidt on the basics of the case. So as he put on a blue one-piece flight suit and leather boots, he already knew he would be taking off into a headwind, looking for a fishing boat with a crew of fifteen almost one thousand miles away. During the two minutes it took him to drive to the hangar, he decided he would take as much fuel as his plane could carry. Schmidt and his copilot then studied the location of the beacon, filed a flight plan, and analyzed weather data while the other crew towed the plane out of the hangar.

Already provisioned with forty-five thousand pounds of fuel, the standard load (a C-130 burns about five thousand pounds per hour), Schmidt's plane took on an extra seventeen thousand pounds even though the additional fuel nearly doubled the normal preparation time of thirty minutes.

"It all pointed to the fact that we could be out there a while," Schmidt said. "And it's just best to have as much gas as you can."

The flight to the position reported by the EPIRB would take more than three hours, as the plane traveled at a speed of about three hundred miles per hour. And because of the headwind, the journey would consume more fuel than normal. Schmidt wanted to be able to stay in the search area as long as possible, since at the time he had to assume that any realistic hope of rescuing the men aboard the *Arctic Rose* rested solely on him and his flight crew. No other ship was within easy reach of the *Arctic Rose* except for the *Alaskan Rose*, which for reasons unknown had yet to answer calls for assistance. Schmidt and his crew were prepared for the worst. But in his heart, he harbored a more optimistic belief, that he would fly out and find the *Arctic Rose* fishing safely, unaware that its EPIRB had fallen overboard. In ten years of responding to emergency beacons as a helicopter and airplane pilot, Schmidt had witnessed only three actual sinkings. His experience taught him the most ordinary of possibilities was the most likely.

The four-engine, propeller-driven C-130, built by Lockheed Martin, is a remarkably versatile airplane, especially forgiving of Alaska's rough weather. During flight, its controls are in constant need of adjustment by the pilot, but it handles turbulence well, absorbing the bumps. C-130s are also popular because they are easy to maintain and ask for very little in return. The Coast Guard's C-130s are between twenty and thirty years old. They can take off with as little as one thousand feet of runway and can fly with just one engine operating. In Alaska, they are the lifeline of Coast Guard personnel posted to the state's most remote stations, transporting four million pounds of cargo and 3,400 passengers a year. If necessary, a Dolphin helicopter, with its blades folded, can be put into the plane's cargo hold.

Schmidt's plane contained two pallets packed with rescue and survival equipment. Each pallet contained two self-inflating rafts and three survival kits lashed together. Steel drums contained portable water pumps and radio sets. The drums are attached to a parachute. The rafts and survival kits are dropped in a free fall to the ocean. A hydraulic ramp opens in the rear of the plane, allowing the crew to drop the equipment from an altitude of about five hundred feet. The plane is also capable of launching flares from near its tail. If they could just find the *Arctic Rose*, they could offer her plenty of help.

Flying with Schmidt was copilot Lieutenant Commander Dan Pike. The rest of the crew comprised enlisted men. Steve Smith was the flight engineer, Bobby Cannon the navigator, and Pete Trappen the radioman. Smith, Cannon, and Trappen sat behind Schmidt and Pike in the cockpit. The dropmaster, Andrew Kasten, and the loadmaster, Aaron Swinford, also acted as spotters and sat below and behind the cockpit next to a pair of two-by-three-foot windows on each side of the plane. They could not see the rest of the crew. Because of this and the thunderous noise inside the plane, everyone communicated through headsets. This crew of seven had flown many missions together.

At 5:10 a.m., its wing tanks full of fuel, Schmidt and his crew took off, punching through a layer of low clouds on its way to a flying altitude of eighteen thousand feet and the rougher air ahead.

At about the time the EPIRB began transmitting, Davey Rundall's father awoke from a terrifying dream. The source of his fear was specific and clear. He remembered waking up with his heart in a sprint. He could feel it pounding through his shirt and blanket. It was less like a dream and more like watching a television show, David Rundall said. He saw the surface of water and objects disappearing below it. The message was so obvious, he took it as a premonition. But all his life he had ridiculed such things. He resumed a restless sleep and awoke later still thinking about the dream. That morning, he ran some errands. One of them was to purchase a DVD of the movie *A Perfect Storm*, about an Atlantic swordfish boat lost at sea. Davey had asked him to buy it. For some reason, David could not bring himself to buy the movie, even though it was discounted $3 that day at the store. He got home at 2:30 p.m. Twenty minutes later, Davey's wife, Kari, called. She was crying. Before she said a word, David knew exactly why she had called and what had happened.

"That dream still haunts me," David Rundall would say years later.

3

The Search for Survivors

The vision that came to him in his sleep had another meaning. David Rundall was sixteen when his father drowned in the Inside Passage while transiting on a ferry between Juneau and Ketchikan. No one reported him missing. One month later, in the spring of 1962, fishermen found his body floating in the water with his wallet and wedding ring. In the paperwork, police called it a suicide, which never made sense to the family. He was traveling alone aboard the ferry *Malaspina*. Because he was relocating, he was carrying a lot of cash and all his possessions, which arrived in Ketchikan without him. He was fifty-six years old. His wife claimed what belongings could be found, but several items, like his stamp collection, were missing. David was living in Seattle with his mother. He hadn't seen his father in four years. His father had asked him to come up and live with him in Alaska. He refused but sometimes wished, years later, that he had.

"Maybe he wouldn't have died if I had been with him," David said.

His mother had become a widow for the second time. Her first husband died when she was very young and pregnant with her first child (David's half brother, Sherwood). He was stabbed three times. Police called that a suicide, too. The family's luck had been cruel. And now it had moved on David's boys.

He loved them all, but Davey was the only one of the five who had his blood. John, the oldest, was Lou Anne's son from a previous marriage. Steven, Norman, and Jimmy never knew their real father, although they tried to find him. David could offer to be their father, but he would never be what they were looking for. But Davey was his own indisputably: a reincarnation of his grandfather, with his unrepentant appetite for Alaska and his prospector's optimism. David was not a particularly superstitious person, but he worried about his sons. He often thought about the 1944 movie *The Fighting Sullivans*, based on the true story about five brothers who all died in battle during World War II and the inspiration for the more recent film *Saving Private Ryan*. Every time he watched it, he understood.

He understood the dream, too. Not all of it. He knew what it was about, but not whom it was about. He hoped it was not about his son, but about his father, a stolen death, a death never fully explained. The vision was his frustration multiplied over the years, of not knowing what really happened, his guilt for not being there. That made more sense than a premonition. He did not believe in curses that stalked a grandson to his death forty years later. Davey was not meant for his paternal grandfather's fate. Davey had Lou Anne's blood, too. Her father was a Bureau of Alcohol, Tobacco, and Firearms agent who retired and built a stone cabin by hand in the San Juan Islands. He and his wife sailed the Puget Sound the rest of their lives without nearly a mishap. He lived to age eighty-nine. That was the kind of ending Davey was meant for. He already had his island cabin, a cottage in Hilo. And he was going to leave Alaska behind before it consumed him. And by surviving this long, Davey had already escaped the curse, beaten it, in fact, six months earlier . . .

It is Halloween in Hawaii, that sublime time of year that means Davey is not fishing and he is home with Kari and the kids. They all set off for the beach for a picnic. He and his middle son, Willy, twelve, are body surfing when a huge wave suddenly crests over them. It tosses Willy to shore and sucks Davey into a nearby lava tube. The waves pull him out, denying him a breath before sucking him back in. The tube fills completely with water. It is sealed in darkness. He cannot feel bottom and cannot breathe and thinks he is going to die. Just at that moment of final submission, the ocean casts him free and this time does not drag him back into the underwater cave. His back is scraped raw, but he is alive.

As a boy, he nearly drowned in a river while hiking with his brother John. Now the ocean had come at him ferociously and then let him go. The family looked at it as a good omen.

"He thought that was his one close call and he survived it," Lou Anne said.

The family would come to discover the ocean had not spared him at all but had merely given him a warning and a brief reprieve.

While David Rundall resumed a fretful sleep, fidgeting beside his demons as he waited for the morning, Lieutenant Commander Todd Schmidt's plane took off into a stubborn headwind of seventy to one hundred knots. Once the plane reached cruising altitude, the ride was relatively smooth, if slow. Ahead of them was a journey whose distance was about equal to that between Seattle and Phoenix. His wife and son were still asleep, now accustomed to his abrupt nocturnal departures. By lunchtime, one way or another, he would be back home and they would have barely noticed his absence.

Schmidt grew up on a ranch near Rapid City, South Dakota, three miles from the county airport. Mesmerized by birds as a young boy, he knew he wanted to be a pilot and developed a habit of looking skyward at the planes taking off near his home. Because his family was poor, he reckoned he would have to devise his own way of paying for flight lessons. After high school, he got a job at a company that refueled and rented airplanes and employed its own flight instructors. He also joined the U.S. Army National Guard and became a flight mechanic with the hope that it would better his chances of getting selected for flight school. His planning paid off, as he was picked to learn how to fly Huey helicopters. He didn't know it for sure but could have easily guessed he was not unlike some of the men he was sent to rescue, boys with good intentions and limited means. Boys who grew up far from cities and poor because the farms, ranches, and mines and the livings they once promised were disappearing.

Schmidt said he joined the Coast Guard in 1989 because he wanted to save lives. Invariably, this is the same reason everyone in the Coast Guard gives for joining, be they pilots or navigators or patrol boat commanders, a chance to be a hero, to be the good guy. They live to find someone clinging to life on the open ocean and pluck them out of the sea. To them there is no more reassuring feeling, and they are driven to it like instinct. It shakes them from sleep and sweeps them into the cockpit of a plane and steers them into the manacles of a building storm, looking for a bobbing head among the whitecaps.

The Coast Guard with its two air stations and various ships patrolling the Bering Sea and Gulf of Alaska oversees an area of land and ocean about as large as the continental United States. The distance between Ketchikan in the southeast panhandle and Attu, the westernmost island in the Aleutian archipelago, equals that between San Diego and Bangor, Maine. Alaska has as many people, about six hundred thousand, as square miles of land, making it more than twice the size of Texas but about as populous as Staten Island. The giant state is entitled to only one U.S. House member but possesses most of the land set aside by the government as protected wilderness. About half the residents of Alaska live in Anchorage. Juneau and Fairbanks have about thirty thousand citizens apiece. Those three cities are the only in the state with traffic lights. Sitka and Ketchikan, the next largest towns, have about eight thousand residents each. Because centers of population are isolated from one another, airplanes are crucial to the state's infrastructure. There are almost as many airports in Alaska (425) as there are miles of railroad track. Most of Alaska's land cannot be planted, or built upon, or inhabited gracefully. The few crops that can be grown in Alaska have very little time. The summer is dreadfully short, but the days are eternally lit by the sun. Even the vegetables in Alaska live desperately, doing all their growing in weeks instead of months. In between the towns are glaciers, mountain ranges, tundra, and, of course, open ocean. If there is trouble at sea, help in the form of the Coast Guard is likely to be hours, maybe days, away. For that reason, seamen learn to depend on one another. Fishing at the edge of the continental shelf, the *Arctic Rose* and the *Alaskan Rose* were wise to stay together, because for all intents and purposes they were on their own.

As Schmidt guided his plane toward the electronic cry for help in the middle of the ocean, he had some reason to be optimistic. The *Arctic Rose* had not radioed for help or sent out a mayday. If it was a true emergency, the boat's captain certainly would have attempted to call for help before activating the EPIRB. He would have at least tried to contact the *Alaskan Rose* by VHF radio, which is reliable at short distances. And in turn, the *Alaskan Rose* would have notified the Coast Guard. In this case, no news tended to be good news, keeping intact the possibility that the *Arctic Rose* was in no danger at all, just unaware that her EPIRB was transmitting.

In the wheelhouse of the *Arctic Rose* was a simple way to call for help if the crew ever needed it. Aboard the boat was a Galaxy model TNL 7001 marine terminal, a satellite communications device consisting of a transceiver and antenna attached to a computer terminal. It can send data and text messages, but not voice messages. It is relatively slow. Data and text have to be stored before they can be sent, so instant communication is not possible. But the terminal can be used to send distress signals. By simultaneously depressing two buttons on the front of the transceiver for five seconds, anyone aboard can send a call for help. An audible alarm sounds. A light flashes. And the machine transmits a message with the boat's identification number, position, speed, course, time, and date. The device can even be programmed to identify the ship's problem. The satellite that receives the signal from the marine terminal orbits the earth at the equator but is designed to pick up any signal below seventy degrees latitude. Only a severe snowstorm would have affected the signal, reducing its strength but not eliminating it. The terminal can be activated from remote alarm panels, but the *Arctic Rose* did not have them. The distress signal would have had to be triggered from the bridge.

As Schmidt flew over the Bering, his radioman, Pete Trappen, continued to call both the *Arctic Rose* and *Alaskan Rose* by high-frequency radio. Like the radio operators at Comsta Kodiak, Trappen received no answer to his calls. Olney also continued, in vain, to call both of his boats. At 6:02 a.m., the Coast Guard icebreaker *Polar Star*, which happened to be working near St. Matthew Island, only 220 miles from the assumed position of the *Arctic Rose*, was ordered to try contacting the lost boat. A radioman on the *Polar Star* tried without success for forty-five minutes. But what was more puzzling was why no one could raise the *Alaskan Rose*, leaving some to wonder if something awful had befallen both boats.

Finally, when the C-130 was within one hundred miles of the source of the EPIRB signal, Trappen reached the *Alaskan Rose*. Answering the call aboard the *Alaskan Rose* was first mate John Nelson. It was about 7:45 a.m.

"Are you fishing with the *Arctic Rose?*" was the first question Trappen asked Nelson.

"Yes," he replied.

Trappen told Nelson the *Arctic Rose*'s EPIRB had gone off four hours ago. Slapped hard by the news, Nelson immediately turned the boat in the direction of the *Arctic Rose*, switched on the boat's powerful sodium vapor lights, the kind used as streetlamps, and opened the throttle. As he steamed full speed toward his mates, he called them on every channel but heard nothing in return. He also woke up skipper Norm Anderson and checked his satellite terminal for any new e-mail. He found one from David Olney and another from the Coast Guard, reporting that the *Arctic Rose*'s EPIRB had gone off. Although he had checked periodically through the night, he had not noticed the e-mail. To this day, he is not sure when exactly the dispatches arrived. Had the weather been bad, he would have kept in touch with Kerry Egan, first mate of the *Arctic Rose*, all night as a precaution. But the previous night had been relatively calm, at least where the *Alaskan Rose* was, and the weather had not been cause for concern.

The plane's navigator, Bobby Cannon, searched his radar for signs of any vessels. He found only the *Alaskan Rose*. Within ten minutes, the plane began its descent to five hundred feet, the standard search altitude. Although a fierce storm front was moving into the area at the time, the seas were still manageable, even improving according to those aboard the *Alaskan Rose*. Weather readings from a moored, weather-data buoy in the Bering also suggested the weather was not too rough. But conditions can vary widely from position to position, making it difficult to say for sure exactly what conditions the *Arctic Rose* experienced that night. The National Weather Service operates a network of data buoys in the world's oceans, all of them located relatively close to shore. In the Bering, it deploys one with a twelve-meter steel hull shaped like a discus. The largest data buoy used by the weather service, it measures barometric pressure, wind direction, speed and gusts, air and water temperature, and wave energy, providing forecasters with a general idea of wave activity, if not specific wave heights. But it was not close enough to where the *Arctic Rose* was fishing to transmit reliable information. Squalls in the Bering can be very isolated. Sailors have seen dead calm seas turn into raging ones in a matter of hours. On the same night, the crew of another ship, about ninety miles to the west of the *Arctic Rose*, reported witnessing sustained winds of forty knots, seas of eighteen feet, and maximum wave heights of twenty-four feet. Storm systems known as occluded fronts can create vastly different weather conditions at locations only ten miles apart.

Nelson estimated he was $11\frac{1}{2}$ miles away, and to the northeast of the *Arctic Rose*'s last known position. No other vessel was closer, which meant the *Alaskan Rose* was the only available rescue vessel. If lives were to be saved on this morning, other fishermen would have to do it. Nelson, however, could not find the *Arctic Rose* on his ship's radar. Worried, he and Anderson woke up the entire crew to help look for any sign of the *Arctic Rose*. Most were groggy, hands numb, still half-asleep, not completely comprehending what was happening. Processor Rafael Olivares, thinking they were looking for one or two men who fell overboard, asked Anderson, "How many of them went over?" Told the entire boat was missing, Olivares' knees went soft and he began to weep. He had worked as the factory foreman aboard the *Arctic Rose* the previous summer and knew many of the men. But the source of his stabbing guilt was the fact that he was the one who helped the three men from Veracruz get jobs on the *Arctic Rose*.

When they were within two miles, Nelson slowed down the boat. They had been transiting for almost thirty minutes. Norm Anderson brought his crew onto the bridge and instructed each of them to watch overlapping fifteen-degree sectors of the horizon. He told them to keep their eyes moving and to imagine the sectors as football fields. Reminding himself that his crew included Vietnamese and Mexicans, he amended his instructions, telling the non-Americans to visualize soccer fields.

Schmidt's C-130 was almost directly above them. At about 8:20 a.m., the plane dropped through the clouds into more darkness.

Descending to five hundred feet, the plane encountered rain and strong winds. In the blackness, Schmidt could see only the lights of the *Alaskan Rose*. The plane's gauges picked up a faint reading from the *Arctic Rose*'s EPIRB. Its signal increased significantly once they were within a mile. After three passes, Schmidt and his crew were sure they had located the EPIRB. Schmidt handed over control of the plane to copilot Dan Pike. While flying at an altitude of four hundred feet and a speed of 180 knots, the crew electronically recorded the spot using a global positioning system (GPS) and launched a flare to mark the spot visually. Nelson was surprised at the brightness of the flare, thinking it looked like dawn breaking on the horizon. Through a mix of rain and snow, he steered the boat toward the shower of light.

Norm Anderson retook the helm, while Nelson began scanning the water with binoculars. The first thing he saw was a baseball bat, used by the crew to break ice off the boat's railings, equipment, and the wheelhouse. It was an ominous discovery, as Nelson knew it must have come from the *Arctic Rose*. Then he saw sealed plastic bags and plastic containers with food in them, and some bottles of ketchup. Nelson's hopes rose as he speculated that if the boat indeed had sunk, at least his friends had had enough time to pack food and therefore probably had plenty of time to put on survival suits and get into the life raft. But his hopes quickly turned in another direction when a deckhand, Paul Headington, reminded Nelson that the *Arctic Rose* carried a food storage locker on its deck and that the containers of food had probably come from there. Headington had been part of the crew of the *Arctic Rose* the previous summer, agreeing to work on the smaller, slower, less profitable boat only because Olney had guaranteed him the same pay he would have made aboard the *Alaskan Rose*. Headington recognized debris from the *Arctic Rose* as it floated by, particularly planks of wood painted white from a box kept on deck to store fresh fruit and vegetables.

Soon, Nelson saw the EPIRB. The crew fished it out of the water, lowering a perforated plastic bucket attached to a rope to retrieve the device. Schmidt instructed Nelson to turn off the EPIRB since they no longer needed it and then dropped a data buoy marker (DBM) out of the plane. A DBM acts as a more capable surrogate to the EPIRB, not only transmitting its position, but recording wind and drift. Search planners use this information to form an educated guess as to where a life raft or a fisherman in a survival suit might drift based on the surface conditions at the time.

Using the DBM as a center, Schmidt charted out a rectangular search area of ten miles by twenty miles. He flew parallel patterns two miles apart, looking for debris or signs of survivors. Dawn was stubborn to break. The light approached in small paces, imperceptibly turning the blackness to a fuzzy expanse of gray. Clouds descended well below eight hundred feet. Winds were blowing about twenty knots. Eight-foot seas were high enough to obscure any debris that might be caught in the trough of a swell. Because of the rough weather, the plane had to fly faster than Schmidt wanted in order to avoid stalling. It made the looking more difficult and survivors easier to miss.

Other than the *Alaskan Rose*, not a single boat showed up on the plane's radar. The crew of the *Alaskan Rose* had been searching for more than an hour. Nelson continued to look through his binoculars. It wouldn't take much longer for him to find a face he knew.

Back at the Rescue Coordination Center in Juneau, a new shift of watch standers had arrived for work. Webb and Pesnell went home to sleep, both fully expecting nothing serious to come of the search they had initiated. The duty officer who showed up that morning was Lieutenant Stacie Fain, a former helicopter pilot who had gained a reputation for drawing more than her share of excitement while on watch. Other watch standers joked about not wanting to share shifts with her because crazy things tended to happen. Once, she directed the medical evacuation of a fisherman who had intentionally cut off his thumb to get out of a contract. She also oversaw the rescue of another fisherman who wrote a suicide note and jumped off a boat but took the counterproductive measure of wearing a survival suit and taking a life ring. He failed in his halfhearted attempt at killing himself. Fain had another bizarre suicide attempt on her watch: An obese fisherman stripped naked before jumping into the Bering. He was rescued forty-five minutes later in such robust condition that he had to be sedated. Probably thanks to his size, he suffered nothing more than cold feet. Later the same year, she would be on watch during the bizarre murder of a Coast Guard officer at the St. Paul radar station and during the terrorist attack on New York and Washington.

Fain's shift started minutes before Schmidt's crew reported it had located the *Arctic Rose*'s EPIRB. Within the hour, the Coast Guard was in full search mode. The discovery of debris meant a boat had almost certainly sunk. But Fain was hopeful that the crew would be found safe in a life raft. The weather had not yet turned life-threatening. Fain's first priority was to send more help. She directed the air station at Kodiak to prepare to launch another C-130 to relieve Schmidt's plane, which would need to return in a few hours. And she ordered the launch of a Jayhawk helicopter, which would be used to pull survivors out of the ocean. It would head for St. Paul, where it would fill its tanks and wait until survivors were located.

A C-130 can only verify a sinking and drop survival equipment. A helicopter would have to perform the actual rescue. With a range of about four hundred miles, the Jayhawk would have to refuel twice before landing on St. Paul, where the Coast Guard maintains a radar station and leases an aircraft hangar. Planning his route in carefully measured segments, the Jayhawk pilot set off on a madman's course. Leaving Kodiak, the Jayhawk would fly northwest to Dillingham, the closest place the helicopter could refuel. But because Dillingham is more than four hundred miles away from St. Paul, the copter would then have to fly southwest across Bristol Bay to the town of Cold Bay, at the end of the Alaska Peninsula. From there it could make the final leap to St. Paul, more than three hundred miles north across the Bering. The fragmented trip would take a total of eight hours. Then the Jayhawk and its crew would face their most dangerous challenge. Because the reported position of the *Arctic Rose*'s EPIRB was a little more than two hundred miles from St. Paul, a rescue attempt would push the helicopter to the limits of its capability. The crew would have barely enough fuel to get there and back and would certainly not have time to stay on the scene for very long.

For obvious reasons, a sea rescue is much easier if the vessel in distress is well within two hundred miles of an air station. In that case, only a helicopter will be launched. During times of heightened fishing activity, the Coast Guard will temporarily post a Jayhawk closer to fishing grounds to cut down on response time. In January, for example, during the crab season in the Pribilofs, the Coast Guard stations a Jayhawk on St. Paul. It also deploys a Jayhawk in Cold Bay during the red king crab season in October, and in Cordova from May to October to watch over the salmon fleet and summer kayakers in Prince William Sound.

The Jayhawk left Kodiak at 9:00 a.m. with a crew of four. Lieutenant Fain's next move was to send a cutter, the largest vessels deployed by the Coast Guard, to the search area. The high-endurance cutter *Acushnet* was on patrol in Bristol Bay, at least two days away and trapped by bad weather. Fain quickly ruled out the *Acushnet*. Another high-endurance cutter, the 378-foot *Boutwell*, was on patrol in Nazan Bay off Atka Island, on the western end of the Aleutians. The Coast Guard keeps at least one cutter on patrol in the Bering Sea at all times. As long as it is not needed for a rescue mission, a cutter's main responsibility is to enforce fisheries laws, so it tends to shadow the fishing fleet, maintaining a discreet distance to keep the fishermen guessing and honest. In general, but not always, a cutter stays close to the greatest concentration of fishing boats. At that time, most of them were near the Aleutians. To join the *Alaskan Rose*, the *Boutwell* would have to cover a distance equal to that between New York City and Tennessee. The *Boutwell*'s top speed is twenty knots. At that speed, it could reach the search area within thirty-six hours. The icebreaker *Polar Star* near St. Matthew Island was much closer, but its captain estimated he would need twenty-four hours to reach the search area. The *Polar Star* would have to break ice for the first hundred miles of the journey, traveling at a top speed of ten knots. Once free of the ice, it could do fifteen knots. Fain made her decision. She dispatched the *Polar Star* at 9:10 a.m.

At the time, the 399-foot *Polar Star*, with a crew of 141, was near the Arctic Circle, serving as a research platform for scientists studying polynyas, or irregular openings in the Bering ice shelf. The holes in the ice tend to develop in the same places every winter, especially near St. Lawrence Island, where the *Polar Star* was working. These holes are formed by strong southerly winds that prevent ice from building up on the leeward side of islands and promontories. The *Polar Star* normally spends winters breaking a supply channel through the ice to McMurdo Station in Antarctica. As an icebreaker, it is not usually summoned to rescue missions. It is nonetheless equipped with rescue equipment and two Dolphin helicopters, the familiar rescue copter seen on television shows like *Baywatch*.

At 9:40, Fain spoke to Olney, who confirmed there were fifteen men aboard. He also told her the *Arctic Rose* had a twenty-man lifeboat and at least eighteen survival suits, more than enough for everyone. He told her all the suits were red, the color of a Santa Claus suit, and came with strobe lights and whistles. He was unsure of the color of the lifeboat but promised to find out. Now on the phone almost constantly, Fain also fielded about half a dozen frantic calls from wives and mothers and friends of fishermen who had heard only that a fishing vessel out of Seattle had been reported missing. It is common for relatives of fishermen to commit to permanent memory the phone number to the Coast Guard's rescue center.

As chief of the search-and-rescue unit, Commander Michael Neussl was expected to speak with and keep informed the families of the men on the *Arctic Rose*. Olney had provided him with a list of the men and the phone numbers of relatives they had given when they signed their contracts. Because the list was so long, Neussl asked Lieutenant Commander Sue Workman to help. The first conversations were generally hopeful in tone, emphasizing the possibility that the men were waiting to be rescued, safe, dry, and warm in the protection of a life raft. In an ideal rescue scenario, a crew abandoning ship would bring the EPIRB with them into a life raft, making it easy for searchers to locate them. But if the boat was sinking fast, they might not have the time. In any case, if there was a life raft anywhere out there, Neussl was confident they would find it.

When a search at sea does not immediately yield survivors, the Coast Guard starts to calculate the shrinking likelihood of finding them alive. A computer software program has made more precise what intuition and common sense tell them, that the chances of surviving the cold Bering waters are better for a young, healthy, large person and much better if that person is in a survival suit. The Coast Guard turns to the computer program only when the outlook is bleak. The program takes into account a person's age, height, weight, body fat, fatigue, time of immersion, how much clothing he's wearing, the water temperature, and the sea state. The latter two factors did not bode well for the crew of the *Arctic Rose*. The Bering water temperature is just above freezing, between thirty-five and thirty-eight degrees Fahrenheit, made more deadly by breaking waves and strong, steady winds. But in a dry suit, a person of average size, health, and stamina could survive in the water for at least sixteen hours, perhaps longer. Without a dry suit, wearing ordinary clothing, survival time is at best two hours and probably much less. The only element the software or an educated guess cannot factor in is the will to live.

"Hang on, Davey!" his stepbrother, John, shouts across the raging Elwha River. But Davey cannot hear because his head is under the water, where it is quiet and voices cannot reach. Davey Rundall is sixteen. His stepbrother, John, is twenty. They are hiking double time through the Olympic National Park, trying to catch up to a group of five other boys who had started off earlier. It is summer, and the Elwha is running very high when they arrive at its bank. The brothers assess the situation and try to figure out how the others had gotten across the river. It looks dangerous. But John has a rope thirty-five feet long and an idea. He makes up his mind: If the other boys can cross, he and Davey can cross, too. They tie each end of the rope around their waists and ford across. After thirty excruciating minutes, the water is up to their armpits. Their limbs ache from the cold, and they are at the edge of hypothermia. The boys' packs fill up with water. John, in the lead, starts to sink. Grabbing desperately at rocks, he manages to pull his way to the shore and stand up.

"Go for it, Davey!" John says. Davey trusts him and goes for the final ten yards to shore.

He cannot manage the current, either. But he doesn't sink the way John did. His head goes straight down. He is pinned in the river and cannot right himself because his pack is too heavy. John can see only Davey's feet kicking above the surface. John pulls on the rope, but Davey doesn't come up. His head stays submerged. His life is now a race against the current and Davey's last breath. John keeps pulling and walking, and after what seems like an impossibly long time, he reaches Davey and lifts him up with all his strength to get his head out of the water. He expects the worst. But somehow Davey had held his breath.

"Thanks, John," Davey says, shocked by the sudden air around him. "You saved my life."

The brothers camp at the shore for the night and reach the other boys two days later. Surprised, the boys ask the brothers how they had gotten to the rendezvous point so quickly. The boys had gone around the river, adding days to their journey. They had decided the river was uncrossable.

Despite his choices, Davey Rundall's will had always saved him and separated him from others. People recognized it immediately. Even those who didn't like him very much felt the reassuring weight of his will. John Nelson comforted himself with this thought. Rundall would fight to survive. He would fight for himself, he would fight to see his wife and sons again.

By 10:00 a.m., the lean sunlight that filtered through thick clouds and beating squalls made much easier the work of the crew of the *Alaskan Rose*. They spotted more bats, garbage, and a crate. The light also revealed pieces of fishing gear sprinkled atop an oval-shaped oil slick, the most concrete proof they had so far that a boat had sunk. Floating with the oil were plastic deck hats, transparent shrink wrap, rags, and more baseball bats. Schmidt used the outline of the oil slick, no more than fifty yards across, to guide his search. The sheen of oil, which grew into an almost perfect circle, was very concentrated, composed of engine oil and diesel fuel. The turbulent sea churned the slick, breaking it up quickly. The tanks of the *Arctic Rose* had been nearly full. They had topped off their tanks in St. Paul one day earlier, anticipating a lengthy trip far from any port.

At almost the same time the oil slick appeared, someone aboard the plane thought he saw a survival suit downwind of where the EPIRB was found. It took several passes to determine that it was a survival suit and that someone was wearing it. From a distance, a fully unfurled but empty suit looks about the same as a suit with a person in it. The spotters were not sure, but they thought they could see a face. Schmidt directed the *Alaskan Rose* toward the body. Then the plane's crew started spotting several more red survival suits, all of them empty. They began circling over the area as more suits appeared downwind, finding at least one suit with each lap over a period of about thirty minutes. All were empty, drifting slowly in relatively close formation, all within a half mile from the line of the wind.

As the *Alaskan Rose* approached the first suit, at about 10:15 a.m., Nelson looked through his binoculars and immediately recognized the face of his friend Davey Rundall. He was completely still, his eyes fully opened. The two men had fished together aboard the same boats and knew each other well. They were about the same age, both married, both fathers of three children. Nelson is a volunteer fireman in his hometown of North Bend, Washington, and is trained in lifesaving techniques. It was decided he was the person best qualified to retrieve Rundall from the ocean. Headington helped Nelson put on a bulky survival suit and attached him to a safety line with a padded strap. Made of thick neoprene, a synthetic rubber, a survival suit is built for insulation, not movement. Nelson climbed awkwardly down a rope ladder thrown over the side of the *Alaskan Rose*. Once in the water, he began a backstroke toward Rundall, who was no more than twenty-five feet from the boat. But waves kept pushing Rundall's body farther away. At one point a wave turned Rundall upside down so that his head was in the water. Rafael Olivares kept shouting at Rundall, telling him to hang on.

The months away at sea had been growing less enjoyable for Rundall, who wanted to spend more time with Kari and the boys, Davyn, fourteen, Willy, twelve, and Max, four. Everyone in his family hoped and suspected this fishing season might be his last. The obstacle was finding another job, suitable work that allowed him more time at home. For so long, Rundall focused his ambitions on just one thing, fishing, and his determination was a difficult thing to call off. Now he was qualified to do little else but work at sea. A few years

earlier, he had found a job with a tugboat crew in Hawaii. He spent
weeks at a time at sea, although he saw his family more frequently
than when he fished. Later, he felt misled about his opportunities for
advancement. Discouraged and not wanting to work his way up the
ladder yet again, he quit and returned to fishing. He still enjoyed the
hunt, but it meant less and less as his sons got older.

Nelson kept swimming and shouting Rundall's name, getting no
response. The length of Nelson's lifeline was spent, but Rundall
remained out of his reach. Nelson made the risky decision to unhook
himself so he could get to Rundall. Once Nelson reached Rundall, he
could tell he was not breathing. He saw that Rundall's dry suit was
fully donned, the hood over his head, although not completely
forward. Indeed, he had fought with his last breath to get his suit
on. Nelson had judged him accurately. The hood was tight enough
around Rundall's face that it restricted blood flow slightly. Nelson
noticed the suit's air bladder was not inflated. The bladder acts as a
built-in flotation device. The crew of the *Alaskan Rose* pulled on the
safety line, now reattached, to help bring both men to the boat.
Rundall was pulled onto the deck as Headington began cutting away
the drysuit, which was oddly bloated at the legs. Water poured out,
revealing that Rundall was completely soaked. Nelson guessed that
Rundall, amazingly, had put on the survival suit after he had fallen
into the ocean, virtually nullifying any advantage the suit would
normally give him. A properly trained fisherman is expected to be
able to put one on in less than one minute, but putting it on in the
water would be very difficult, if not nearly impossible. That Rundall
accomplished the feat was testimony to his concentration and
strength. If a fisherman is already submerged in water, putting on
a suit might give him only one or two more hours of survival time at
most. Rundall usually kept his boots and a survival suit next to his
bed. He was a compact man with smaller than average feet. Small feet
generally make it easier to put on a suit.

Rundall and his suit reeked of diesel fuel. He was wearing
sweatpants, a T-shirt, a sweatshirt, and rubber slip-on boots still
splattered with paint. Olivares recognized them as Rundall's favorite
boots, a pair he had owned for five years and took meticulous care of.

He immediately thought of an incident one year earlier. While painting the boat, Olivares and some other men had accidentally spilled some paint on Rundall's boots, and he had scolded them for it. Now he looked at the familiar splatters still on Rundall's boots. Rundall's eyes were glazed over, turned back into his head. The capillaries in his eyeballs had burst, turning the whites of his eyes blood red. Nelson and three others carried Rundall into a hallway below the wheelhouse. Rundall's arms were locked in an upright position, elevated ninety degrees from his body.

He was cold, not breathing, and had no pulse. Trained to administer cardiopulmonary resuscitation, Nelson worked on Rundall for more than fifteen minutes, watching his chest rise and fall as he blew into his lungs. Nelson noticed rigor mortis setting in and saw that Rundall's lips were becoming cyanotic, or blue from lack of oxygen. Nelson asked Schmidt if he should stop trying to resuscitate Rundall. After consulting a Coast Guard flight surgeon, Schmidt directed Nelson to continue for ten more minutes. When he reported no further success, Nelson was told to stop.

"I feel sure in my mind that Dave did everything he could to survive," Nelson said later. "He was the person with the most experience. He was a tough, young guy who had been on the sea a long time. He has three boys, and I know that drove him to survive."

Several days later, in Anchorage, the chief medical examiner for the state of Alaska performed an autopsy on Rundall. Dr. Franc Fallico determined Rundall died of saltwater drowning, likely near the surface of the ocean, as his body did not show any signs of having been submerged deep in the water. Rundall's blood and urine showed no signs of alcohol or drugs. His lungs were greatly expanded. Consistent with long exposure to cold temperatures, his skin was discolored a cherry hue. Fallico found no evidence of blunt-force injury.

"They told us his lungs were almost touching each other," his father, David Rundall, said.

While Nelson attempted to resuscitate Rundall, Olivares shouted that he had seen another person in the water who appeared to be wearing black or dark pants, a white T-shirt, and a dark jacket with purple trim. He was not wearing a survival suit. Other crewmen saw him, too. But as the *Alaskan Rose* approached the body, it disappeared into the waves, never to be seen again. Norm Anderson suspects the added turbulence of his approaching boat helped sink the body. No one is sure whom they saw. Olivares thought it might have been Kerry Egan because he believed Egan owned a black-and-purple jacket. Egan would have been in the wheelhouse at the time of the sinking. He would have been closest to the survival suits and the only one above deck. The mother of deckhand Eddie Haynes, however, would later say that she believed it was her son because he owned a purple jacket.

"I hope it was Eddie because I just hate to think he was trapped in that room in the boat," Rose Workland would say later. "It makes me feel better somehow."

At 10:55 a.m., about ten minutes after Nelson stopped trying to resuscitate Rundall, the crew of the C-130 made another hopeful discovery, the orange canopy of a life raft. It was the copilot, Dan Pike, who first saw it. He couldn't get the words out as quickly as he thought them and tripped over them for a second.

"Life raft!" he shouted.

The crew marked its position with a flare and dropped the plane to an altitude of two hundred feet to make sure of what they saw. Not all the survival suits had been retrieved. They were becoming distractions for the spotters who were looking for a raft among the suits. Some were still rolled up, while others clearly had been unrolled and unzipped. The partly deployed suits suggested a frantic rush by some of the men, who must have realized that getting into the suits meant the difference between life and death. What they must have thought in the seconds that followed, sinking into the sea, unable to get into their suits, was too horrifying to consider. At one point, the rescue crew mistook a survival suit for a second raft. Thickening rain and snow were affecting visibility. They continued to fly over what they thought was the raft as they directed the *Alaskan Rose* to it. Much of the early hours of the search followed this pattern. Someone in the plane would spot debris, mark it, and guide the *Alaskan Rose* to it. The plane acted as eyes, the boat arms, in a hunt for life.

The raft appeared to be fully inflated, its orange canopy deployed. The canopy, however, was partially collapsed by the weight of seawater that had gathered on top of it. It was evidence that the raft had inflated itself underwater. Like the EPIRB, it was activated by water pressure, inflating itself as it sank into the water. The opening to the canopy was visible, and someone on the plane thought he once saw a person's face in the opening. Schmidt asked Anderson if someone on the boat could reach the raft. Anderson agreed with some trepidation, afraid of the worsening seas. This time, Headington was designated to put on a survival suit and swim to the raft. The *Alaskan Rose* reached the life raft at about 12:30 p.m. Headington found the raft empty except for a survival kit, a canister that comes with the raft, containing food and water and first-aid supplies. It showed no signs of ever having sheltered people. It did not appear that anyone ever reached the raft. Schmidt asked Anderson to pull it aboard. But Anderson judged the task too dangerous under the weather conditions, so he told Schmidt they would sink the raft instead so as to remove it from the search field. Nelson lowered a knife to Headington, who punctured the raft.

In total, six survival suits were recovered, as well as two flotation vests, the kind worn by deckhands while working. The six suits were not in their storage bags and had been unzipped. It appeared as if the men had had enough time to get their hands on the suits and attempt to put them on before a sudden rush of water prevented them from completing a task they knew their lives depended on. A portion of some netting was recovered, as was a bucket, a pylon, a piece of plywood, and an empty survival suit bag with "*Arctic Rose*" written on it. Although the search would last for five days, at a cost of $1.74 million, almost all traces of the boat and her crew were discovered within the first eight hours.

Schmidt's plane covered an area five miles upwind from the oil sheen to ten miles downwind from where the raft was found. He flew parallel patterns, whose total width measured ten miles. At about 1:00 p.m., with barely enough fuel remaining to return to Kodiak, Schmidt and his crew were relieved by another search plane as they began their flight back home. The mood swings among the crew of the C-130, Schmidt remembered, were the most severe he had experienced. The crew began its mission with very high expectations of finding the boat and its crew perfectly safe. The debris erased that hope, which the crew replaced with the very reasonable expectation that they would find survivors in a raft. That was usually what happened in these rescues. With each new discovery, the prognosis changed drastically. Information was passed with surprising efficiency between the plane, the *Alaskan Rose*, the rescue center in Juneau, and Olney in Seattle. But a few details got lost in the intricate relay. For its entire flight, the crew of Schmidt's plane was convinced it had seen two rafts. The men did not learn until well after they landed that the boat had only one raft. And for several hours, Fain believed two bodies, not just one, had been recovered.

By the afternoon, both the *Polar Star* to the north and the *Boutwell* to the south were on their way to the debris field. The *Polar Star* would spend nine hours breaking ice before hitting clear water at 6:23 p.m.

Now, as the planes kept flying grids, the people in charge cannot wait any longer. The phone calls must start, to mothers and fathers and sisters and sons. There is no good news to tell any of them. The same awful details are repeated, the same despairing questions asked and answered with solemnity. They are trained to speak this way. The life raft was empty. No survivors located. Only one body. Planes are still searching. We are very sorry. Everyone is doing everything possible. We don't know what happened. We'll call you as soon as we hear something.

Another phone call goes out to Lacey, Washington, to the two-story home of David and Kathy Meincke. He sells pharmaceuticals. She is an accountant. Their home has a vaulted ceiling and a well-tended garden. From the Boy Scouts, Jeff Meincke learned the Latin names for the plants that grew and the birds that might land there. Jeff's Jeep is parked in front of the house. The houses in the subdivision are new, the asphalt fresh, the lawns without a single weed. It all says what everyone knows when they meet Jeff, that he is a nice kid from a nice family who lives in a nice home. It doesn't matter that he has a pierced tongue or tattoos or that he smokes and curses or that he fishes. The "nice" comes through. Jeff cannot help it. He seems different. For one of his Eagle Scout projects, he helped restore a walking path next to a creek near Olympia.

The awful call to the Meinckes arrives on opening day of baseball season. The Athletics will play the Mariners in a night game at Safeco Field, and David and Kathy Meincke are going to the game with friends. David is getting ready to leave when he hears the phone ring sometime around 3:00 p.m. The ring on the Meinckes' phone is customized, so David knows it is a call from out of the area code. He decides not to answer, because he is in a hurry, but listens to the message on the answering machine before leaving for the game. The call is from John Casperson, a good friend of David Olney's and a maritime lawyer who knows the Alaskan fishing industry well. The message is simple: I am calling from Arctic Sole Seafoods. I have information about your son. Please call back as soon as you can.

David is not alarmed. He is almost glad. Because he is sure the call means Jeff broke his arm or broke his leg and that he will be coming home early. The phone call is good news. It means his son's experiment with fishing is over and his mother can stop worrying about him. David calls Casperson back and does not know what to do with what he hears. He gives Casperson the number to his mobile phone. He gathers his things, walks out the door, gets into his car, and drives. He picks up Kathy at work and picks up their friends. He drives them to the game in Seattle. He tells Kathy nothing.

Kathy thinks David seems preoccupied but doesn't question him about his mood. He gets up often. The Athletics go ahead 4–0. Kathy thinks he is in the bathroom. But he is really checking his cell phone. No one has called. The Mariners score a run in the fourth and another in the fifth. The game is sold out. It is the debut of the Mariners' sought-after star hitter from Japan, Ichiro Suzuki. He fails to get a hit in his first three at-bats. David gets up again to buy a drink. He doesn't know what the score is. The game is, for David, a convenient opportunity not to talk about the obvious. Jessica calls him. She is crying. She heard the news from Jimmie Conrad's girlfriend. David goes back to his seat and wonders why he is watching a baseball game. In the seventh inning, Ichiro hits a single to center, his first Major

League hit. The historic ball is taken out of the game. Ichiro scores. The Mariners tie the game. David decides not to tell Kathy anything until tomorrow. She is enjoying the game. It is cold, thirty-nine degrees. The Mariners go ahead in the bottom of the eighth on a sacrifice fly. They win the game 5–4, the first of 116 victories that season, more than any team in baseball history except the 1906 Chicago Cubs. The Meinckes drive home. It is as if David never went to the game. The next day, Kathy is sitting on the edge of the bed when he finally tells her.

Kathy is angry, angry that he knew and didn't tell her, angry that he carried something so terrible by himself all during the game, all through the night. Years later, she would still be angry about that.

"It was like it didn't sink in," David said later. "I didn't believe it, not until I sat Kathy down and told her."

Aboard the *Alaskan Rose*, about the time the baseball game ended, Norm Anderson convinced Nelson he should get some sleep since he would have to be on watch later that night. Nelson slept for a few hours, waking up at 10:00 p.m. The weather was as good as ever. That evening, David Olney provided physical descriptions of the men aboard the *Arctic Rose* to Fain so she could insert the information into her cold survival computer program. Just before midnight, Fain spoke with John Kivlin, the son of the *Arctic Rose*'s cook, Ken Kivlin. Then she called the Dutch Harbor Police Department and updated an officer on the search, sending her a copy of the crew list and an 800 number for any other relatives who might call.

After midnight, the winds at the search area shifted and intensified. By 3:00 a.m., they were blowing more than forty knots and the ocean spray was freezing on contact. At about this time, the *Polar Star* finally arrived and took charge of the search.

Within twenty-four hours, four inches of ice coated the ship's deck and rigging. This amount of ice is a concern even for a craft as big as the *Polar Star*. It was built to be on top of ice, not under four inches of it. The ship's blunt, rounded bottom and spoon-shaped bow make it efficient at breaking ice but become a liability in rough seas, causing the ship to roll more drastically. Gusts peaked at twenty-five knots, blowing over ten-foot seas, and it would get worse. No one was permitted on deck of the *Polar Star*, so all available eyes looked out the windows of the eighty-four-foot-wide bridge, sixty feet above the waterline. Because the ship rolled violently, helicopters could not safely be launched. So the C-130 planes, one flying in after another at a rate of three per day, were the only aircraft that could search for survivors.

By the next afternoon, the weather became unsafe for the 124-foot *Alaskan Rose*, so it departed with Rundall's body aboard. The *Boutwell* arrived on the third day, already beaten by storms. It had also contended with an emergency of its own.

Shortly after exiting Nazan Bay, the *Boutwell* was hit by a storm that caused deck gear to come loose. While trying to secure the loose equipment, two crewmen were nearly swept overboard by a rogue wave. One grabbed on to a railing with one hand as he was about to fall into the sea and had to be pulled back onto the deck. The other crewman, eighteen-year-old Darrell Strickland, struck his head on a bulkhead, suffering deep cuts around his eye and on his forehead. The injury required more care than the ship's facilities could provide. The weather was so rough, the ship's doctor was afraid to stitch the wound for fear of injuring Strickland further. Winds blew at thirty-five knots, with waves up to twenty-five feet. So the *Boutwell* had to alter its course to the *Arctic Rose*, in order to move within helicopter range of St. Paul island. The weather was too rough to launch the ship's helicopter. So the Jayhawk helicopter waiting on St. Paul to rescue the crew of the *Arctic Rose* had to rescue a member of the search party instead. And the C-130 working the search area had to be diverted to fly the injured crewman from St. Paul to Anchorage.

The *Boutwell* had no sooner joined the search before six inches of ice accumulated on its deck. Although it was a slimmer, more stable ship, even its helicopters could not be launched.

On the fourth day of the search, the seas finally calmed a bit and the crew of the *Polar Star* was allowed on deck. They struck at their vessel with baseball bats and ax handles to remove ice. At this point, rescuers were not expecting to find survivors. Every empty drysuit represented a person who was surely dead.

Water conducts heat away from the body up to twenty-five times faster than air of the same temperature. As hypothermia sets in, basic body functions like breathing, heartbeat, and metabolism slow down. Thinking and speech become impaired. Reflexes are slowed, and muscles become stiff and unusable. Eventually, irreversible and dangerous heart rhythms develop. By then, drowning is inevitable.

After four days of searching, the mission was called off. The brewing storm hit the *Polar Star* with full force as the ship left the search area. The icebreaker pointed headfirst into seventy-five-knot winds and fifty-foot seas. One wave hit the bridge so hard, it knocked out an inch-thick window. Another knocked out the windows of a crane box about forty-five feet above deck. Yet another tore the jack staff off the bow. At times, the ship rolled as much as fifty degrees, making it easier to walk on the walls than the floor. Off the mainland coast, such a storm would make headlines. In the Bering, it was just another spring blow.

Miles away, the crew of the *Alaskan Rose* had to contend with the same storm. They abandoned plans to take Rundall's body to St. Paul because the rough waters made it unsafe to enter its harbor. In order to enter, the boat would have to expose its side to the storm, a risky move. A wave hitting a boat broadside could cause it to capsize. So instead, the *Alaskan Rose* turned south to Dutch Harbor, 250 miles away. With the storm at its tail, the *Alaskan Rose* had little trouble reaching Dutch. The crew arrived April 5 in Captain's Bay, docking a few hundred feet from where the *Arctic Rose* had docked only weeks before. Anderson turned over Rundall's body to a state trooper, who escorted the body to Anchorage, where it would be autopsied. The men were given a few days off. A local church arranged to take the crew by bus to a short service at the United Methodist Church of Unalaska. Later, the men paid respects to their drowned mates at Unalaska's Memorial Park, where wreaths were laid at the foot of a monument to dead seamen. After taking two days off, the crew of the *Alaskan Rose* went back to sea, returning to the spot where the *Arctic Rose* sank. They rang a bell for each of the fifteen dead men, many of whom they never knew. Then they steamed farther north to resume fishing. They had no heart or stomach to fish the Zhemchug. While in Dutch Harbor, all the men had been told they could stop fishing and go home if they wanted to. To a man, all had refused.

On the last day of the search, the officer in charge at the rescue center in Juneau received a phone call from a house painter named Bobby Croome who lived in Chignik, Alaska. He sounded agitated. He claimed that several years ago, he used to be a deckhand on a boat called the *Tenacity*. He said the boat was known to be a dangerous and unstable vessel, that it almost flipped over when he was aboard. He described a fish hold he thought was too big for the boat and the boat's slow, hanging roll that had made him and other crew members anxious during rough seas. He said during some hard weather, the boat once sprang a leak where the propeller shaft exited the boat. The packing around the gear box had deteriorated and come apart. The stream of water entering the hull resembled a fully opened garden hose, dangerously flooding the engine room. Water came within six inches of the main electrical box. He had reported his concerns to the Coast Guard years ago but was not taken seriously, he said, because he had been fired from the crew and was considered a disgruntled employee. He had just read about the sinking of the *Arctic Rose* in the paper and after thinking for a while decided he should call the Coast Guard. The owners of his old boat never made enough money because it was too small and too slow. Debts went unpaid, and eventually federal marshals repossessed the boat for the bank holding its loan. A new owner had bought the boat at auction, fixed it up, and renamed it the *Arctic Rose*.

4

The Investigation Begins

The chambers of the old boat smell of wood and brine. She is navy surplus, a minesweeper of obsolete vintage, traded for an industrial lathe to a retired machinist and his wife, who have converted the hulk into a floating home by the docks of Bellingham. The boy clambering through her compartments and passageways is the couple's grandson, a boy of eleven or ten or perhaps younger. His name is David Olney, and to him the boat must be a thousand feet long. It is his favorite place to be. All his life he remembers the smell from the boat, the smell, he will know later, of his destiny.

Most of the boys who grew up in Deming, Washington, near the western rise of Mount Baker, stuck to the land. Theirs was a logging town that accommodated a few dairy farms and chicken ranches. But the Olneys had only a few acres. The men in the family were mechanically inclined. David's father was an auto mechanic, and cars and boats being similar enough, he somehow became the port engineer for a seafood cannery and its fleet of eighty gill netters, generally small, one-man fishing vessels that cast nets of large mesh. Gill nets hang like a curtain from the surface of the water. Salmon swim into the holes of the net. The small ones pass through, but those that are suitably large cannot swim completely through. They get stuck at the gills, hence the name. David Olney first learned from his father how to properly winterize a fishing boat, how to scrutinize an engine and repair rotted planks. He also fished with his uncle Harvey, who ran a small purse seiner in southeast Alaska. Purse seiners catch salmon by setting a huge net of smaller mesh. The net is attached at one end to a skiff, which is launched some distance from the boat. The skipper of the boat encircles the school of fish before meeting the skiff. The two ends of the net are then joined, and the bottom is cinched closed like a purse, trapping the salmon. A purse seiner needs a small crew of four to seven. Uncle Harvey gave David, at age seventeen, his start in fishing as a deckhand aboard his boat. When David was nineteen, he bought his own boat, a salmon gill netter he used in the local waters as a way of making extra money in the winter. Every few years, he traded in the boat he had for a better one. It was a modest living, but one that stuck. He bought his first full-time trawler in 1979, dragging the waters off Washington and Oregon with a crew of four, for cod and rockfish.

The *Arctic Rose* was his reward for years of smart fishing and careful investing. She was a boat that failed her previous owner, but Olney thought he could change things. He bought her a new life, spending hundreds of thousands of dollars, restoring every foot of her. He had a mind to lengthen her once she started making money. He never felt she was unsafe and never experienced the dangerous rolls that Bobby Croome spoke of. In Olney's mind, that just couldn't happen unless you loaded the cargo incorrectly. He had enough faith in the boat to put himself, his brother, and his son to work on the *Arctic Rose* at one time or another.

"I liked the way it handled," said David Olney, forty-eight. "I liked the ride better than the ride on the *Alaskan Rose*. It didn't roll much side to side. When we were in twenty-to-twenty-five-mile-an-hour winds, we rode straight and bobbed up and down. With the *Alaskan Rose*, if the ocean moved, the boat moved with it."

The sinking was an agonizing puzzle to Olney. He was regarded by other owners and fishermen as a conscientious and experienced operator who was not too stubborn to spend money to keep his boats running well. A hands-on owner, he always served aboard his own vessels. In the industry that is a good sign, indication of an owner's commitment and trust in his equipment. He had, in fact, taken three trips on the *Arctic Rose* one month before she sank.

The loss of the *Arctic Rose* was one of the worst fishing disasters in modern history. The Coast Guard had very few ideas of what caused it.

Weather, although always a hazard in the Bering, was not unusually rough and certainly not the worst the boat had experienced. The *Arctic Rose* was relatively new, only twelve years old, and had been recently refurbished. Moreover, she had passed an impromptu, at-sea Coast Guard inspection in February. The inspection found everything aboard the boat to be in good order. Her skipper and mate were both experienced seamen who had put in years running boats like the *Arctic Rose* in Alaskan waters. What was especially perplexing was why no one aboard had called for help or reported a problem the night the boat sank. Or at least no one heard such a call. The scant evidence suggested that a catastrophic force hit the boat with little (if any) warning, sinking it very quickly. On that order, only a few events, perhaps a collision, an explosion, or a fire, could have occurred. Only one man, it appeared, had time to don a survival suit and then only after he had fallen into the water. A full net of fish weighing ten tons can potentially destabilize a boat, acting as a giant counterweight. If the net were to sway off center to either side of the boat, it could cause it to roll sharply and capsize. But as far as anyone knew, Rundall had decided his crew was not going to fish any more that night so that his processing line could catch up and put away the fish that had already been caught.

Fishermen had some of their own theories, that the boat was struck by lightning, rammed by a giant freighter, unaware it had maimed a fishing boat, sucked under by a Russian submarine tangled in its net, or sunk by a sudden explosion belowdecks. Some suspected a rogue wave, which is improbable but always possible and difficult to identify as a cause without any witnesses. Rogue waves have been known to capsize even large ships in otherwise calm weather. A rogue is a one-in-a-million wave reaching heights of up to two hundred feet. Rogues form during storms when the crests of several different trains of waves, each with a unique speed and path, converge at exactly the same time, forming one giant wave equal to the sum of the heights of the individual waves. Since the trains are moving at different speeds, a rogue quickly disassembles itself, breaking up into smaller waves again, leaving little trace of the giant it once was. Or it destroys itself by cresting. It is a terrifying, if unlikely, prospect.

The number of lives lost on the *Arctic Rose*, fifteen, was unusually high. Among all American fishing boats, it was the most lives lost in the previous fifty years. (In the history of fishing off Alaska, three accidents involving Japanese trawlers took more lives. In March 1981, the *Daito Maru No. 55* sank 380 miles off Adak, killing twenty-six. In January 1982, the *Akebono Maru* sank 50 miles north of Adak, claiming thirty-two lives. And in February 1984, the *Kyowa Maru No. 11* collided with another vessel and sank 120 miles off Atka at a cost of sixteen lives.) Although fishing boats frequently sink in Alaska and fishermen die every year, in most cases only a few lives are lost at a time. Someone falls or is washed overboard or gets trapped below the deck of a sinking ship. Or perhaps in a particularly bad accident, three or four succumb to the elements and do not survive the rescue attempt. But even the worst stories end with the saving of a few, if not many, lives. That is because ships tend to sink slowly, developing a problem that is at least detected early, giving a crew time to call for help, work on the problem, maybe even arrest it and in the process buy more time. Even when a ship is lost, there is time to prepare for the worst. The *Arctic Rose*, it seemed, had virtually none. The loss of life was high because of the number of people required to run the ship. The boat needed extra hands to process the fish it caught. While not the smallest boat in the Bering, the *Arctic Rose* was a relatively small vessel with an inordinately high number of crewmen who fished far from shore. That is the burden of the head-and-gut fleet.

Head-and-gut boats are anomalies of the fishing industry, small boats that do the work of big boats. Boats that do similar work can be as big as tankers. And boats of comparable size usually catch fish but do not process them, staying close to shore for frequent unloading. These catcher boats deliver fish to shore plants or in some cases mother ships that process the product. Small boats generally do not go very far out or stay out long and do not require large crews. Crab boats, dangerous in their own right, typically require a crew of six or seven to set and retrieve crab pots. No processing is done on board. Once full of live crab, these boats return to port to sell their catch. Fishing boats generally do not require large crews unless they intend to process fish at sea. Such work is the domain of factory trawlers. They are the backbone of the Bering Sea fishing industry. These are giant ships with cafeterias, big-screen televisions, Jacuzzi tubs, and a crew of dozens. Some fish. Some just serve food. They are floating cities and among the safest vessels working in the Bering. Most of the growth of the U.S. fishing industry over the last twenty years can be attributed to factory trawlers.

The crew of the *Arctic Rose*, it can be argued, had to do the same work as the crew of a factory processor, but with a much smaller boat and a much slimmer margin for error. Half of her crew ran machines and cut fish and put them in freezers. They were not fishermen, they were factory workers whose factory happened to be fastened on the deck of a ninety-two-foot boat in the Bering Sea. They were not so much seamen as passengers, a liability on a four-month fishing trip. That being said, the fleet to which the *Arctic Rose* belonged had a relatively good safety record. No head-and-gut boat had ever sunk before. No one, it seemed, really expected accidents on the scale of the *Arctic Rose* to happen anymore.

Regulations requiring lifesaving equipment on commercial fishing vessels had been in effect for the past ten years and seemed to be saving lives. During that period, an average of seventeen fishermen have died every year fishing in Alaska. And the number of deaths had been dropping. In 2000, only seven fishermen died. Still, fishing remains the most dangerous job in America. A fisherman is about ten times more likely to die on the job than a policeman or fireman, according to the Bureau of Labor Statistics.

Fishermen are humbly comfortable about the risk of dying. Fishing, they know, is dangerous enough that they all can tell of a friend or acquaintance who died at sea. And most can recall at least one incident in which they faced the possibility of death. Statistics show that fishing is in fact safe enough that, although death is not uncommon, one can reasonably expect to survive: A 1998 report by the Bureau of Labor Statistics calculated that a fisherman in America has a 99.86 percent chance of completing a year of fishing without fatal injury. The chances of surviving a forty-five-year career of fishing is 93.89 percent. Those odds are somewhat worse in Alaska, where most of the country's fishermen die. Between 1992 and 1996, Alaska accounted for 112 fatalities, or 29 percent of all fishing-related deaths in the United States, almost four times the number of deaths in Massachusetts and Texas, which tied for second. While the Coast Guard reports that the number of fishing-related deaths in Alaskan waters has decreased, this does not necessarily mean fishing itself has become safer; it is more the result of the decrease in numbers of fishermen as the industry contracts and consolidates. In 1995, fishermen died at a rate of 104 per 100,000, the highest of all professions. The rate reached an all-time high of 178 per 100,000 in 1996. In 1999, the rate fell to 162.5 deaths, for a yearly average of 140 since 1992. The bottom line is that fishing remains the deadliest job in America despite the fact that the past ten years have been the most regulated in the history of U.S. fishing. The leading cause of death on the seas is vessel sinkings, followed by wave action and diving underwater to untangle nets or lines.

Until 1991, boats were not required to keep lifesaving equipment aboard. The change in fishing regulations was largely the result of the death of one young fisherman whose father happened to be a well-placed diplomat in Washington, D.C.

In 1985, a seventy-five-year-old purse seiner called the *Western Sea* departed Kodiak island with a six-man crew to fish for salmon. Like the *Arctic Rose*, it sank with no warning. Back then, emergency beacons were not required equipment, so no one even realized the vessel was missing until the body of one of the crew, Peter Barry, was found by fishermen. Barry happened to be the son of Robert Barry, a U.S. ambassador who was then head of the U.S. delegation to the East-West conference on disarmament in Europe. His influence helped persuade Congress to introduce three bills in 1986, which among other things made lifesaving equipment mandatory aboard commercial fishing vessels. The Commercial Fishing Industry Vessel Safety Act was finally signed into law in 1988, the year the *Arctic Rose* was built, requiring life rafts, survival suits, beacons, and firefighting equipment aboard all vessels. It went into effect three years later.

A recent Coast Guard report questioned the value of the 1988 act. Prompted by a spate of sinkings within a three-week period in early

1999, in which eleven died, the Coast Guard assembled a task force to determine whether or not fishing had actually become safer. Its conclusion was less than reassuring. In his report, called "Living to Fish Dying to Fish," Capt. James Spitzer wrote that the "level of fishing vessel safety standards is analogous to requiring parachutes for an airplane crew, but only marketing voluntary measures to encourage a mechanically sound aircraft and a competent pilot and crew." The 1988 act, Spitzer wrote, "focuses on surviving a casualty rather than preventing one."

News of the mysterious sinking of the *Arctic Rose* and the presumed deaths of her crew incubated slowly but was disseminated by most major U.S. news outlets. It was neither initially nor eventually the biggest story of the week, because one day before the sinking a U.S. Navy spy plane collided over China with a Chinese jet fighter sent to intercept it. The plane landed safely, but its crew of twenty four, which coincidentally was based at the Whidbey Island Naval Air Station near Seattle, was detained by the Chinese for several days. Sadly, it is not a shocking or even surprising story when a fishing boat sinks in the Bering Sea. In the grand scheme of things, the end of the *Arctic Rose* was a minor industrial accident that occurred too far off the grid. Television cameras did not broadcast live images of the search. That far out, a news broadcast would have been a nearly impossible technological and logistical feat. The sinking was not attached to a larger event like an epochal storm or a violent collision involving vessels of competing superpowers. There were no survivors or witnesses to help tell the story. The men aboard were not famous or influential. The *New York Times* and *Newsweek* ran stories about the sinking. So did the *Washington Post*, albeit weeks later. The media was slow to digest the story of the *Arctic Rose*, treating it as more novelty than news, a story that appealed to a natural fetish for disasters on the high seas. The ABC news program *PrimeTime* set out to produce a segment on the *Arctic Rose*. CNN commissioned a documentary for its series *CNN Presents*. All would air about a year after the fact, owing in part to the media vacuum created by the Sept. 11 attack on New York and Washington. By far, the story received the most coverage by the Seattle media.

Perhaps more than any other city in the United States, Seattle and its fortunes are tied to the sea and the lands beyond it. Seattle and Washington State earn more money per capita from foreign trade than any other state, almost $6,000 in 2002. Few other states even come close. An estimated one out of every three jobs in Washington State is tied to foreign trade, responsible for about $35 billion in exports a year. Seafood is but one of those exports. Eight of the crew of the *Arctic Rose* came from or had family ties to the Seattle area, where most of the Alaskan fishing industry is headquartered, even though the boats work primarily out of Dutch Harbor, Alaska, in the Aleutian Islands. The natural deepwater port is where boats receive fuel and deliver fish and where a vast amount of fish is processed. Its airport is the only one near the fishing grounds where jets can land. There, minor repairs can be made to boats and men. And between rounds of fishing at the edge of the earth, the port is a semblance of civilization, an artifice of a gentle suburban life. Out of the fog and the ice comes a chapel, a supermarket, a museum, a library, a schoolhouse, and a softball field. But the fishing industry's true infrastructure, its banks, insurance brokers, naval architects, shipyards, suppliers, and lawyers, is located in Seattle, as is the industry's most important resource, fishermen.

More often they come from the towns around Seattle, the flannel belt communities that seem to have little to do anymore with the Seattle of popular imagination, places like Roy and Spanaway and Arlington, in the woodsy extremities of the concentration of cities and towns known as the Puget Sound region. Men who fished once lived in the city before a critical mass of California money and Ivy League degrees raised the price of the ante and transformed Seattle. It happened sometime in the last ten or twenty years. Local rituals like Seafair, the maritime-themed festival held every summer, became less relevant. A community of one sensibility splintered into several, each one indifferent to the next. Outsiders began to dictate fashion and custom. A local boy named Bill Gates dropped out of Harvard and started a software company. Barney's and Tiffany opened stores downtown. Laboring men could no longer afford homes within the city limits. The clock punchers were replaced by stock option types with fetishes for bookstores, granite countertops, and shade-grown coffee. Like many cities, Seattle was drained of its middle class, transformed into a city of poor and rich, of servants and intellectual and creative elites. Families gave way to childless professionals. According to the *Seattle Times*, the city has about the same population it had in 1960 but about half as many children, a correlative effect of the boutique-ification of Seattle. The laboring men moved north and south mostly. Soon Tacoma resembled Seattle more than Seattle. It was no coincidence that a large chunk of the *Arctic Rose* crew came from Pierce County, where Tacoma is located, and Thurston County to the south.

Rundall grew up in the Seattle of old, in the neighborhood of West Seattle, a hilly, windswept community of beautiful vistas at its waterside edges, but very ordinary looking in the gully blocks near its center, like the precinct of Delridge where Rundall's parents, David and Lou Anne, still lived. Their son, at age five, caught his first fish, a salmon, from the Duwamish River, which passes through many of the city's industrial lots. Once a peaceful slough that was home to shellfish and marsh birds and a passageway for spawning salmon, it has become the final destination of storm drains and sewer overflow. When salmon spawn, they do not eat. Their appetite vanishes, as they spend their energy on the single-minded mission of reaching the spawning grounds. So using bait is useless. However, the spawning salmon are easily agitated and will bite at anything that irritates them, like a spinning lure. The twenty-pound salmon was a marlin to the forty-five-pound boy. Salmon are fighting fish, charging and thrashing until the bitter end and more than capable of ripping a rod and reel from a youngster's grip. The fish might even be able to yank a small boy over the edge of the boat. His father gave him only this advice: "Don't let go of the pole!" Davey didn't. He didn't whimper or speak or smile but focused only on the pole. The elder Rundall loosened the drag on the reel and held his boy tight. After fifteen minutes, the courageous fish tired and the boy had landed his first big one.

Though the 1980s and 1990s were the time of Seattle's cultural and commercial ascension, the city's proximity to nature remained its defining quality, a metropolis of creeping, flowering vines, ringed by jagged volcanoes, ancient forests of giant cedars and firs, and, all around it, the water. Seattle is bounded and severed by lakes, waterways, and bays. A great number of Seattle's boys, for this reason, grew up to work in shipyards, lumber mills, and fishing boats, more than those who became software engineers, Internet entrepreneurs, or rock stars.

David Olney's only brother, Mike Olney, forty-six, was a pipefitter at the Todd Pacific Shipyard. The shipyard was a giant place, taking up all twenty-six acres of Harbor Island in the middle of Seattle's Elliott Bay, not far from where Rundall caught his kindergarten salmon. The kind of work done at Todd is of a mammoth scale, like repairing aircraft carriers or building the giant automobile ferries that make up Seattle's commuter ferry system, the nation's largest. But the work was unreliable, and slow economic cycles meant fewer jobs. Layoffs caused Mike to turn to his brother, David, for work aboard his boats. Working for his older brother was better than collecting unemployment.

Much of the money made fishing Alaska ends up back in Seattle or Washington State somehow. And it was the same for the *Arctic Rose*. The cook, Ken Kivlin, and deckhand Eddie Haynes, both consummate wanderers who have lived all over the country, were looking to settle down in the area, where Kivlin's grown son and Haynes's mother and sister lived. Kivlin wanted to open his own restaurant and brewery in the city and run it as a family concern. He would cook. His son could make the beer and keep the books. He dreamed of buying a large lot with trees and a meadow, perhaps near the water on the Kitsap Peninsula, across the bay from Seattle. There he would plant a double-wide trailer, the family's own Shangri-la. Haynes, thirty-nine, had less ambitious plans. He said he wanted to use his fishing money to pay for tuition at a vocational school in Seattle, where he would learn how to repair computers. Whatever he had left, he would spend on renovating his mother Rose's basement into a small apartment where he could live. He was a talented mason, carpenter, and craftsman who could build anything from a patio to a guitar.

Jeff Meincke, Jimmie Conrad, and G. W. Kandris were connected by overlapping circles of co-workers, siblings, and girlfriends. They lived near Tacoma and Olympia, the state capital. Three days before the *Arctic Rose* departed, Meincke rented a room at the Ameritel Inn in Lacey and threw a small party, which Conrad and Broderick attended. They swam in the pool, jumped on the beds, had a pillow fight, soaked in a hot tub, watched pay-per-view movies, and stayed up most of the night. It seemed an auspicious start to a winter of fishing. Meincke had been naïve about what lay ahead. He had brought his snowboard and encouraged Conrad to do the same. When exactly they had intended to use them was not clear. It was probably just part of some dreamy notion of what an adventure in Alaska should include. Their travels took them nowhere near a ski resort and afforded little time for frivolous excursions. Furthermore, the boards took up valuable space belowdecks, where there was barely enough room to turn one's head. Shortly after hearing about the sinking, Conrad's girlfriend, Christina, in a fit of delirium and a desperate wish, opined that Jimmie and Jeff had used their snowboards to save themselves and were riding waves to a safe shore.

"That is the most stupid thing I've ever heard," Jessica told her. And unable to witness Christina's bout of denial any longer, Jessica left for the company of Jeff's family, with whom she spent a lot of time in the days after the sinking. Although she had known Jeff for only a few months before he went to Alaska, she felt close to his family. She did not yet know just how close she had come to becoming part of them.

When she arrived at his family's home, his sister Jennifer was there. So was Jeff's best friend, Jeremy Busby. His other sister, Jana, was on her way from the airport. Jessica and Jennifer exchanged glances, and Jennifer walked over.

"I'm sorry for being distant earlier today," Jennifer said.

"Don't apologize," Jessica said. "You're going through it, too. He's your brother."

"I shouldn't be mean to the girl that Jeff was going to ask to marry."

Jessica's silence and stunned expression conveyed her surprise.

"You didn't know?" Jennifer asked.

Jessica looked at Jeremy, who simply nodded. And again Jessica broke down in tears. She sat shaking as Jeremy revealed that Jeff had told everyone he had planned to propose when he got back. He was trying to surprise her. In that, he had succeeded.

Jeff was her first love. Her parents bought him Christmas presents. Never before had they made this gesture for a boyfriend. As sad as she was, she was angry, too. Angry that he had gone to Alaska, angry that no one saved him, angry that he hadn't instead gotten that job on the caviar barge, which would have been much safer, angry that he had loved her and then left her. Sometimes it seemed he was still there somehow, because they never found his body and no one saw him die. They had simply said good-bye and promised to see each other in May. May had not yet arrived. So she could still pretend. He was, in some form, still very much around her. His phone number was still a reflex of her fingers, his voice still alive in the audiotape of her mind. She had kept some of his things, his CDs, his cell phone, and his black Billabong sweatshirt. Huge when she wore it, it came down to her knees. Because she wanted them to, every song on the radio reminded her of him. On April 4, while she was at work at the pizza parlor, the last batch of his letters arrived at her house.

"I didn't want to open those letters," Jessica said. "I didn't want to know what was going on, on that boat. I forgot I had those letters coming. My dad called me and said his letters came today. I was so upset, I got sent home from work again. I waited until the night, until I was by myself, so I could cry by myself, because I knew that I would. I didn't want anybody around, not even my parents."

She read his letters and got angry again. He had not told her exactly how dangerous the work was. But now here it was, written in his own words. She wished he had never told her. On March 26, 2001, he wrote:

Dear Princess. Haven't said that for a while. Well things are still shitty. It's a never ending roller coaster, up and down, back and forth. This storm just won't quit. It's been three or four days and all we have is half a freezer. This trip is sucking my will to live. I've had way too much down time. All we do is watch movies and wait till the morning to break ice. I've got the fun job of breaking the ice on the wheel house. There's about three inches of ice and no one else will go up there. In this weather, you just slide around the roof. I almost fell off the boat but I grabbed a light before I went all the way over. Don't worry we weren't going that fast so they could have picked me up quickly. And the weather isn't that bad. It's just bad enough where we can't set our net. Well anyways, there's absolutely nothing going on, on this Savage Rose. We're going to paint our motto on the side soon, "if it makes sense we don't do it." Ha ha . . . The moment I step off the plane it will be the best moment I've had in four months. I miss you so much. Not much longer honey. Love, Jeff.

The loss of the *Arctic Rose* created a gravity in the industry not felt since the sinking of the A-boats in 1983. The *Americus* and *Altair* were identical crab boats, designed by the same architect, built in the same Anacortes shipyard, and owned by the same man. The sister boats both sank within hours of each other on Valentine's Day, in calm waters near Dutch Harbor, killing a total of fourteen. The casualties were especially devastating because all the fishermen were from the same small town of Anacortes, Washington, on the northern tip of Whidbey Island in Puget Sound. Many were related. Thousands attended a prayer vigil for the crew of the *Altair* in downtown Anacortes, as another memorial service was being planned for the crew of the *Americus* at the town's high school. The sinking of the A-boats, known by their initials, was also a mystery. The boats were state-of-the-art vessels, designed by reputable, experienced shipbuilders. Those boats also sank without a prior call for help and left no survivors. But investigators had more clues, as well as complete blueprints. And they had full access to a third boat identical to the two that sank. The builder was still in business near Seattle. Investigators determined with certainty that the A-boats had been mistakenly loaded with more weight than they could safely bear.

With the *Arctic Rose*, the Coast Guard had an even bigger challenge. The lost boat had no stand-ins, no sister boat (the *Alaskan Rose* was a sister vessel only in spirit, as she was structurally unrelated), and no blueprints. Her builder would be nearly impossible to locate. Because of the great loss of life, and the national media attention, the Coast Guard convened a Marine Board of Investigation, reserved for only the worst accidents at sea. Several officers are appointed to the board, which conducts a formal investigation. The investigation into the sinking of the *Arctic Rose* would eventually become the Coast Guard's costliest ever for an accident involving a fishing boat.

Lieutenant Jim Robertson, the Anchorage office's senior investigator, was put on the board, along with Commander John Bingaman from District 17 headquarters in Juneau and Captain Ronald Morris, who headed the Marine Safety Office in New Orleans. Bingaman is a 1984 graduate of the Coast Guard Academy. He spent his first sea duty aboard an icebreaker in the North Atlantic. Assignments took him to Puerto Rico, South Carolina, and Juneau. While in the Coast Guard he earned an M.B.A. at the University of Maine. Morris enlisted in the Coast Guard in 1972 as a college student and moved from one Marine Safety Office to another, from Buffalo to New Orleans. Morris was named chairman of the investigative board. The chairmanship would normally have gone to the captain in charge of the Juneau office, but he was due to retire soon, so Morris got the assignment. They were teamed with a representative from the National Transportation Safety Board (NTSB), Robert Ford. The board was formed within one week of the sinking.

When the news of the *Arctic Rose* hit the Coast Guard's Marine Safety Office in Anchorage, a controlled frenzy took over. The office is on the ground floor of a glass building in downtown Anchorage, with a clear view across the water of Knik Arm. Anchorage is the only place in Alaska that has mimicked the conventions of the mainland, with indoor malls, highway interchanges, and enough traffic and sprawl that locals have come to call it Los Anchorage. It is a hub of civilization for the state's outer communities that must come to Anchorage for appendectomies, graduate degrees, or a flight to Hawaii. But by mainland standards, the city is a homely outpost, small and drab, its structures built low and without flair, whimsy, or optimism. Most of downtown Anchorage was severely damaged after Alaska's great Good Friday earthquake of 1964. What Anchorage does have are spectacular views and access to incredible wilderness, thousands of rivers, millions of lakes, and glacier-fed valleys. For that reason, it is a coveted post in the Coast Guard.

It is where Lieutenant Robertson had spent most of his career. He received his first reports of the search in the form of e-mails that began coming in at 10:00 a.m. on April 2. His world changed significantly.

"It was very clear to me, right away, that this was not going to be a normal week or a normal month," Robertson said. "What I did not realize is that the next two years were not going to be normal. I had an immediate sense this case was going to be very important. Not to sound morbid, but there was also a sense of excitement. When you're given that kind of a challenge, if you're not excited about doing this, you're the wrong person for this investigation . . . It's a commitment."

The investigation of his life did not come at an opportune time for Robertson, then thirty-seven, the youngest member of the board and the one who would be chiefly responsible for drafting the report. When the *Arctic Rose* sank, Robertson's wife was four months pregnant, their baby due in September. Both previously married, he and his wife had brought one child each into the marriage. This would be their first together.

"I knew what a daunting task this was," Robertson said, "but I had no clue just how overwhelming and consuming the investigation would be. I was very fortunate to have an understanding wife and family, who allowed me to disappear and be gone for months at a time."

For most of the rest of the year, from April to the end of November, Robertson was home for only about sixty days.

On top of Robertson's bookshelf at his desk are the various remains of investigations and disasters averted, the glove compartment of his seventeen years of work as a Coast Guard investigator, where he keeps sheared bolts and shafts, rusted rivets, suspicious fuses. Among the more prominent of his keepsakes is a burst expansion joint, a thick rubber sleeve used to join two pipes. This particular expansion joint was once a working piece of the luxury cruise ship *Regent Star*, whose engine room caught fire in 1994 in Prince William Sound with 2,200 aboard. The potentially serious fire was serendipitously extinguished when this expansion joint failed, burst, and created an accidental sprinkler system in the engine room when it most needed it. It is a reminder that disaster is created and sometimes averted by the smallest detail, things you don't or can't plan for. In Robertson's drawer is something that looks like a piece of string. It was once a carrot. Robertson keeps it around to remind him of how many weeks and months sometimes pass while he is out of the office working.

With no survivors from the *Arctic Rose* to speak to, Robertson needed the next best thing, anyone who had recently been on the boat. David Olney was one, but he had already taken the advice of lawyers and declined to discuss matters related to the boat. He had retained attorneys at the Seattle firm of LeGros Buchanan & Paul, which had represented the ownership of the *Aleutian Enterprise*, which sank in 1992 and whose owners were criminally prosecuted. Anyway, Olney had not been on the boat in the weeks leading up to the sinking. As it happened, however, there was a woman, a fisheries observer named Jennifer Eichelberger, who took leave of the boat only days before it sank.

An observer's job is to work aboard fishing boats, or in some cases fish-processing plants, and monitor their catch. They weigh and tally the kinds and amounts of fish caught, taking a sort of inventory used by ecologists and marine biologists. Large boats must have an observer on board at all times. But boats the size of the *Arctic Rose* are required to have one on board only 30 percent of the time.

Eichelberger got off the *Arctic Rose* on March 21. She was the last person to walk off the boat alive. The next day, she caught a flight to Seattle for a week of meetings with fisheries officials. These meetings, known as "debriefings," during which she reported details of her assignments, were typically pleasant. While in Seattle, she stayed at a company apartment in the neighborhood of Wallingford only a few blocks from her favorite sushi restaurant. All the hours spent in the company of dead fish did not dim her appetite for the same. On March 30, she flew to Arizona to spend time with her boyfriend in Prescott. A few days later, on April 2, she got a phone call from the Coast Guard. Charlie Medlicott, the Fishing Vessel Safety program manager in Anchorage, called to confirm that she had indeed gotten off the boat and was alive. He told her the *Arctic Rose* had sunk. After a long silence, Eichelberger began to cry. Once she had regained her composure, she was asked to verify the number of crewmen on board and was asked how many life rafts were on board. Two days later, she flew back to Anchorage on her way to her next assignment. She met with Jim Robertson and was shown a list of the crew. She was asked to draw a diagram of the boat. She had remembered it well and sketched the details for Robertson. She was the first to draw attention to the discrepancies involving the men from Mexico. She said the given ages of the men didn't seem consistent and that the names seemed off. She said they spoke very little English.

"A lot of people said to me in the weeks and months after the sinking, 'Oh my God, you're the luckiest person I know,' or, 'Oh my God, if you had stayed on that boat one more trip, you'd be dead,'" Eichelberger said. "Everyone had a very dramatic reaction to it. When they saw me, they'd embrace me. But I felt completely hollow, completely empty. I lacked that feeling completely. I didn't feel in any way lucky. That was the farthest thing from how I felt. My emotions were centered on the event, thinking about each of the guys, recollecting conversations. I remember at the time thinking of contacting family members of the men on the boat, but I failed to follow through on any of those instincts. I remember in particular feeling incredible grief for Kerry's daughter. I related to her grief because I lost my father in a sudden tragic accident and I just wanted to tell her she was the center of his world."

Eichelberger understood losing a father. She was seventeen when the small plane her father was piloting crashed on takeoff. She has often been told she is most like her father, stubborn and independent, the type who prefers the itinerant life of an Alaskan observer. After the sinking, her employers offered her counseling, which she declined. They did make sure her next assignment was on a larger boat, the *Northern Glacier*. So about one week after the sinking, the same time Robertson arrived in Dutch Harbor to begin the investigation, she was on another fishing boat in the Bering Sea. She boarded the *Northern Glacier* on April 11 for a two-week trip that ended April 25. Then she went to Seattle again for a meeting with upper-level officials of the National Marine Fisheries Service (NMFS) who tried awkwardly to prepare her for the Coast Guard hearing that was sure to follow.

Eichelberger became a fisheries observer because there were few other ways for biologists to earn good salaries. She was the first member of her family simply to attend college, let alone earn a graduate degree. She is also the only one in her family who left Brown County, Illinois, where she grew up. The idea of working in Alaska was conditionally recommended to her by a colleague she had worked with in Tallahassee, Florida. The work was steady and well paid, but the working conditions were awful and the fishermen poor company, Eichelberger was told. She never envisioned it as more than a one-or two-year job, a way, in essence, of getting paid to travel in Alaska. In March 1998, out of work after having followed her boyfriend to Colorado, she trained for one month to be an observer in Alaska.

She had worked on just about every kind of factory trawler in Alaska by the time she was assigned to the *Arctic Rose*. But because she had taken more than one year off, in 2000, from fisheries work, and because she had started the 2001 season posted to a fish plant, she was again unaccustomed to working at sea. The time on land showed as she battled seasickness throughout the trip. She spent about three weeks aboard the *Arctic Rose*, enough to get to know most of the crew. When she left, she would think to herself that although the boat itself was "the crappiest" she had worked on, the job was made much more tolerable because she had gotten along with the crew and had found them on the whole likable and interesting.

"No matter how good or bad your sampling is, it's the crew that makes your trip miserable or not," Eichelberger said. "I was a little surprised that it turned out as good as it did because I had very low expectations. My first impressions were all very negative."

Observers are trained by the NMFS, an arm of the National Oceanic and Atmospheric Administration (NOAA), employed by a private staffing agency (in Eichelberger's case, Alaskan Observers), and paid, albeit indirectly, by the fishermen whom they police. Fishermen in Alaska spend about $13 million a year to pay the agencies that supply their boats with observers. The thinking is that it is better to pay for your own monitors than to face unwanted regulation down the road. And theoretically, at least, fishermen have an interest in preserving fish stocks, a goal shared by the observers.

Nonetheless, there is a natural tension between observers and fish-ermen, who feel constantly and unfairly scrutinized by scientists, environmentalists, and conservationists. Observers are neither adver-saries nor allies but are still viewed by fishermen with suspicion.

Captains of trawlers are perhaps particularly sensitive to this kind of scrutiny because their boats are thought of, even by other fisher-men, as the most gluttonous operators on the sea. Rather than surgically removing fish with hook and line, the nets of trawlers devour without discrimination, sweeping the sea bottom clear of life. The pollock fishery has been blamed by some for the dramatic reduction in the Steller sea lion population in the Bering. In the last twenty years, their numbers have dropped 80 percent. Some scientists say the drop is due to natural fluctuations of climate and habitat. Some speculate that killer whales, not so much the factory trawlers, are doing in the sea lions. In a study published in 2003, scientists theorized that commercial whaling in the Bering and North Pacific, outlawed in the 1970s, is indirectly responsible for the drop in the sea lion population. Because the giant humpback, sperm, and bowhead whales were hunted to small numbers after World War II, the study concluded, pods of killer whales turned to other, smaller sources of food, eating sea lions, seals, and sea otters. In turn, the drop in the otter population led to an increase in the urchin population, a big part of the otter diet. At the same time, killer whale populations are thriving. Whatever the cause, scientists agree that any mass extraction of sea life will usually lead to a change in the food chain that might not show up for years. In general, no one can prove fishing stocks are down. But many fishermen feel that they are, and the trawlers are easy scapegoats. Fishing industry executives claim the Bering fishery is extremely well managed, which it is. But conserva-tionists continue to insist that sea life in the Bering is in grave jeopardy. The rift is predictable and not particularly interesting. The truth most likely falls somewhere in between. A consequential number of fish are removed from the Bering every year. But depletion is not imminent. The industry has many safeguards to protect the supply of fish. But it is also probably disingenuous to suggest fishermen are thoughtful and conscientious protectors of the sea just because their livings depend on it. Perhaps some captains have achieved a holy communion with the sea. Some may plan or hope to fish their entire lives. But fishermen are opportunists at heart. And like all the other opportunists who came to Alaska before them, they are here to take what they can, while they can, and before everyone else does the same. They might hope it lasts forever. But more important, they are in it for the here and now. Next year is for retiring in Mexico.

An observer certainly has more formal education than the average fisherman and probably a more nuanced view of marine conservation, but even an observer's motivations are not pure. Honest observers will tell you they like the quick money and the free time their jobs provide. They work hard in the winter and spend the rest of the year traveling. While they are counting cod, they too are probably day-dreaming about a hammock in Belize. In that respect, they are not so different from fishermen.

Observers in Alaska generally prefer to work in shore plants or aboard large factory trawlers, which provide the most comfortable working conditions. In both cases, two observers each work twelve-hour shifts. The job of counting and cataloging is easier on factory trawlers, as they tend to catch pollock and little else, leaving very little by-catch (incidental catch they are not allowed to keep) to keep track of. Living quarters are more comfortable, and the food better, on large ships. Shore plants have the obvious advantage of being on land. Eichelberger, then thirty, had spent most of the winter of 2001 at the Westward Seafoods plant in Dutch Harbor, living in a company dormitory. Two months into the assignment, she began to wonder if she would be lucky enough to spend the entire season on land, a scenario she knew by experience to be unlikely. As she suspected, she was told at the end of February that she would be leaving the plant and assigned to a head-and-gut trawler, just about the worst kind of assignment an observer can get.

Head-and-gut boats tend to be smaller, and their method of fishing produces lots of by-catch to keep track of. The by-catch also creates a greater potential for conflict between a captain and an observer. The ride on smaller boats is rougher, making the workspace even more uncomfortable. And because observers work alone, sleep is irregular and hard to come by. When she saw the *Arctic Rose* for the first time, Eichelberger's first reaction was, "You've got to be kidding me."

Only one observer has died working in Alaska, in 1992, aboard the *Aleutian Enterprise*. Eichelberger's boss, Michael Lake, knows David Olney well. Lake is a former fisherman who quit in 1987 to start the observers agency. He described Olney as a hard worker, "a good and honest man . . . salt of the earth.

"I talked to Dave when I heard about the *Arctic Rose*," Lake said. "The first thing he said to me was, 'Thank God we didn't have an observer on board.' I told him, 'That's just like you, Dave.'"

Jim Robertson arrived in Dutch Harbor on April 10, wearing his full dress uniform. He had approximately two months to gather information and secure witnesses for a hearing scheduled in June, in Seattle. Dutch Harbor, because of its proximity to the fishing grounds and to the Pacific shipping routes, is the busiest fishing port in North America. The industry has made Dutch Harbor and its accompanying town of Unalaska the most populous community in the Aleutian Islands. Robertson got off the plane and started knocking on doors, starting with the row of businesses on the main road leading to the airport. Most had never heard of the *Arctic Rose*. Others remembered doing business with its crew, but further conversation revealed the transactions as forgettable and inconsequential. Robertson estimated he visited forty businesses in Dutch Harbor, speaking to an average of two people at each business for at least five minutes each. He was particularly interested in finding anyone who had recently worked aboard the *Arctic Rose*.

It did not take much time for Robertson to discover that a young processor named Nathan Miller had worked on the *Arctic Rose* earlier that winter and that he was now part of the crew of a crab boat named the *Shishaldin*, which was still out at sea when Robertson first arrived.

"Mr. Miller is a very private person, and he made sure he was protected by a circle of friends," Roberston said. "We had to assure these people we were not out to arrest him, that we just wanted to ask him questions."

Miller, twenty-five, was fiercely self-possessed—to the point, some would say, of paranoia. He had a prickly disposition but could be equally as engaging. He grew up in Livonia, Michigan, and attended Asbury College, near Lexington, Kentucky, for a few years before dropping out to live the life of a dilettante. He worked as a carpenter, chauffeur, nanny, bartender, martial arts instructor, smoke jumper, cowboy, knot-tying instructor, house painter, and, in the winter of 2001, fisherman. The *Arctic Rose* was his first boat. He made $1,587 for about six weeks of work. Hired as a processor, he was, more than anyone on the boat, shocked by the smallness of the factory space. He had been warned the *Arctic Rose* was not a moneymaking boat, but about this he seemed unconcerned. The job was more of an adventure for him. He was what some fishermen called a "Discovery boy," novices lured to Alaska by glamorous documentaries like those on the Discovery Channel. Miller was comfortable enough with the label.

When the *Shishaldin* came into port, Miller warily returned a message left by Robertson. After a short conversation on the telephone, Miller and Robertson agreed to meet in the public library in Unalaska, a setting Robertson supposed Miller would find the least threatening. Robert Ford of the NTSB also joined the meeting, which was held in a private room at the library. Miller appeared leery and nervous, aware that as someone who spent part of the season aboard the *Arctic Rose*, he was a unique source of information. While Robertson wore a uniform, Ford wore jeans and boots and posed a fatherly presence to Miller, who seemed more comfortable with him and began to open up. What he had to say got the attention of his questioners. He painted a picture of poor morale and questionable attention to safety, although it was hard to tell at the time exactly how relevant his information was. He seemed credible and sincere. Miller's testimony at the hearings in Seattle would later be judged as revealing by some, colored and unreliable by others. He met with Ford and Robertson twice in Dutch Harbor, promising to appear at the hearing in Seattle in June. Among the information Miller provided was that yet another crewman left the *Arctic Rose* before it sank, a burly man with a thick accent whom everyone knew simply as "Big Mike." For nearly two months, Big Mike was the boat's chief engineer.

Not fond of the captain and hopeful of a better-paying job working on a Russian vessel, he had left the *Arctic Rose* at the end of February when the boat off-loaded in Dutch Harbor, the same time Miller and the owner, David Olney, departed and a few days before Kerry Egan joined the crew. In his search for the engineer, Robertson had only a general physical description and the vague-sounding nickname, which he hoped was at least his actual first name. It was not. He found no one in Dutch Harbor matching the description.

He continued his search for Big Mike one week later in Seattle, where he joined Bingaman, who had already begun interviewing potential witnesses. The fishing community in Seattle is relatively small and its regulars well known. A few hours on the docks yielded a full name, Milosh Katurich, which they felt sure belonged to the man known as Big Mike. With it, Robertson found former employers and acquaintances, all of whom promised to put out the word that the Coast Guard was looking for Katurich. Little did Robertson know that Katurich spent most of every day sitting on the same street corner in front of a coffee shop in the Seattle neighborhood of Ballard, where much of the fishing industry is based.

"Lo and behold, he called us," Robertson said. "We didn't know what we were getting into."

Robertson and Bingaman arranged to meet Katurich on a cool, breezy Sunday morning at his favorite haunt, Tully's, a local chain of coffee shops modeled after Starbucks. Tully's general business strategy was to open up a shop across the street from every Starbucks, a strategy that worked well enough to get the attention of executives at Starbucks. Tully's did innovate the practice of putting living room furniture in its stores; soon, Starbucks did the same. But Katurich rarely made use of the comfortable furnishings inside. He was a chain smoker and sat outside on a metal chair, no matter what the weather, to indulge his habit. While Ballard is still a neighborhood of old salts and a few moldy bars, gentrification has overwhelmed the local habitat, creating a cultural tension in places where the old-timers mix with the new arrivals. At Tully's, young, affluent couples with their expensive baby strollers pass the old drunks sitting outside. The scene is but one symptom of the changing Seattle, an allegory of fishing and its shifting place in the city's culture. Bingaman and Robertson waited inside for Katurich, who stood out from the usual crowd of graduate student types who sat in the store's leather club chairs. Before long, the effects of thirty years of working in engine rooms became apparent. Hard of hearing, Katurich spoke loudly.

"He's getting louder and louder and using very colorful language," Robertson remembered. "I'm guessing he must have 50 percent hearing loss. People are filling up the place, there's more background noise, he gets louder as he talks, and he's getting excited, using more and more colorful language. By now he's dropping the F-bomb every third word. This is a Sunday morning, and there are families with kids in the place. After about an hour, the place has cleared out. We figured we needed to take the conversation outside, which he was happy about because he wanted to smoke. We sat outside for ninety minutes, but we didn't have jackets and had had enough of the cool weather, so we moved back inside. I guess we didn't expect such a colorful character."

Milosh Katurich was the son of a shepherd from Montenegro, Yugoslavia. It turned out he lived in Ballard, not much more than a mile from Fishermen's Terminal, paying $250 for his half of a two-bedroom apartment. His nickname, Big Mike, spoke to his girth, not his height, a modest five feet eight. He appeared taller because he had large shoulders and a thick chest and neck. When he sneered, he resembled Robert De Niro. When amused, he resembled Buddy Hackett.

Violent death was part of his family history. He was named after an uncle who died at age eighteen after he was gored by a bull. Katurich's grandfather married several times, beating one of his wives to death over a suspected infidelity. Katurich's older brother, Uglyesha, died in 1958 at age twenty-six on a ship crossing the Black Sea. The family never found out why. They were told only that he had been drinking.

Born in 1948, Katurich graduated from a maritime college in Yugoslavia at age twenty-one, working on ships that supplied oil rigs in the North Sea. American companies based in the South are heavily invested in the North Sea, so it was not long before Katurich found himself working in the Gulf of Mexico. He worked on freighters, tugboats, and other supply ships. He first glimpsed Alaska in 1986 when his Gulf-based company was contracted to transport jet fuel from Vancouver, Washington, to Kodiak and Dutch Harbor. Along the way, he was plied with stories of jobs on fishing boats, jobs that could earn an experienced engineer like himself up to $15,000 a month, triple what he was making. The pollock boom was well under way in Alaska, and such salaries were not necessarily exaggerations. After delivering the fuel, he flew to Seattle in the summer of 1986, as he tells it, with two duffel bags and checked into a motel under the Ballard Bridge. He found his first job, aboard another tugboat, from a phone book he borrowed from a barkeep at the Valhalla Tavern. That job, and another as a mechanic at a Seattle seafood plant, kept him employed until the crab season opened in January. His first fishing job was, coincidentally, on the *Shishaldin*, the same crab boat that now employed Nathan Miller. After the job ended, he flew back to New Orleans, where he had been living, sold and gave away most of what he had left behind, and moved permanently to Seattle. The next year, he was sworn in as an American citizen.

He never married, a fact he blames on arriving in America at age thirty-four, too old in his estimation to truly assimilate. He was, he believed, too long on the vine and too set in his ways to be loved or to find love. He would return to Yugoslavia only a few times for heartbreaking visits he will talk very little about, except to say he contemplated suicide after his most recent visit in 1997. His ease toward drinking and his taste for cocaine "made a mess of my life," he said, and led to ten months in jail. By the time his one-year probation ended in December 2000, he had lost his engineer's license, all his savings, and the deed to his condominium in the north Seattle neighborhood of Greenwood. He was desperate for work and considered it a great stroke of luck that his employment agency found him a job within a few weeks aboard a fishing boat called the *Arctic Rose*. He did not think much of the boat, but until he could reinstate his license, he could not get jobs aboard bigger boats.

Katurich would prove to be a valuable witness. His skills and expertise with the mechanics of a boat were evident. He had a savantlike facility for remembering dates. He was not necessarily an honest man, as much as being convicted of a crime excludes one from that category, but he was a very truthful man, forthcoming about the facts of the boat, about his life, his mistakes, about everything. He had nothing to protect anymore. People who lie tend to have something to lose. Of this particular commodity, Milosh Katurich had very little.

Within a month of the sinking, Robertson and Bingaman had assembled a list of about fifty witnesses who had all promised to testify, either at a hearing in June in Seattle, or at one later in the summer in Anchorage. It included former crewmen of the *Arctic Rose* as well as crew members of the *Alaskan Rose*, all twenty-seven of whom Robertson had interviewed on a second trip to Dutch Harbor in May. Naval architects, welders, surveyors, and meteorologists were among the experts asked to testify. But already some unsettling revelations had become public and sprouted into amateur speculation about the cause of the sinking. Much of it focused on the propeller shaft. It was well known that overheating of the shaft and shaft bearings had delayed the start of the trip in January. Now stories circulated that it led to the sinking, that it might have broken, or that the seal around the shaft disintegrated, allowing water to flood the engine room. For obvious reasons, Katurich was questioned thoroughly on the subject by investigators.

Another troubling revelation was the boat's origins. The *Arctic Rose* was built without blueprints by a Vietnamese fisherman on a rented piece of beachfront in Biloxi, Mississippi. No one could locate the builder. Constructing a boat freehand was a common practice among Vietnamese immigrants and grudgingly accepted among the community of established builders and fishermen in the Gulf. It was simply the result of the changing dynamics of the industry. After the end of the Vietnam War, shrimping became the favored enterprise of thousands of Vietnamese who immigrated to Texas, Louisiana, and Mississippi. Many had earned their living in Vietnam by catching shrimp. And many had experience building fishing boats or were quick to learn. Some established boatbuilders conceded that some of the Vietnamese-built boats were as good as those built by established builders. But the Vietnamese builders were also known to cut corners in construction—for example, using lighter welding rods to fasten the seams of the hull. And some wondered just how strong some of those welds were. Had the rigorous conditions of the Bering caused a seam to burst? If so, the resulting flooding would have been catastrophic. In any case, why was a boat designed to work the relatively shallow and gentle waters of the Gulf of Mexico trawling in the Bering Sea? The answer would prove complex, but the implications sounded serious, perhaps reckless, and, to some, downright criminal.

"That isn't the kind of fishing they should have been doing," said Kathy Meincke, Jeff's mother. "They were trying to make money, pushing it, they made so many modifications . . . I know someday I've got to forgive him. But not today. As far as I'm concerned, David Olney murdered my son."

Jeff's death was the end of so many things, the least of which was the Meincke name. He was the only male Meincke of his generation and the only hope of continuing his father's family name. The job Jeff accepted was a deception, the contract he signed a con, the Meinckes believed, the empty promise of money and adventure aboard a boat and in conditions Jeff had no ability to imagine. He knew nothing of labor statistics and safety regulations, or how to judge a boat's stability and seaworthiness, or what true risks he would be taking for what amounted to much less money than he expected. He didn't know a Gulf boat from a Bering boat. Fishing was just a phase for Jeff, one his family was sure had ended. In his letters and phone calls, he showed no enthusiasm for it anymore.

"He was trying to find himself," David Meincke said. "To him, fishing looked real romantic. You don't realize you're just waiting a lot. He liked being outside, working hard. He talked a lot about working hard and building his muscles. But the reality was, it was cold up there, they weren't catching any fish, and he was bored a lot of the time. I don't think he had any idea how bad it could be. But he would've stuck it out. It's not Jeff's nature to complain. If he started something, he was going to finish it. We didn't like it, but we decided he was an adult and could do his own thing. If we had known what actually goes on . . ."

The Meinckes met David Olney for the first time one month after the sinking, at a memorial service for the crew. With her husband trailing slightly behind, Kathy approached Olney. He backed up until it was obvious she was determined to find him. Olney seemed wary and uncomfortable when confronted but felt more at ease once he realized the Meinckes were not there to assail him. Kathy asked him if Jeff was a good worker, if people on the boat liked him. Olney said Jeff constantly asked questions, that he had to know how everything worked. Kathy recognized her son in Olney's observations. She hated Olney as he stood there but also desperately wanted something from his memory, something only he could give, a precious little part of her son. David Meincke stood by silently, letting Kathy ask the questions. She did not weep or smile over them. The answers were short and unsentimental. The conversation lasted only a few minutes. Kathy said she felt as though she were able to touch Jeff one last time. Olney stopped talking. Kathy asked no more questions. He didn't volunteer any information. They didn't say good-bye. They didn't shake hands. No one said "Thank you" or "I'm sorry." They just stopped talking and walked away.

5

Dying for Sole

Eddie Haynes steps out of his mother's car and into the weather, into a peculiar kind of cold. Seattle in January. It is not quite freezing. The air is saturated, on the verge of rain. The cold is penetrating, a submerged kind of cold, the winter air so heavy and vaporous that it steals warmth. It is the night of January 15, 2001, one day before the *Arctic Rose* is to depart for a season of fishing off Alaska. Haynes spent weeks helping prepare the boat. He walked the dock one day prospecting for a job and got one as a deckhand, on the strength of his experience as a welder in the navy. His mother, Rose Workland, waits in the car. She keeps the engine running while Haynes goes into the QFC supermarket to buy candy for his crewmates. The store is next to Key Arena, where the Seattle SuperSonics play. The parking lot is nearly empty. Haynes draws the suspicion of a security guard. He does not look like the kind of person who usually shops at this particular store, located at the bottom of Queen Anne hill, one of the city's toniest, most expensive neighborhoods. Haynes is wearing high rubber boots, dirty work clothes. His long hair is tied in a ponytail. The guard approaches him in a friendly manner in an obvious attempt to read his eyes, perhaps to thwart him from stealing, to discourage him from staying too long. Instead of taking offense or reacting defensively, Haynes greets the guard like a best friend. This is his natural reaction, not a rehearsed plan to win the trust of the guard. Haynes is sweet, indiscriminate, and guileless. He obliges the guard with some friendly chitchat and purchases ten pounds of candy. The treats are a surprise, and he can't wait to get on the boat and pass them out.

He has a few tangible dreams, which he has yet to fully realize, to be a musician, to play guitar in a band, to be a graphic artist, to design computer games. He joined the navy after high school and worked aboard a frigate that steamed across the Atlantic. He has no real roots, no plans to marry, and is a contrast to his older brother, Don, who dresses conservatively, wears his hair short, and has a stable job as a wine distributor. His older sister, Heidi, is a bookkeeper for a construction company. She and her husband have homes in Seattle and Yakima. Eddie is different. He is like a big kid who, for better or worse, never quite grew up. He assumes the best in people. He thinks things will get better. He travels the country by hitchhiking. He is tall and can look imposing, but for some reason people always pick him up. He does not keep a home or a job for any length of time. Most of the time, no one knows where Eddie is or what he is doing. Eventually, after many months, he calls or shows up. That is Eddie. He comes. And now he is going. He will be gone for about four months. At the moment, he is happy about the trip, happy around his shipmates. On the boat, which he helped put in good repair, he feels needed and valued. The men quickly come up with a nickname for Eddie. He is tall and gangly, and they too see the kid in him. He is Big Bird.

The drive to Fishermen's Terminal is short, about five minutes. The *Arctic Rose* is moored at what is called the western wall, and it is exactly that, a concrete wall that draws the western boundary of the marina. It is the terminal's longest continuous mooring. The *Arctic Rose* has spent weeks here while the crew prepared her for the season. Rose Workland is able to drive right up to the water's edge. Eddie invites her to take a closer look at the boat. She is immediately taken aback by the sight of the boat, sitting low in the water. To her, the *Arctic Rose* looks fragile and neglected, unsteady even in the still waters of the wharf. She sees more rust than she expects or is comfortable with. The boat seems covered in it, and looks very small. She wishes Eddie were working on one of the larger boats nearby.

Eddie's legs are so long, he steps with ease over the gunwale and onto the deck of the boat. He is carrying a guitar and a yellow comforter his mother insisted he take. He had relented to a haircut, too, also at his mother's insistence. They compromised. Rose cut it short in front and on the sides, leaving it long in back. But now she doesn't care about his hair or his clothes or whether or not he stays warm. Rose is worried about the boat and tells him so.

"Are you sure you want to do this?" she asks. "You know you don't have to go out on this boat."

"Don't worry, Mom," Eddie says. "Look at the name. With a name like *Rose*, I can't go wrong."

The next time Rose drove to Fishermen's Terminal, it would be for a memorial service honoring the dead crew of the *Arctic Rose*.

Fishermen's Terminal is located in the neighborhood of Ballard, a few miles north and west of downtown Seattle, joined to a canal that leads to the Puget Sound and eventually the open ocean. The terminal is the original home of Seattle's fishing industry, which began a century ago on inland waters and those off the Washington and Oregon coasts. As proximate fishing grounds were depleted of stocks, the industry moved farther north to Alaska. The Port of Seattle, which owns and operates the terminal, wants to open the place to pleasure craft, from which officials figure there is more money to be made. Fishermen want to keep it the working harbor it has always been. Fishing boats are repaired and outfitted at these docks. Even when most boats are out working, the terminal looks full, resembling a low, deciduous forest in winter, with masts, outriggers, antennae, and various polings resembling naked trunks and branches. Amid the welding and the scraping and hammering, tourists and weekenders shop at the fish market and arrive for brunch reservations at Chinook's restaurant, which has a view of the harbor. As fishermen go about their maintenance, shoppers ask about the best preparation for king salmon fillet and the price of line-caught halibut, oblivious to the real and terrible cost of Saturday dinner.

The statue nearby is of a fisherman standing in the classic pose of a Greek god, one arm hoisting a giant halibut hooked to a long line, the other arm wielding a club. His hair is swept forward by the wind so that it resembles a crown. One forearm is bare. He stands atop a twenty-foot stone pillar. Sculpted into its base are all species of sea life hunted in Alaska. The nameless fisherman stands in remembrance of the real, human fishermen killed at sea each year in Alaska. It is chiseled proof of the hazards of the profession, an unintentional and subtle warning. The bronze fisherman is hard to miss, planted by a railing in the middle of an open plaza. He is the myth, the heroic fisherman, always standing, never aging. The unchangeable facts are cast on bronze plates mounted on immovable granite a few feet away from the statue. Here are the names of dead fishermen, dating back more than one hundred years.

In October 1988, a committee of fishing industry insiders dedicated the Seattle Fishermen's Memorial. Because so few bodies of fishermen are recovered from the seas off Alaska, the committee had decided that families and fishermen needed someplace to go to mourn, a wailing wall for people bound by a different kind of faith. A board of fifteen oversees the memorial's upkeep and solicits donations to provide grief services to families and pay for safety training for fishermen. The board hosts an auction, a banquet, and a festival in the fall to raise money. The industry is so dreadfully reliable, it is never a matter of whether or not fishermen will die this year, but a matter of how many. Names of the dead, now more than five hundred, are engraved on ten vertical plaques. The names keep coming. The committee recently planted a second granite block across from the first to accommodate more plaques and names.

On the first Sunday of every May, the committee hosts a memorial service to honor the year's dead. Not all are from Seattle, but most have come from a place nearby. They worked for boats crewed out of Seattle and for companies based here, and they died somewhere off Alaska. They happen to all be men. The men of the *Arctic Rose* were remembered on the afternoon of May 6, 2001, a spring day of rare clarity. The sky was scrubbed clean. The unobstructed sun gently warmed the mourners, but a persistent breeze made sure they kept sweaters and jackets on.

Individually, the men had been eulogized by their own families, who held their own wakes and funerals. But the ceremony at Fishermen's Terminal intended to claim the men as part of something larger, a community of fishermen. Some had been a part of this community for only months. But in death, they were made part of it forever. And as part of the community, their deaths meant something more. There was, already, a sense bought into by the families and fed by news reports that the cause of the catastrophe was more than bad luck or bad weather. Surely it was the result of a fundamental flaw of the industry, evidence of its systemic disregard for safety. To believe otherwise was to believe the sinking was completely unpreventable. The cause, it would eventually be known, was complex and the result of the fatal alignment of many small and large circumstances, some preventable, some a matter of luck, some well in motion years before the men stepped aboard.

The committee arranged wreaths of flowers and set up white folding chairs in diagonal rows for the short service. As parents of the captain, David and Lou Anne Rundall greeted and comforted guests. They offered condolences and received the same. Poems were recited. The Lord's Prayer was sung. Speeches were given, filled with flowery, trite sentiments. The men knowingly worked a dangerous job and died providing for their families, one speaker said. Part of the service was recited in Spanish for the benefit of the families from Mexico. They were polite and well-meaning even if they spoke little about who the men really were. A ship's bell was rung as each dead man's name was announced. Cake was served for the departing crowd of about one hundred people. While using the restroom, Kathy Meincke heard a woman crying in the toilet stall next to her. She waited for the woman to stop crying and come out, wanting to meet and talk to her. She expected it to be a wife or perhaps, like her, a mother of one of the men. Instead, it was the wife of John Nelson, first mate of the *Alaskan Rose*. He was taking it all very hard, and she was worried he would soon go over the edge. Only the family of Davey Rundall took the time to console David Olney. Some lingered about the granite block, staring at the newly stamped names. They left notes and jars of flowers in the fashion that has become so familiar in the public expression of grief. Old women stood silent, and young men wept with their arms around each other, some of them unable to conceal inebriation.

"To be honest, I've had twelve drinks," said Jeff Meincke's friend Jeremy Busby, confessing through dark sunglasses. "You know this was supposed to be Jeff's last trip. He was going to get an apartment, go to school, go completely straight."

The friends preferred marijuana. But Jeff had learned a lesson about drug tests, failing one a year earlier when he applied for a job at Home Depot. He took it hard and, a bit embarrassed, promised himself to be smarter. He tested clean before departing on the *Arctic Rose*. Jeremy was also supposed to be on the trip but failed his drug test. Perhaps the failure translated into foreboding. Or perhaps it was nothing, just a coincidence or the grief-stricken fiction of a drunk and shattered friend. In any case, Busby said he'd had a frightening premonition about the boat and tried to warn Jeff, Jimmie, and Aaron. Jeff and Jimmie met through Jimmie's stepbrother, Richard. Their friendship took off when they started snowboarding together.

"Guys, I have a bad feeling about the boat," Busby said he had told his friends. "Guys, I don't think we should go on this fucking boat. I think we should just wait and chill . . ." Reflecting on his premonition, Busby later said, "It pisses me off that I couldn't have enough influence on him."

That power of persuasion belonged to Jimmie Conrad, a skinny and fearless kid able to talk his way out of trouble and into any conversation.

"He was like gravity. Shit just goes to Jimmie," said his younger brother, Brandon, whom Jimmie had also talked into going on the trip that season. "After just two weeks, my crew of friends became his crew of friends, just like that. I was pissed and way jealous. But I couldn't do anything about it."

On sight, Brandon and Jimmie were carbon copies, identical in their lingo, their gait, the kinds of cars and women they liked. Jimmie was the runt of the litter, however, weighing only 130 pounds. He lived with his father, Bernard Conrad Sr., and his stepmother, Barbara Conrad, in Roy, near the county line between Thurston and Pierce counties, a rural hamlet of one thousand people and a single red schoolhouse. When it was founded early last century, the railroad ran through it and its early inhabitants mistakenly thought their town was destined to become an important stop.

Jimmie was the only one of his three brothers who had attended college, studying psychology at New Mexico State. When he came home he worked as a cashier at the Little Park Restaurant in Spanaway. He wore a large shirt to hide his tattoos because he didn't want to offend the elderly customers who frequented the restaurant with their grandkids. Had he not found a spot aboard the *Arctic Rose*, Conrad would have spent the winter working at the Little Park, where steak and eggs cost $5.95. It is styled after a mountain lodge, with a ceiling of exposed rafters. There are model trucks, and mounted on the wall is an out-of-place swordfish.

Jimmie took the job aboard the *Arctic Rose* to do something different. He also needed more money than he could make at the restaurant. Jimmie had a student loan in default, various unpaid traffic tickets, and an unpaid fine for driving drunk. Additionally, he owed the IRS back taxes for underreporting his income from the restaurant. He and his brother Brandon helped repair and clean the *Arctic Rose* for the trip. The men helped weld ballast, ground old paint off the hull, and changed lights on the ship's gantry. Brandon, whose aspiration was to own his own car repair business, worked hard repairing pumps and painting rusted water tanks. But Brandon had smoked marijuana and knew he risked failing the drug test. So he purchased a concoction from a head shop that claimed to conceal any traces of marijuana use in urine. But it didn't work. Like Jeremy Busby, he flunked the test by a considerable margin. He already had all his stuff on the boat, his television, VCR, about forty of his movies, a hundred CDs, his Sony PlayStation, and dozens of video games. He didn't feel like dewiring the equipment, so he told Jeff and Jimmie to use it. Anyway, he planned to test clean for the next trip. He still keeps the paper showing the results of his failed drug test in his glove compartment, a reminder of what could have been.

After the boat departed, Brandon got himself arrested for stealing a car. He said it was his friend who actually stole it, but the police found Brandon with the car keys. He spent two months in jail. He was still in a cell when he was told his brother had died. He broke both his hands hitting them against the wall.

"I'm so glad I was in jail," Brandon said. "When our shit hits the fan, me and my brothers, we all tend to see black and everything and everyone becomes targets. If I was in a bar drinking, and I would have been, I would have gladly picked a fight and stuffed my fist down someone's throat for any reason. Maybe I would have beat someone up and he would have shot me."

As his family mourned his brother's death, Brandon prepared to become a father. The family was convinced it was going to be a boy. Brandon wanted to name his son Jimmie Lee after his brother, although he was afraid the name was cursed.

"I'm going to give the name one more chance," Brandon said. "My fear is that I'm going to have to bury my son."

The first Jimmie Lee was Bernard Conrad Sr.'s best friend. The two went to high school together and then to war. Jimmie Lee was killed in action in Vietnam at age twenty-two when he was struck in the face by a ricocheting bullet. So Bernard named his middle son after his friend. (The younger Jimmie was almost the same age, twenty-four, when he died.) The family was a little bit relieved when Brandon's baby turned out to be a girl. They named her Olivia.

Jimmie's death seemed to shock the family into closeness, driving everyone toward one another. Trust came grudgingly in the family, but old pain and anger disappeared when Jimmie died. His older brother, Bernie Jr., had been living in Abilene, Texas, with his wife, estranged from the family. Bernie Jr. saw his father for the first time in years at Jimmie's funeral.

"If we had not lost Jimmie at the time, Bernie wouldn't have left Texas," Barbara said. "In a way, Jimmie brought the family together. Now Bernie and his dad are close. They're friends. They have a relationship again."

After Jimmie's death, Bernie Sr. had three sons left, one a stepson from his second marriage. And for the time being, at least, they were all close by.

"My father always told me, 'Your boys will always find you.' I didn't know what he meant," Bernie said. "I do now."

In the woods of giant firs just beyond his house, where he takes his two old dogs, Bernie Conrad prays and he listens and for a few hours he has his boys. The dogs, they are his boys, too. Jake and Oscar. They don't let Bernie out of their sight. The big dog, Jake, will tear out the throat of any other dogs who get near Bernie, even if they approach with tails wagging. He has been walking Jake and Oscar on these trails on Fort Lewis for years. The land belongs to the army. The dogs chase raccoons and eat blackberries off the vines like deer. The walk lasts an hour, three on the weekend. The army uses the ungroomed land for training. They look the other way when people use it. It's too much land to fence off. Guards do not keep watch. People ride horses and hike there and occasionally run into soldiers training. The dogs are love simplified. The walking loosens the pain. And the woods are the place he can leave it behind.

"A lot of people go to church," Bernie said. "A lot of people have to go to places like that. I go to the woods."

Bernie Sr. works for an insurance company at the Port of Tacoma, examining cars as they are off-loaded from freighters. He walks the docks, looking for scratches and dents on Mazdas, Mitsubishis, and Isuzus. Like his dead son, he makes his living from trade with Japan.

For most of his life, Bernie Sr. made a career of the army, getting out in 1989. He had traveled around the world a dozen times, lived in South Korea and Germany. He did a tour in Vietnam, reporting for duty in 1971 when he was eighteen. It was the first time he had ever left home in rural Ohio. He spent a year in Vietnam on a dangerous assignment, as crew chief of a helicopter used for airlifting injured soldiers off the field of battle. They flew low and slowly into hostile territory. The enemy fired surface-to-air missiles, rocket-propelled grenades, and bullets. Flying into DaNang harbor, he would see kites flying with hand grenades tied to them. Those were meant for him, too.

Most medical helicopters landed only in secure zones. Bernie and his crew had to go in no matter where they had to land. He flew with a medic, a commanding officer, and a pilot. Bernie sat on the floor of the bird, next to an eighteen-inch door through which they hoisted the wounded. Bernie's seat was armor plated and bulletproof. When the bullets started flying, Bernie made sure he got as small as that square of lifesaving metal.

"Bullets would be bursting through the top of the floorboards. It sounds just like popcorn," Bernie Sr. said. "It was a job. We were taught how to do it. You were told to keep your ass down, and your mind open, and you just did what you did. We were young and vulnerable and being educated. The first thing that came to your mind when the shooting started was that you were young and you still want to live."

His tour lasted one year, the standard length for a kid sent to Vietnam. About six months in, his copter was shot down, hit in the tail by a missile. The strike took out the tail rotor. Bernie sat with his toolbox, behind the pilot, back to back. With nothing to counteract the action of the main rotor, the bird spun out of control and hit the ground bouncing. On the second bounce, the copter started rolling. The helicopter's inverters, like the alternator of a car, sat on top of the fuel tanks. The violent rolling sheared the tanks open, exposing them to the red-hot inverters, which produce current for the chopper. The heat instantly ignited the fuel, and the whole mess turned into a roiling fire. It wasn't the crash that killed everyone, it was the fire.

"If it hadn't been for a good friend of mine," Bernie said, "if he hadn't been flying behind us and seen the crash and jerked my ass out, I'd've been dead, too. It would have been seconds. I was already making my peace. I had given up. You couldn't get out. I was pinned in. Everything was on fire. I was already there. I thought I was dead."

The hand of the angel was a soldier named Kim Kadlowec, who happened to also be from rural Ohio. He lived in Bedford. Bernie was from Maple Heights, only eight miles away. They met in training at Fort Dix, and both became crew chiefs.

"I don't know how he did it," Bernie said. "All I can remember was hearing his voice, 'Not like this you ain't,' and he lifted me out. He kept saying something about me owing him four cartons of cigarettes and how I wasn't going to get out of it that easy."

Bernie was the only one who survived the crash. He finished his tour with a rookie crew. He didn't let them know he was a short-timer because that was something so precious, you didn't brag about it. He kept his mouth shut until the day came. He packed and got his paperwork cleared. He jumped on a helicopter and didn't even say good-bye. The next time he ever talked about it would be decades later, when Brandon chronicled his dad's military history for a school project.

He first glimpsed the Northwest in July 1972 on a cool summer day. He was returning from Vietnam. His plane landed at McChord Air Force Base near Tacoma. He put both hands, palms down, on the tarmac and kissed the ground. He looked up at Mount Rainier, which looked very close at that distance. And he swore to himself that he'd come back one day. It happened to be the first glimpse he got of his country, and the mountain was just what his heart needed to see. Had he settled somewhere else, Jimmie might not have fallen into the circumstances that led him to fish. But the memory of the sun against his face, the towering pines, and the mountain pulled hard and years later pulled him all the way back.

Jimmie Conrad's family held a service in Tacoma at a meeting hall for fishermen. Brandon made miniature life rings with Jimmie's name on them and passed them out. They played his favorite song, "Only God Knows Why," by Kid Rock, the song Jimmie always sang at karaoke bars. His father and his brothers swear Jimmie sends them little signs. When Bernie sees a penny in the sand outside his house, or an eagle in the woods behind it, he wants to think it's Jimmie giving them a sign. One day, Bernie realized the Kid Rock CD in his car's CD changer was disc number nine, and "Only God Knows Why," was the eleventh track. Nine eleven. Jimmie again trying to say, "Hey, it's me."

The newspapers and television stations eulogized the men too in their own way, describing them in the simple and gentle terms reserved for obituaries. They became devoted dads and war heroes and Boy Scouts and devout Christians. They were absolved of their flaws for having died at sea, defined by their final choices, much the way an athlete's virtue is measured by his greatest game or an artist's capacity for love is measured by the beauty of his masterpiece. So it was for the crew of the *Arctic Rose*, not so much the truth as it was comfort to those left behind. To say he died doing what he loved, and that the most important thing in his life was his family, the people who loved him, this was a gesture to the survivors. It was all true enough.

Soon, death would be weighed and measured in less elegant ways.

Days before the memorial service, the mothers of G. W. Kandris and Shawn Bouchard had filed wrongful death lawsuits against Arctic Sole Seafoods, asking for an unspecified amount of monetary compensation. Representatives of the company's insurance carrier, the Polaris Group, also attended the service. Polaris paid travel expenses for family members flying in from out of town and cut several checks to help some families with funeral bills and other expenses. Ostensibly, it was a gesture of goodwill, a courtesy extended by the boat's insurer. Of course, Polaris also had a financial interest in earning the families' favor. It wanted all the families to agree to insurance settlements rather than taking matters to court. Polaris wanted to avoid a trial if possible. The company encouraged family members to work with its own probate lawyer. A few weeks after the memorial service, Rose Workland, Eddie Haynes's mother, and Ken Kivlin's son, John, each hiring an attorney, also sued Arctic Sole Seafoods for wrongful death. Eventually, the families of all but one of the men, Justino Opoll Romero, would be represented by legal counsel in a lawsuit against Olney and his company. Romero's widow, Maria Sanchez Rendon, guided only by a court-appointed guardian, settled out of court for $200,000. She had two children and a seventh-grade education, without so much as a bank account to her name.

Publicly, Rundall's parents were supportive of David Olney, sympathetic to his losses. They did not view his relationship with their son as custodial. They were peers, in their minds, both holding positions of responsibility on the boat. They trusted Olney had done his best to operate a safe vessel, just as they believed their son, the captain, had done the same. Rundall's wife, Kari, did not file a lawsuit. But she hired an attorney nonetheless to represent her in negotiations for her share of the insurance settlement. Kari was represented by Paul McFarlane, Davey Rundall's old fishing buddy.

McFarlane met Rundall in 1985. He was then twenty-four, a processor on the factory trawler *Ocean Bounty*. Rundall was nineteen and the youngest deckhand aboard. They had drawn different lots in life, and it showed. McFarlane was the son of a doctor, the nephew of a lawyer, and if he didn't exactly know it yet, he probably wasn't going to fish or live on boats forever. School and serious jobs awaited him somewhere in his future. He listened to Neil Young, the Grateful Dead, and Devo. Rundall liked White Snake. Rundall made fun of McFarlane's crew cut and the polo shirt he changed into after showering. McFarlane made fun of Rundall's mullet haircut.

Rundall wanted to be a captain someday. McFarlane wanted an excuse to postpone college. But both worked hard at their jobs on the ship and admired each other for it. They were men who never waited to be told to do something. They looked for things to do. Unlike other deckhands, Rundall did not come up with excuses when he was asked to help on the processing line. To him, work was work, and he liked it all. And if he said he couldn't process fish because he had to repair gear, he really did have to repair gear. While waiting for the net to come up, the other deckhands usually watched television. But Rundall helped McFarlane run the fillet machine or stack boxes in the freezer. Rundall's goal was the wheelhouse, and everyone around him knew it. He was always asking questions, learning as much as he could. When he read, he read fishing journals. McFarlane read trash novels. A lot of fishermen he knew could be hard drinkers, but Rundall wasn't one of them. He didn't enjoy alcohol very much. Before hard hats were required on deck, Rundall wore one.

"He was like the nerdy kid with bicycle helmet," McFarlane said. "And he wore a safety line."

After about five years of fishing, McFarlane was the veteran of many tours on trawlers and crab boats as a factory foreman. But he did not feel a desire to ascend higher, so he quit in 1989 and enrolled in school. He went to Portland Community College for a year, then attended Lewis & Clark. His days of fishing turned him on to maritime law, which he studied at Tulane. He joined the boutique maritime law firm of Madden, Poliak, MacDougall & Williamson, moving into an office on the twenty-eighth floor of a Seattle high-rise. He last saw Rundall in 1987.

"I had no sense I was never going to see him again," McFarlane said. "I thought I would see him around."

McFarlane was driving to work when he heard a public radio news report about a fishing boat that sank off Alaska. He did not recall the name of the boat. The report did not mention any names. An hour later, he was getting coffee in the break room of his office when he spotted a newspaper on a table. He opened it up and there he saw a photograph of Davey Rundall.

Seattle is sandwiched by Lake Washington to the east and Puget Sound to the west. Joining the two bodies of water is a canal and a saltwater inlet called Lake Union. It is impossible to drive any direction for more than a few miles without encountering a bridge of some kind. The prevalence of water encourages the city to remain compact and discourages sprawl. The water is also evident in the city's quaint rituals, its powerboat races, milk-carton derbies, the crew races that mark the opening day of boating season. The quintessential romantic Seattle dwelling is a houseboat. Other cities have their lofts, brownstones, villas, and bungalows, but Seattle has its floating cottages.

The watery, economic artery to Alaska begins here in Ballard in the terminal. To get through the short canal and out to sea, vessels must wait their turn in the locks. The line of workboats and pleasure craft becomes a parade and an attraction for tourists when the weather is warm. Built on the banks of the canal are neighborhoods of sloping parks and homes with expansive decks and large picture windows. A railroad trestle bridge, part of the rail line that connects Seattle to Canada, marks the point where the canal opens into Shilshole Bay, the last sight of the world of salad bars and cable television. There is a marina for pleasure craft, a boat launch, a public park, and a beach, Golden Gardens, where Milosh Katurich, the Slavic engineer, spent many of his idle hours feeding pigeons. Around the marina are seafood restaurants and condominiums. Past the Shilshole Bay marina and the embrace of land, the water opens up wide.

Historically, Ballard was a working-class neighborhood, cleared of trees by the first immigrants from Scandinavia. They brought their fishing skills and quickly put them to use. They found the new world familiar, with its tall evergreens, rocky coast, and long, exquisite summer days. Already expert fishermen, they were well suited to the Pacific Northwest. The oldest names on the fishermen's memorial are almost all Scandinavian in origin. Fishing money built the neighborhood's simple homes. Because of Alaska and fishing, Ballard is Seattle's last true working industrial neighborhood, one that best defines the city.

The old fisherman's demeanor is the template for the character of the city. It is practical, introverted, full of Scandinavian reserve, austere, stoic, the kind that patiently breeds ulcers and unspoken grudges. Its religion is Protestant, lean on ritual and melodrama, steady if not devout. It is passive-aggressive, indirect, a bit repressed, loath to brag, and uncomfortable with flamboyance. As Seattle changed, as it catered to popular culture, it did not completely shed this core character. Grunge music, poetry of the misunderstood and disaffected, stayed true to its roots, mixing pain with glamour. The drug of choice was heroin, the drug of introspection and inspiration, the injectable muse, magnifying glass on the soul, a drug that needed to be taken seriously. The popular television shows that came out of Seattle, *Twin Peaks* and *Northern Exposure* (the show was set in Alaska but filmed near Seattle), also reflected the old fishermen, dark and sarcastic by nature, polite but suspicious, hard to read. When prosperity came to Seattle, displays of wealth were allowed, but the money had to be spent on appropriate trophies, on Gore-Tex not fur, on gadgets not jewelry, on SUVs not Porsches, on private school educations not time-shares in Cancún. Even if extravagant, it had to be a life the old fishermen would approve of. And Ballard, where the fishing boats repair before winter, as much as it has changed, remains a reminder of that. The old haunts, however, are not what they used to be.

On the north side of the canal is Ballard Avenue, once the main strip for local fishermen and the place to indulge their vices. The street has undergone a transformation, taken over by expensive shops whose esoteric wares would rival any found in Beverly Hills or on Madison Avenue. There is a pet store that sells fleece coats, tribal print collars, ice cream, and carob-peanut truffles for dogs. There is a studio that models food destined for glossy magazine pages, a plant show-room specializing in rare palms, a shop that sells $20,000 French stoves. Even businesses that attempt to reflect the area's blue-collar origins have upmarketed themselves. The local tavern serves rosemary hummus and cod dusted with Japanese bread crumbs. The tattoo parlor is as clean, airy, and bright as an art gallery, decorated in wholesome hues of pale blue. No dingy windows or sleazy neon. The parlor, open to view through its huge plate-glass windows, displays a collection of vintage bicycles. During the 1990s economic boom, Ballard was one of the first Seattle neighborhoods to gentrify. The places where old fishermen can loiter are becoming few and fewer.

Across the canal is Ballard's last bona fide shipyard. Marco is considered the biggest among the small shipyards in the Puget Sound area. Once a prolific builder of Bering Sea fishing vessels, it hasn't built a new one in years. Instead, it works on Gulf boat conversions similar to the one that bore the *Arctic Rose*. Marco began operating in the 1950s as a builder of wooden yachts. It reinvented itself during the Alaskan fishing boom of the 1970s and 1980s. And when the industry contracted, it reinvented itself again, building tugboats and other nonfishing work vessels. New regulations required oil tankers to have tugboat escorts, providing a new market for Marco. Yet another was created by the superfreighters bringing foreign goods for American consumers. The giant ships needed pilot boats, shuttles that take boat captains from ports out to waiting vessels. Marco builds those, too. Marco also builds boats designed to clean up oil spills. And it has a sister operation in Chile that builds purse seiners that catch anchovies and sardines.

At the height of the crab boom in the 1970s, Marco employed seven hundred and produced a new boat every six weeks. The company got rich. But it has not built any new fishing boats since 1990, because owners can no longer afford them. A cheaper and preferred option is to take an existing boat, usually an oil industry boat from the Gulf of Mexico, and convert it into a fishing vessel. They are called "mud boats," flat-bottomed workboats used to drill pipes for oil platforms. They are exceptionally stable on flat water but have little ability to right themselves if rolled to an angle approaching forty-five degrees. By comparison, steep-bottomed boats tend to rock more but can generally recover from steep rolls. Nonetheless, many Gulf boats have been successfully and safely converted into crab boats and trawlers that work in the Bering.

The *Arctic Rose*, like most shrimp boats in the Gulf, had a relatively flat bottom. Small and built out to its limits, it was subject to many restrictions relative to its safe operation. The Coast Guard must review and approve stability reports of passenger vessels and larger ships. But the *Arctic Rose* and other fishing boats are exempt from such reviews. Nonetheless, when Olney purchased the *Arctic Rose*, he had it examined by a well-regarded naval architect, David Green, considered an experienced and conservative practitioner in the field of boat conversion and stability. He looked at the boat's recent modifications and made recommendations for its safe operation.

"With all naval architects, there is a temptation to make the numbers work," said Charles Cannon, vice president of naval architecture at Marco. "You want to make it work for the owner. It's just human for a guy sitting in an office to want to say that under a certain set of conditions, the boat will work for you."

The incentive is huge. By revenue, fishing is the number two industry in Alaska, behind oil. In sheer volume, no other fishing ground in the world compares with Alaska. In 2000, 4.5 billion pounds of seafood was landed in Alaska, three times the amount landed, by weight, in the second most productive state, Louisiana. Salmon is the U.S. seafood industry's number one export, followed by lobster and surimi, a fish product made from pollock. Surimi is a sort of fish paste and the main ingredient in fish cakes, imitation crab, and imitation scallops. Surimi can be flavored and adapted to mimic just about any kind of seafood. For that reason, it has sometimes been called "the turkey of the sea." Because of pollock, the remote port of Dutch Harbor is the most productive in the world. Among the world's harvested wild fish, pollock is a close second only to anchovies in tons caught per year.

Because of the Bering fishery, U.S. fish exports have tripled in volume and doubled in dollar value over the last ten years. Americans still consume far more seafood than they produce but have closed the gap. Strangely, during this time, fishing employment in the United States has decreased from an estimated fifty-nine thousand employed in 1992 to forty-seven thousand in 1996 even though demand for seafood has grown. This is because of the declining supply of fish. The boats still in business now have to travel farther and stay out longer to catch the same amount of fish, increasing the risk of injury and death for fishermen.

Despite the amount of seafood landed in Alaska, an accompanying processing industry never evolved there on a large scale. An attempt to build an industry in Anchorage failed mostly because it became too expensive to bring in the needed supplies, the batter, the boxes, the bread crumbs. Shipping, flying, or trucking those ingredients to Anchorage and operating factories there was more expensive than simply transporting the fish to the mainland United States or to other markets like China, where the fish can be more cheaply turned into fillets or fish sticks. Alaska also generally suffers from a lack of labor. There simply aren't enough warm bodies to support large-scale, labor-intensive industries.

The number one fish crop in Alaska is pollock, the generic white fish of the American fish industry. It was once thought to be unfit for human consumption. It is still not very valuable per pound, which is why it must be caught by the ton by giant trawlers that fish around the clock. In addition to surimi, pollock becomes fast-food fish sandwiches and frozen fish sticks. The fish served in the company or school cafeteria, the fish served at McDonald's or Burger King, is almost certainly pollock from Alaska. Pollock is sold in frozen blocks of standard size, much like lumber. A standard fish block weighs sixteen pounds and is perfectly rectangular.

It did not take long for all the world's profitable fishing grounds to be identified and exploited. Because it was so remote and inhospitable, the Bering was the last of them. These days, new markets for fish are not so much discovered as they are invented. Fishermen are not going to find new fish, or new fishing grounds, but they might find or create new markets for fish that are already there. One example is Chilean sea bass, a familiar item on the menus of most upscale restaurants. The name is purely the result of clever marketing, intended to give the fish an exotic appeal. The fish might not be as appetizing known by its actual name, the Patagonian toothfish. Its popularity has seriously damaged stocks of the fish, which grows slowly. When king crab stocks dwindled, the crab fishery turned to the smaller but marketable snow crab, now a staple of seafood buffets and restaurant chains like Red Lobster.

Seafood markets are somewhat arbitrary, rising and falling with fashion and tastes. Lobster, the prized crustacean, was centuries ago considered slop fit only for inmates and beggars. Today's dog food might be tomorrow's delicacy. And what doesn't sell in one market might be valuable in another culture's diet. The American groundfish industry created a market for itself in a similar way, identifying a demand for flatfish that are in plentiful supply in the Bering and relatively easy to catch. The Japanese had fished for sole for decades off Alaska. But when the landmark Magnuson Act was enacted in 1976, keeping all foreign fishing boats at least two hundred miles from American shores, Japanese companies needed American surrogates to land the sole for them. Now American trawlers would satisfy Japanese appetites, supplying the raw material for Japanese processors. In American waters, sole fishermen had little competition, with everyone else chasing crab, salmon, halibut, and cod.

In the mid-1980s, a Japanese buyer met the head of Arctic Alaska Seafoods in a Ballard restaurant. Arctic Alaska had made a fortune in the king crab boom and was a pioneer of frozen-at-sea cod fillets. But cod could not be fished for year-round. The market for pollock did not yet exist. Arctic Alaska needed something to fish for outside of cod season. The Japanese buyer needed sole. In each other, the men found solutions to their problems. And the American groundfish industry was born.

The first year of the head-and-gut fishery was 1986, the first boat the *Bering Enterprise*. Olney was one of the pioneers in the head-and-gut fishery as part owner of the *Arica*, a former Gulf workboat converted at the Marco shipyard into a groundfish trawler. He ran the *Arica* and eventually sold his minority investment in the company, parlaying it into Arctic Sole Seafoods. He ran the small company with his wife, Ann, whom he had married in 1992. They met through mutual friends in Singapore, where she grew up. Both had children from previous marriages. With the living he made fishing, Olney successfully steered his children away from it. His daughter studied architecture and joined the Peace Corps after college. His son went to culinary school to become a chef. He tried fishing on both his father's boats but decided it wasn't for him. David Olney was not disappointed.

More than five hundred species of flatfish from several families are found all over the world, including the tropics. Sole and flounder are types of flatfish, as is halibut. All flatfish are designed by nature for life at the sea floor. They have asymmetrical skulls, with both eyes on the same side of the head, so they can essentially swim on their sides with their eyes facing up toward the surface. The upfacing or eyed side is richly colored, sometimes speckled, the bottom-facing or blind side pale and white. As the name suggests, flatfish do appear flat. Their color camouflages them well against the sea bottom. Their dorsal and anal fins surround almost their entire bodies. From side to side, flatfish have very narrow bodies. Small flatfish eat marine worms and clams, nipping off the ends of their siphons. Flatfish do not have many natural enemies, and their rate of mortality is slow. They adapt well to temperatures and are opportunistic eaters, able to make a meal out of almost anything. As a species, they are durable and successful and therefore good fish to harvest. The only drawback for fishermen is that with the exception of halibut, most people do not love to eat flatfish. The flesh of flatfish is white and mild, and they are generally not prized as a food crop.

Flatfish spawn in inland waters, dropping their eggs in sandy shallows. A typical egg is about three millimeters wide and yields larvae about twice that size. Good spawning seasons for flatfish depend on the Bering winds that deliver plankton to hungry larvae. The formation of sea ice each winter is also important. It reduces ocean salinity and encourages the bloom of plankton. Flatfish are born with symmetrical skulls, with eyes on opposite sides of their head. They look like traditional fish. But almost immediately after they hatch, one of the eyes begins to migrate toward the other. Fin growth begins around the circumference, and the differential coloring begins. Within four months they look like adult flatfish except that they are the size of potato chips. They live inland for three to four years, feasting on plankton before venturing out toward the edge of the continental shelf.

The business of harvesting flatfish is steady and fairly reliable, but tedious and unspectacular. Salmon and crab fleets have had boom years when stocks were especially rich. But there will never be a flatfish boom. The catch is too strictly regulated, and unlike salmon and crab, flatfish will never be a coveted delicacy.

Halibut is the biggest impediment to the head-and-gut fishery, which catches a lot of halibut but must release them whether they are dead or alive. They must record the amount of halibut caught, and once the fishery as a whole releases its limit of halibut, all fishing must stop. Unfortunately, halibut share habitat with the kind of sole the head-and-gut fleet is after, so it is a challenge to avoid catching both. There is a limit to the amount of sole that can be caught, but it is usually never reached. It's generally halibut that determines the length of the season. Head-and-gut captains have lobbied the North Pacific Fishery Management Council to institute individual halibut quotas rather than one quota for the entire fleet. Captains believe quotas for individual boats will allow them to fish more safely, at their own pace, reducing the pressure for boats to fill up before the season ends.

Limits on fish caught are not effective without a limit on the number of licenses issued. Until 1995, licenses were unlimited. So many boats fished the waters that seasons became ridiculously short. Halibut season lasted two days. Now a fixed number of licenses are available. The only way to get one is to essentially buy someone else's. And they are expensive comparable to the cost of buying a home. Fishermen are often invested by tens, even hundreds, of thousands of dollars before a season begins. The house is literally at stake. The intention of the quota system is to give all fishermen ownership of a fixed share of a limited resource, encouraging them to conserve the resource, because if fish populations rise, their shares grow. Quotas are also supposed to curb the risks fishermen take to catch fish by moderating the incentive to catch as much as you can. But quotas go only a small way toward removing the risk and in some cases encourage fishermen to take more. As the head-and-gut fleet nears its quota of halibut by-catch, captains are under pressure to make the most of their final hauls.

Japan is the main customer of the head-and-gut fleet. The head-and-gut industry's most valued product is pregnant rock sole. They can be caught only in February, since rock sole spawn in early spring. Roe season is short but is responsible for the bulk of profit for the fleet, since Japanese consumers will pay a premium for a headed-and-gutted rock sole laden with eggs. (Small male rock sole are typically discarded; close to half of the rock sole caught is usually thrown away. By the winter of 2003, a new rule took effect, requiring the head-and-gut fleet to keep all rock sole it caught.) Presentation of roe is important to the Japanese shopper. The fish might end up in a *depachika*, a giant food hall usually located in the basement of a department store near train stations in Japan. Attractively displayed in a grocery case, the fish is cut so that part of its egg sac shows through the clear plastic. Rock sole with roe will fetch up to $2 a pound at the dock, a relative fortune compared with the twenty cents a pound that yellowfin sole gets the rest of the year. Roe fish can account for up to 80 percent of a boat's yearly revenue. By volume, however, yellowfin accounts for three quarters of the fish caught, by weight. So the most important part of the season is the dead of winter, when bellies are full of roe. The rest of the season is spent just breaking even. One thing is certain: Without the Japanese market, there would be no head-and-gut fleet. Japanese buyers almost always insist on putting a fish technician on board to monitor the roe season. They are usually retired captains who possess encyclopedic knowledge of the Bering, since the Japanese fished these waters long before the Americans. Like tempered steel, they are famously impervious to the rigors of the Bering. They wear shower sandals and shorts on deck and work the factory twice as fast as men half their age. And with little more than a calendar and a wristwatch, they can point to a spot on the chart and find fish.

The head-and-gut fleet generally begins the season in late January, fishing for Pacific cod until the roe season begins. By March, rock sole roe is generally overripe and the big-money portion of the season is over. And most head-and-gut skippers worth their salt go after Pacific cod again. In March, cod school up, prepare to spawn, and fatten up. Cod also brings a respectable price but is more labor intensive than sole. It must be bled before it is frozen or the flesh will be red instead of the pale white consumers are accustomed to and fond of. The roe, which has little value, is pulled out. As stocks of Atlantic cod become more scarce, Pacific cod has gained value even in countries that favor the Atlantic variety, which is considered to be more delicate. Pacific cod is thought to be rubbery if you don't like it, firm if you prefer it. South Americans like large cod, the bigger the better, because its size indicates the prosperity of the family that serves it. The Japanese prefer the flavor and texture of small cod, which they eat mostly in the winter, dipping strips of the flesh into a pot of boiling broth heated on a tabletop stove, fondue style. The colder the Japanese winter, the higher the price fetched by cod caught in the Bering.

Another important component of the Alaskan cod harvest is North America's market for refreshed cod, which is frozen cod that is thawed and filleted and sold as fresh in supermarkets. Cod purchased in supermarkets in Boston or New York in the winter was likely caught in Alaska, frozen immediately, then shipped to plants in the Northeast. The refresh market is possible because of the freezer technology available on board boats like the *Arctic Rose*. Bacteria counts (the measure of freshness in fish) taken from refreshed cod have shown that it is often fresher than locally caught fish, which is generally never frozen. Flathead sole is also a big part of the North American refreshed fish market, often sent to East Coast stores and sold as flounder.

The highest price for cod, more than $1 per pound, is paid for line-caught cod. Some Japanese buyers purchase only line-caught cod, whose flesh is not as bruised. Cod caught in a net, the kind harvested by the head-and-gut fleet, is more prone to damage and thought to be of lower value. As a result, some head-and-gut boats don't even bother with cod. Mistakes in handling show easily in the form of bruises. If the fish is not skillfully bled, the flesh loses its firmness. And it must be beheaded properly. David Olney sold relatively little of the high-maintenance cod. He sold his fish through a fish broker who negotiated prices with established customers. That way, owners like Olney do not have to deal and haggle with several buyers. His broker took care of all that. Olney concentrated on the fishing.

Yellowfin sole is the fish of last resort for the head-and-gut fleet.

Not particularly large, its flesh bland, it never commands a high price and must be caught in very large quantities to make the effort worthwhile. Sometimes called "dish rags" by those inside the industry, yellowfin yields small profits and is often a break-even proposition. Almost all yellowfin goes to China, where it is further processed into frozen fillets, typically sold to Canadian distributors for less than $2 a pound, and then sold retail for about $3 a pound, often back in the United States. If you purchase frozen fillets of sole in the supermarket, it's almost certainly Bering Sea yellowfin. When no other fish is running, head-and-gut boats can almost always go after yellowfin. The fleet usually ends the A season fishing for yellowfin in May and June and spends a large part of the B season, in the summer, landing yellowfin.

The head-and-gut boats have little else worth catching. The bigger, fleshier rex sole has value in the Asian market as a whole, unprocessed fish. But it is harder to catch, tends to inhabit deeper waters, and is not found in great numbers like yellowfin. The arrowtooth flounder, commonly known as turbot, is an even bigger flatfish, weighing up to seventeen pounds and growing almost three feet in length. But an enzyme unique to the species begins to break down the flesh almost immediately after the fish dies. The flesh of a turbot has been likened to fish-flavored mashed potatoes. Fishermen have a test for turbot they catch. If they can bend its body so that its nose touches its tail, the flesh is too soft and they toss it back.

The boats in the head-and-gut fleet are between one hundred and two hundred feet long. They catch fish by stirring up the muddy sea bottom, agitating and herding them into nets that can be as long as four hundred feet. A full net on a large boat can hold fifty tons of fish at a time. Once brought up, it is dumped belowdecks into a container called a "truck," where it is sorted. Fish that the fleet are not allowed to keep, such as halibut, are released immediately. The rest are sent to the processing line. The fish are beheaded by circular blades. Bellies are slit by hand and the guts removed. The headless, gutted fish are then put into shallow metal pans, which are put into plate freezers. Each pan holds about sixteen kilograms of fish and is frozen to minus twenty-four degrees Fahrenheit. After a few hours, the processors "break" the pans, remove the frozen slabs of fish, and put them in paper bags, which are stored in the freezer hold, usually in the bow of the boat. The biggest boats can hold up to four hundred tons of frozen fish in their freezers, which are as large as truck containers. Processing the sole on board allows the boat to catch more fish per trip, since whole fish weigh more and take up more space. Once rid of the valueless heads and guts, the fish command a higher price at the dock. Since sole is generally not very valuable, it is especially important to maximize volume.

After a year of good fishing, a processor on a large head-and-gut boat can earn up to $40,000, the deck boss twice that. Deckhands might earn $60,000. So does the cook. The captain of a profitable boat can earn between $150,000 and $200,000 a year, the first mate about $50,000 less. Paul Ison, forty-eight, is captain of the *Unimak*, a 160-foot head-and-gut trawler. He has made good money running the boat, although he has certainly paid for his choice of career with two divorces. In addition to two ex-wives, he has an adolescent daughter in Oregon whom he sees only a few months a year.

"Most people who fish are escapists," Ison said. "We don't think about what's going on in the real world. I've done this over thirty years. It's hard to think of doing anything else. And by now, I'm probably not qualified to do anything else. It's one of the few jobs where you get out of it exactly what you put into it. The gratification is instant. When you see that big floating bag of fish blow out of the water like a submarine, it's the biggest thrill. I live for that rush. It's like a drug."

Fishermen like Ison remember the perfect hauls the way athletes remember a perfect shot.

"I hit this one spot, and I hit it perfect," Ison said. "I hauled up a net full of snapper, every one of them three feet long. These are long-lived fish. And fish that big are probably one hundred years old. I just looked at those fish. It makes you go "Wow." It really makes you think."

6

The Hearing Begins

Accused of nothing, David Olney, owner of the *Arctic Rose*, sat between his lawyers, his back to the room of about thirty people there to witness and record the first day of formal hearings into the sinking of Olney's boat. His expressions revealed little. He had a way of seeming cheerful in the most grievous situations. It was read as grace by some, rigidity or aloofness by others. He was seated at a table near the front of the room, taking the position and posture of a defendant, although this was not a legal proceeding, the room not a courtroom, and Olney not on trial.

In some ways, the hearing did resemble a trial. Witnesses had been subpoenaed, and they would be questioned by the members of the Marine Board of Investigation. A stenographer would record everyone's testimony. Olney's lawyers, David Bratz and Doug Fryer, were allowed to question every witness as if they were undertaking a cross-examination and working in Olney's defense. In a sense, they were. Owners have been prosecuted in criminal court before, and it was still possible Olney could face criminal charges, although none had been filed. U.S. attorneys were following the investigation but had not yet decided whether or not to charge Olney. He had already been sued by several families, and their lawyers were among those sitting in the auditorium. Ostensibly, Olney attended the hearing because he was asked to testify. Whether he intended to or not wasn't clear at the start of the hearing, which would last for two weeks. He was scheduled to testify on the third day, but already his lawyers requested that he answer questions later in the proceedings.

Although the Coast Guard had little or no sense of what sent the *Arctic Rose* to her doom, it already had ordered an upgrade of its satellite communications as a result of the sinking. With the upgrade, rescuers could send urgent, encoded e-mail that would trigger alarms aboard vessels when the mail arrived. An audible alarm accompanying e-mail, the thinking went, would go a long way to ensure the e-mail would be read immediately. The night of the sinking, an e-mail requesting help was sent to the *Alaskan Rose* at about 4:00 a.m. But no one saw it until hours later. To this day, no one knows for sure exactly when the e-mail arrived. John Nelson, the mate on the bridge of the *Alaskan Rose* that night, said he read the urgent e-mail only after he was contacted by radio by the Coast Guard at about 7:45 a.m. Had an alarm gone off aboard the *Alaskan Rose*, its crew might have responded to the distress call sooner. Olney's two boats were only one hour apart. But the *Alaskan Rose* did not reach the site of the wreck until five hours after the *Arctic Rose*'s emergency beacon was activated. Those hours might have cost Davey Rundall, and possibly others, their lives. Rundall survived the sinking itself and was able to put on his survival suit as he struggled in the icy water. Already subjected to extreme cold, he probably did not last very long. His only chance to live was the swift arrival of the *Alaskan Rose*. An audible alarm accompanying the e-mail, if it arrived promptly, might have saved Rundall's life. The Coast Guard did not need to interview anyone to know that much.

An open hearing is about the worst thing imaginable to a fisherman, independent by nature, beholden only to his own decisions and opinions. Fishermen are not accustomed to scrutiny. Their ship is their world, so to suddenly have it become the object of a public proceeding is something of a psychological nightmare.

"I wouldn't wish it on any vessel owner," said John van Amerongen, editor of *Alaska Fisherman's Journal*, a former fisherman and among the journalists covering the hearing. "How would you like to sit there in that chair and have someone interview all your former crew members, the ones that liked you and the ones that didn't."

Captain Ronald Morris opened the hearing the morning of Tuesday, June 12, 2001, by asking for a moment of silence, calling the

hearing a "solemn process" intended to bring closure to the "tragedy." The hearing was held in a small auditorium in Building 9, part
of a complex of government buildings used as the offices of the
National Oceanic and Atmospheric Administration, adjacent to the
derelict naval air base on the north shore of Lake Washington. Unlike
buildings downtown, the low-rise NOAA headquarters had the
feeling of a community college campus, plain and far less official
seeming than an office building. Investigators questioned witnesses
on a raised stage as a court reporter transcribed the testimony. The
Marine Board members, dressed in full uniform, sat side by side
behind a long table covered by a white pleated table skirt, like a row
of judges at the state fair.

Listening to the testimony were family members of some of the
crew, seated in flip-up chairs. Eddie Haynes's mother and sister were
there. John Kivlin attended, as did his wife's mother. David Meincke
and one of his daughters, Jennifer, went. So did Shawn Bouchard's
mother, Joan Branger, who had driven to Seattle from Harlowton,
Montana. As a rule, the relatives sat in different rows, keeping a
comfortable space between them. Sitting near the front, attorney
Joseph Stacey kept thorough notes. He represented several of the
families. His firm specialized in maritime injury, paying for a large
advertisement on the wall of the Dutch Harbor airport, next to the
only gate. The ad for Beard Stacey Trueb Jacobsen & Stehle LLP is one
of the last things a fisherman sees before leaving Dutch Harbor, and
one of the first when he arrives.

The investigators wanted to know everything they could about
how the boat was used before it sank. It was a relatively new boat, so it
had a short history, much of which had been revealed before the
hearing began because of the media interest in the sinking. It had not
been a moneymaker and had been put up for auction twice. It was
now widely known that the *Arctic Rose* began life as a shrimper and
was modified for the Bering fishery. It was also now common
knowledge that the crew of the *Arctic Rose* was not very experienced.
And most guessed that inexperience played some role, small or large,
in the sinking.

"All those processors weren't seamen," said John van Amerongen.

"They're essentially fast-food workers. When everything's fine, things are going to be a challenge. When things are shit . . . When you're not making money, everything looks like shit. Your friends don't look like your friends. You can't wait to get off the boat."

The first witness called to testify was Tom Neikes, who had last worked aboard the *Arctic Rose* in 1993. He oversaw the vessel's conversion from an East Coast scallop boat to trawler and was its first captain in its new incarnation. Robertson and the others had tried and failed to locate the boat's builder or its original blueprints. Neikes was the best they could do.

The *Arctic Rose* was born on the Mississippi bayou, an environment about as opposite from the Aleutians as can be imagined. The air is like velvet and stubborn to move. In this air, puffs of cigarette smoke hang an eternity, as if drawn onto a page, dissolving slowly into limbs and then fingers. In 1988, the boat that would become the *Arctic Rose* was assembled on a sandy, littered lot next to the marsh in Biloxi, Mississippi. In U.S. Department of Transportation records, the builder is listed as H&P Inc., a company that no longer exists. Its first owner and the man who built the vessel appeared to be a Vietnamese immigrant named John Van Nguyen. H&P Inc. likely consisted of Nguyen, perhaps a spouse or relative or two, a crane, an arc welder, and a rented space in a boatyard. He likely borrowed building plans from another fisherman. The plans might have been used or adapted by several builders, passed around and borrowed like a cookie recipe. The construction of a shrimp boat was simple and uniform enough and did not require unique, complex designs. Department of Transportation records show Nguyen initially borrowed $95,000 in October 1988 toward the construction of the boat. One month later, he borrowed $350,000 from a different lender and paid off his first loan. He named his boat the *Sea Power*. Within less than a year and a half, three companies, L. D. Armory, Biloxi Hardware and Marine Supply, and Pier VII Corporation, had liens against Nguyen totaling $33,477.87, not including interest.

Biloxi sits on what some call the rectum of America, where the Mississippi River empties itself into the sea along with all the pollutants it has picked up during its long, southward journey.

By the time Nguyen built his boat, gambling began to displace shrimping as the preeminent industry of the region. Casinos were opening in Biloxi and would soon become the area's economic engine. Because Mississippi law allowed riverboat gambling, casinos were built over the water, qualifying them as boats. Giant Las Vegas–style casinos now line the main street along the oceanfront and along the bayou, consuming wetland as they go up.

Most of the Vietnamese immigrants lived and worked in the oldest, most run-down section of town, backed up to the marsh and away from the beachfront. They worshipped in both Buddhist and Catholic churches. They opened Vietnamese restaurants and groceries and stores that rented Vietnamese movies. Nguyen was one of many Vietnamese immigrants who decided shrimping was the surest way to a better life, a springboard to maybe a general store and later a nicer house north of town. They pressed their children into schoolwork, and soon the kids with strange, unpronounceable names ended up valedictorians and National Merit scholars. For some of those families, it all started with a shrimp boat. They had learned to fish in Vietnam and put their experience to use in their new home. In large part, the Vietnamese saved the shrimping industry in Biloxi because they were willing to work longer hours on cheap, lousy boats in order to make the slim profit margins work. Vietnamese shrimping concerns turned a profit by employing family members. As these operations prospered, owners built larger boats, staking family reputations on the size of their vessels. Their labors were important in the face of mounting competition from foreign countries, which sold cheap farmed shrimp to the United States. Ironically, a lot of this farmed shrimp was coming from Southeast Asia.

The Vietnamese were doing in Mississippi what Balkan immigrants had done decades earlier. Slavic surnames are still common in Biloxi. One of the finest homes along the bayou belongs to the Covacevich family, which owns a boatyard across the street. It was here that Nguyen rented space to lay the keel for his boat. The steel he used to frame and sheathe the boat probably arrived on a flatbed truck at a price of about twenty cents a pound from a plant in New Orleans or Mobile, Alabama, fabricated from steel recycled in South Korea. In a previous life, the steel might have been a washing machine or a Toyota before it was rendered back into liquid metal and stamped into a three-eighths-inch-thick plate that became the skin and bones of a boat. Nguyen probably could not have afforded to buy a boat made by an established builder. He probably did not have the money to hire an architect. With some basic plans, some experience, borrowed labor, and good advice, he could do it himself for less money. Reducing start-up costs was one way of getting a leg up in an increasingly competitive market.

For as much seafood as Alaska produces, the United States still imports far more seafood than it exports, largely because of its huge appetite for shrimp, most of which is imported. The value of shrimp imported from Asia every year is about $3.7 billion, accounting for more than half of the U.S. seafood trade deficit of $7 billion. All signs point to that gap growing. For instance, while salmon exports have dropped slightly over the last ten years, the amount of salmon the United States imports has tripled in the same time. But the disparity is greatest in the shrimp market. Driving the deficit are the giant, man-made shrimp farms in Asia. Shrimp are raised in shallow ponds in Thailand, Vietnam, and China, where they can be produced more cheaply. The ponds are usually carved from wetlands or dug out of cleared forests. Some are twice the size of a football field. By the early 1990s, Thailand became the world's largest producer of farmed shrimp. Within ten years, China surpassed Thailand, and Latin American countries mounted a serious challenge. Farming led to a glut in the supply of shrimp and drove down prices worldwide. Gulf Coast shrimpers couldn't compete without cutting some corners, and the Vietnamese immigrants figured out how to do that.

Men like Nguyen were the bane of established builders like Michael Toche, whose family has been building boats in Biloxi since 1934. While most of the Toches have gotten out of boatbuilding, Michael and his sons continue to run the business his grandfather started. These days, the business depends on Coast Guard contracts to refurbish patrol boats. It just doesn't pay to build shrimp boats anymore. The Toches found it especially difficult to compete with the Vietnamese builders. They learned quickly, Michael Toche recalled, copying measurements from already constructed boats with wooden sticks, then transferring the measurements, freehand, onto their designs. The replicas looked remarkably similar from the outside and inside and seemed to make for sound vessels once put to sea. There were dozens of Vietnamese building their own boats. Some of the men were old and seemed to have some experience with the trade. Others had less. The main difference between his boats and the Vietnamese boats, Toche said, was in the welding. An improperly welded seam might have a narrow void in its core. It cannot be seen or detected, but it compromises the strength of the hull. Toche would never begrudge a man for trying to make an honest living, but the Vietnamese-built boats, he said, undersold his boats.

"They were just building them for themselves to run for maybe a year and then sell to someone looking to buy a cheap boat and retrofit it," he said, describing the somewhat dubious practice inflicted upon some of the Vietnamese themselves when they first got into the business.

"I don't wish anyone bad luck, but I wish they'd play the same ball game," Toche said. "It makes it hard for us to do what we do."

The 1980s were boom years as local fishermen built as many new boats as possible. Workboats from the oil platform industry were also converted into shrimp boats. The rush to build quickly created a surplus. Toche recently built a new shrimp boat in his family's shipyard in Gulfport, located on the road named after the family, across the bay from Biloxi. Michael's new boat is top-notch. But he is worried he won't be able to sell it for the $1.5 million he needs to make a profit.

Until 1960, shrimp boats were made of swamp cypress, mahogany, and cedar and air-dried for four years before being used. Michael's father doesn't even know how to weld. Now, all boats are made of steel. There is not much, really, to the design of your basic shrimp boat. The pilothouse was built up front and slightly elevated. The aft deck was left open. Here, the shrimp would be dumped before being stored in a refrigerated fish hold below the deck. An average boat would have two side fuel tanks, two generators, one compressor, a hydraulic pump, a hot-water heater, and a freshwater tank. With its flat bottom, it can sit empty in as little as seven feet of swamp water. Boats with freezers can stay out for months at a time, packing up to sixty thousand pounds of frozen shrimp.

Gulf shrimpers go after one of three species, brown shrimp, white shrimp, and pink shrimp. Despite the names, their colors differ only faintly. Gulf shrimp are born in the marshes. Within one month they can double in size. They generally spend their days in the mud, coming out at night to feed on algae and worms. They propel themselves by popping their tails, moving backward in a sudden burst of speed when they sense danger. They travel on the tides. The bottom of the Gulf is mostly flat and featureless. Close to shore, the water is no more than thirty feet deep. Even twenty-five or thirty miles offshore, the water is less than one hundred feet deep. Most shrimp are caught in these shallow depths. About 80 percent of the shrimp harvested in U.S. waters comes from the Gulf, although it makes up a small part of all the shrimp eaten in the United States. Virtually all of the shrimp we eat is imported from farms abroad. Of the nearly sixty million pounds of shrimp that is processed into institutional, five-pound boxes in Biloxi every year, only a few million actually come from local waters.

Too many boats are chasing too few shrimp in the Gulf. Like much of the American seafood industry, the Gulf fishery is overcapitalized. Meanwhile, the flood of cheap, imported, farmed shrimp from Asia threatens to end commercial shrimping in the Gulf, a proud family tradition for decades. Nowadays, for a Gulf fisherman to make a living, he needs to have a second or even a third job. No longer a living, shrimping only augments an income. Even the resourceful Vietnamese struggled. This climate, in part, probably drove John Van Nguyen and his boat out of the business. He tried harvesting scallops in the North Atlantic to offset a bad season of shrimping. It appears he wisely might have planned all along to use his boat in northern waters. The *Sea Power* was not built as a traditional Gulf shrimp boat. Its pilothouse was set slightly back. It had a substantial forecastle deck for crew quarters and generous freeboard. But fishing two oceans wasn't enough. In 1990, the company holding the $350,000 mortgage, Cummins Financial Inc., filed suit against Nguyen because he had defaulted on the loan. About that time, the *Sea Power* was involved in a collision at sea that guaranteed its owner's ruin.

The boat was under way late one night in the Gulf, presumably towing. All its crew had fallen asleep, unaware it was on path to strike a smaller, oil supply boat moored to the bottom. The collision occurred at a slow speed, but the impact was powerful enough to seriously injure the captain of the supply boat. He filed suit against the owner of the *Sea Power*, whose insurance had lapsed. The company that carried its policy was one of many wiped out by the hefty claims filed after Hurricane Hugo in 1989. Without insurance, the owner's only substantial asset was the boat itself. Meanwhile, the boat was repossessed for nonpayment on its mortgage and placed in the custody of a federal district court in Massachusetts, which ordered it sold in 1991. John Van Nguyen simply walked away from his boat. He did not bother to hire a lawyer or negotiate an alternative to losing the *Sea Power*. He left it for others to devour. The boat was sold at public auction June 28, 1991, for $303,000. In the end, Cummins Financial received reimbursement only for what it called "administrative costs," $18,116.25, most of which was spent docking the boat for eight months at the D. N. Kelley & Son shipyard in Fairhaven, Massachusetts, while it was in custody of the court. The injured supply boat captain received virtually all proceeds from the sale of the boat. In the pecking order of lien holders, an injured seaman has priority over a bank or other creditors. The foreclosure was a bust. The bank's lawyer, Norman Peloquin, never got paid. He did not know about the collision or the injury claim before he took the case. Once he discovered it and understood the claim to be legitimate, he too walked away and advised his client to give up the case. In Peloquin's practice, the *Sea Power* represented an air ball.

"Every now and then you'll pull an abstract [a record of a boat's ownership] and you'll see one seized and sold by a U.S. marshal three or four times," Peloquin said, "and you've got to scratch your head and wonder whether there is or is not such a thing as plain bad luck. This was a nice boat, fairly well constructed."

While pursuing the foreclosure, Peloquin had put an ad in *Boats and Harbors*, an internationally distributed periodical advertising vessels for sale. He remembered many people expressing interest, in particular an obstetrician from California. It was sent to auction and purchased in July 1991 by the North American Fish Company, owned by two doctors from Eureka, California, a husband and wife named Deepak and Kusum Stokes. The couple operated a thriving clinic and owned a few fishing boats (one of them named after their daughter, Sonya) as an investment. The doctors' side business had done very well in its first season, probably a case of beginner's luck. It encouraged the Stokeses to purchase another boat. To acquire the *Sea Power*, the Stokeses took out a mortgage for $391,000.

Tom Neikes thought about buying it himself and using it as a catcher boat out of Kodiak. But he decided against the large responsibility and instead helped broker its purchase by the Stokeses, who hired him as the captain. He supervised its conversion into a trawler because he had done similar work before. First he piloted the boat, still called the *Sea Power*, to a shipyard in Pascagoula, Mississippi, where a factory was added to the boat. The boat was virtually gutted. Bigger generators and refrigeration equipment were added. The owners hired Bruce Culver to design the factory space. Culver, a marine architect since 1967, was for most of his career the chief engineer for Tacoma Boat Building, which built small military vessels, tuna boats, Coast Guard cutters, tugboats, and barges. Culver first saw the boat in dry dock in Fairhaven, Massachusetts, and remembered the boat looking "scruffy and run-down" and badly needing a paint job. The factory took up almost all of the exposed deck, leaving ten feet open at most. The boat, Culver found, had no original plans, and he could not consult John Van Nguyen because he could not find him. Culver designed the factory to be weather tight. In his plans, Culver made clear the hatches should remain closed and that water should not be allowed to collect in the factory. Standing water, when allowed to slosh from one side to the other, could destabilize the boat.

The fuel tanks were subdivided into smaller tanks. Water tanks were moved. Heavy refrigeration equipment was installed. A crane was added to the top of the factory deck. The modifications took about five months to complete, from July to December 1992. A new stability test was performed after the conversion, and the boat passed. The conversion, repairs, and upgrades were costly. In January 1993, North American Fish Company borrowed $870,000 from a lender called Pacific Coast Farm Credit Services, part of a federal program created to grant farmers, and later fishermen, low-interest loans backed by government bonds. The money was used in part to pay off the Stokeses' initial $391,000 loan. Six months later, North American refinanced its debt, borrowing $890,000 from Northwest Farm Credit Services and paying off Pacific Coast Farm Credit.

The Stokeses wanted to try fishing in the Indian Ocean with their new boat. Neikes talked them out of it, at least at first, recommending Alaska instead. Neikes took the vessel through the Panama Canal and up to Oregon, where more work was done on the boat. It fished for the first time as a Bering Sea factory trawler in March 1993 with a crew of no more than eleven, most of them processors. It handled well and experienced few mechanical problems but seemed to get stuck almost every hour, owing to its relatively small engine, then a 675-horse-power Cummins that averaged about three knots when towing a net. The underpowered vessel could not fish around the clock and didn't make a lot of money. From the start, it seemed the boat struggled. Neikes recognized a losing proposition and didn't stick long with the owners.

"They were kind of an unorganized operation," he said. "They didn't really know what the fishing industry was all about, and it never worked out after that."

Meanwhile, North American was falling behind on its bills. Magone Marine Services of Dutch Harbor filed a lien against North American for $5,425.09 in September 1993. It was paid off within a month. But Harbor Enterprises of Seattle filed a lien for $12,010.98 one month later.

Her owners decided to try their luck in a different ocean. North American's second captain, Kevin Ward, whose brother was a part investor, was hired to take the *Sea Power* on an eight-month fishing trip to India, where a small company also owned a stake in the boat. Ward made the trip across the Pacific with just an engineer and a deck boss, stopping in Hawaii, Guam, and Singapore on the way to the port city of Cochin in the Indian coastal state of Kerala. The trip took forty-five days. Trawling off the west coast of India for four months, the boat "didn't catch enough fish to make a good chowder," Ward said. Like many inshore fishing grounds, India's was overfished. Tens of thousands of registered trawlers work along the west coast of India. One can only imagine how many unregistered trawlers cut into the business. The waters of the Indian Ocean were calm, but Ward still felt the boat was tender, using outriggers while steaming to give the boat some stoutness and balance.

"If you didn't keep the fuel tanks evenly balanced on the forward and starboard side, the boat had a heeling problem, I guess," Ward said. "The heel almost felt unnatural from boats that I'd been used to fishing on . . . an unnatural roll to it, almost like a shimmy."

The venture in India was a failure and sent its owners further in debt. In September 1994, Kodiak Oil Sales filed a lien against North American for $9,982.84; in August 1995, Western Pioneer Inc. filed a lien for $35,103.33; in September 1995, Fishermen's Boat Shop in Everett, Washington, filed a lien for $34,765.65. About that time, the owners hired a professional management company in Seattle called Scan Sea Fisheries. Prior to hiring Scan Sea, the owners allowed a relative to manage financial affairs and relied on the captains it hired to deal with day-to-day matters. Management companies are common in the fishing industry, as owners are often not fishermen but merely investors who need to hire those with fishing expertise to run the boat. Companies like Scan Sea, operated by four people, hired crews, insured the vessel, arranged for repairs and maintenance, and marketed and sold the boat's catch. It had no financial liability in the boat. It got paid whether the boat made money or not.

North American Fish Company soon took out another mortgage, this one for $150,000, which it used to settle some of the liens against the company. And under Scan Sea management, the boat's name was changed from *Sea Power* to *Tenacity* on February 8, 1996. David Bauman, who managed finances for Scan Sea, remembered the hard-luck boat needed an engine replacement after fishing the winter season of 1996. The engine was flown to Dutch Harbor at great expense. Scan Sea ordered the exact same engine to hasten the change-out. The Stokeses applied for an emergency advance of $75,000 against their mortgage for the new engine. The repair had to be made quickly so the boat could resume fishing the B season from late spring until early fall. Bauman often spoke to Kusum Stokes about getting even more money for the boat. It was the last thing Stokes wanted to hear. She already was behind on payments to creditors.

Complicating matters further, one of the boat's crew, a fisherman named Charles P. Stewart, sued North American for injuries he sustained after being washed overboard February 7, 1995. He claimed the company ran an unsafe boat. Stewart settled on May 9, 1996, for $50,000.

That same month, North American took out its largest mortgage, for $1,151,000. The company now had more than $2 million invested in its struggling enterprise. Meanwhile, unpaid bills continued to pile up, as the boat couldn't earn enough money to pay even its own operating costs. The boat itself had negative equity since it could never be sold for the amount of debt it carried. Only the boat's fishing rights were worth anything.

Fisherman Todd Wheeler was among the *Tenacity*'s first crew. He last worked on the boat in February 1996 as its factory foreman. An employee of another boat Scan Sea managed, he was asked to help get the *Tenacity* into good running shape. Wheeler knew it would be a challenge with such a small boat. Instead of the ten-ton bags of fish it was expected to take per tow, the boat often hauled up two- and three-ton bags. The crew never made much money. Water accumulated in the factory, and the pumps sometimes had trouble removing it. The boat rocked in heavy weather and never felt reliably stable to some. "I didn't like that," Wheeler said, "but that's the way the boat was designed." He had one particularly frightening experience while the boat was pulling up a full net of fish. As the deck boss winched the bag onto the top of the factory, the stern suddenly went under the water. The sea burst through what were supposed to be sealed hatches in the factory. The water penetrated the seams and came out the other side as a tight spray. The captain released the bag and turned sharply, avoiding what could have been a catastrophe.

"I don't know if the sea was hitting us wrong or if the bag was too heavy, but we were pulling it up and the back of the boat, the whole stern, was basically under the water," said Wheeler, who quit not longer after that. "I wasn't happy with the boat. The factory was small, it was cramped. I didn't like the way the boat rode when we were full. I felt unsafe in it, and I had an opportunity to leave and I took it."

Hiring for the boat was always a challenge. Annemarie Todd, who handled personnel for Scan Sea, said the company never advertised or used employment services because they were usually not worth the expense. Experienced fishermen typically asked how big the boat was and how many plate freezers it had and upon being given the answer would hang up or walk out of the office. So she usually had to settle for friends of former crew or an occasional walk-in who didn't know any better. These were usually not the most dependable types.

"For them, fishing isn't a career," Todd said. "It's a point they go through to get to their end, where they use it as a vehicle to either get some money together, get away from home, or get away from problems at home until they can figure it out in their minds and are mature enough to come back and deal with living on land."

Although she was not describing the crew of the *Arctic Rose* in particular, the description fit.

Within a year of replacing the engine, the boat needed a new propeller shaft and bearings. Seawater leaked through the worn bearings. The repair would cost up to $50,000, which the owners, perhaps still weary from the engine repair, never came up with. So the boat remained tied up at Fishermen's Terminal in Ballard, not earning any money. Its lame shaft sat in a shipyard in Lake Union, north of downtown Seattle. More funding was promised by its owners, but the money never came. By the beginning of 1997, the *Tenacity* had been seized by federal marshals yet again for nonpayment of debts. The number of liens filed against North American was staggering: It owed Aleutian Fuel $52,217.74; it owed Offshore Systems $20,365.05; it owed Triple B Corporation $22,600.94; it owed Western Pioneer $92,545.83; it owed Cummins Northwest $27,402.78; it owed Frontier Fluid Power $4,038.27; it owed World

Express Travel $5,611.03; it owed Maritime Industrial Center $5,791.52; it owed Net Systems $5,673.87; it owed Harris Electric $14,650.69; it owed Lunde Electric $5,915.24; it even owed its own management, Scan Sea, $23,400.97. More than once, Stokes paid a bill to get authorities to release his boat, only to have another creditor come forward and get the boat arrested again.

"This was the only time in my life I had been involved with a vessel arrested three times in one summer," said maritime attorney Charles Stanley Loosmore, who represented Northwest Farm Credit Services. "Most vessels go through their entire useful life without hearing the word *U.S. marshal*."

The boat's principal creditor, Northwest Farm Credit, foreclosed on its loan on July 22, 1997. By this time, the Stokeses had already sold the *Sonya S.* to cover their debts. A U.S. District Court judge in Seattle ordered the *Tenacity* sold at auction.

"Everyone came out of the woodwork," said Loosmore. "There were crewmen who hadn't been paid, all sorts of suppliers."

The Stokeses could not keep up with their creditors and eventually filed for Chapter 7 bankruptcy, which meant near total liquidation of their assets. The Stokeses spent years resolving the bankruptcy caused by their investment in the *Tenacity*. As recently as 2003, creditors and lien holders were still waiting to be paid, among them the lawyer the Stokeses hired when their boat was first seized.

Scan Sea momentarily considered bidding themselves on the *Tenacity* but decided it could not take on the added financial responsibility. At the time, Bauman thought the boat might be able to successfully fish off Mexico, where it wouldn't be considered small and where it could go after high-value fish instead of fish that must be caught at high volume, something that had always seemed to be a problem for the boat. The *Tenacity* had only one passable season in the Bering, 1996, when it caught about 1.7 million pounds of fish, about eighty-five full nets. On September 9, 1998, the *Tenacity*'s mortgage holder, Northwest Farm Credit Services, purchased the boat for $125,000.

If any owner could have made a profit from a boat like the *Tenacity*, it was David Olney. He had been fishing for thirty years, buying and running several boats. He always owned at least a piece of the boats he fished, plowing his profits into larger ventures. He started Arctic Sole Seafoods by selling his 12 percent share of the *Arica*, a successful, 180-foot factory trawler named after the southernmost city in Chile. Cashing out in the late 1980s, he bought the *Alaskan Rose* at a marshal's sale for about $500,000, putting in twice that amount to widen and repair the boat. He understood the expense and commitment needed to run a boat and spent whatever the business required.

As an operator and owner, Olney understood the market and the work. He understood the mechanics of fishing. Best of all, he knew the groundfish industry. As one of the first American fishermen to exploit the market, he was responsible for helping start it. He quickly turned the *Alaskan Rose* into a profitable business.

Olney was only peripherally familiar with the *Tenacity*. He had fished around it. He boarded it once, four years earlier, at the invitation of a former mate. He knew it had been in financial trouble. When the boat was repossessed in 1997, Olney was not inclined to buy it. He was not yet ready to enlarge his business, even though he recognized potential in the small boat with a rough history. He did not participate in the marshal's sale. About two years later, Olney saw the boat advertised for sale in a fishing magazine for $450,000.

Fishing with the *Alaskan Rose* had been profitable for Olney, and by the time he saw the ad, he had saved some extra cash. With it, he began looking into possibilities of modestly expanding his enterprise. The market for sole was good. It was still relatively easy to catch the fish and even easier to sell it. The crews tended to be smaller, the overhead lower. And most of the owners, like Olney, also ran their boats, a practice he liked and was accustomed to. By the time Olney formed Arctic Sole Seafoods, fisheries regulations prohibited new boats from entering the market. The fisheries council hoped the rule would stem the overwhelming rush of investors and fishermen who made quick work of fish stocks. An owner had to buy a boat that already was working in Alaska, a process that resembled a game of musical chairs. The only way to acquire another boat was to wait for another owner to sell or replace a vessel that was taken out of service.

That left Olney with few choices in 1999. Only one boat, the *Tenacity*, was available. In February of that year, Northwest Farm Credit Services sold it to Olney for $440,000. And on February 25, he renamed the boat the *Arctic Rose*.

"He bought himself a hard job, and he knew it," said Graham Redmayne, a seafood marketing executive who has known Olney for years. "It ain't a big boat. The *Arctic Rose* was a stretch, but it was about the only boat out there. If there was a better boat out there, he would've bought it."

Olney spent another $1 million repairing it. A port engineer who had inspected it in 1997 found it to be filthy and neglected. Dirty oil seemed to cover everything. The engine appeared to be leaking, and it too was smeared with oil. Spare parts sat in milk crates. Dirty filters and rags, belts, and tools were scattered all over the engine room. The hull looked to be corroded in places. The propeller shaft needed to be replaced or rebuilt, as did the shaft bearings. By all accounts, the boat was in the same condition when Olney bought it a few years later. He devoted the winter of 1999 to repair work.

By the time marine surveyor Carl Anderson saw the boat in June 1999, it looked almost like an entirely different vessel, he said. Anderson was hired by the insurance company covering Olney's new boat to independently assess its condition. He found the boat at a Seattle boatyard, its repairs almost complete. The engine had been overhauled. A five-inch stainless-steel shaft had been installed, along with a new sixty-eight-inch propeller and new bearings. A kort nozzle was attached to the propeller for extra power while trawling. (The nozzle acts as a sort of turbo booster.) The factory had been refurbished, its hydraulics inspected. The hull had been sandblasted and painted. Ballast was added to the keel in the form of a lead shoe six inches thick and one hundred feet long. Additionally, twenty thousand pounds of steel and concrete had been poured into the bottom of the hull for even more ballast. The additional weight, low in the vessel, would help the crew safely hoist heavier loads of fish onto the deck above. Even new mattresses and cushions were put in the living quarters. Anderson was impressed, although his general impression of boats constructed in the Gulf of Mexico was that they were light of frame and not built to last. He noticed that the boat, now called the *Arctic Rose*, was framed with four-by-three-inch angle iron spaced two feet apart and did not have longitudinal framing. That is, all the framing ran one direction like a rib cage, instead of running perpendicular like a web. The framing, however, did not overly concern him at the time.

A new stability test was performed on the boat by an architect working for Jensen Maritime Consultants of Seattle. The firm passed the boat, provided it traveled with a certain amount of cargo aboard (the amount differed depending on how much fuel was in the tanks) and adhered to limits on how much fish it could place in the hold before unloading. In general, the more fish the crew put in the hold, the more fish they could safely bring up in the nets. The fish in the hold acted as ballast or a counterweight to fish on deck. The more fish stored below, the more fish the crew could catch at one time. But the formula also posed a dilemma: Before it was safe enough to catch a lot of fish, the crew needed to catch a lot of fish.

"I would say that the *Arctic Rose* had more restrictions on average than boats that I have experience with," said Eric Blumhagen, who worked on the stability report. "But it didn't necessarily have more than all the boats."

The report also required the boat's main forward fuel tank to contain some fuel at all times. The weight of the fuel was needed as ballast. It meant the *Arctic Rose* would have to refuel more frequently and make slightly shorter trips, cutting into its profit margin. The *Arctic Rose* had a total fuel capacity of seventeen thousand gallons, three thousand of which had to remain in the main tank at all times to keep the boat stable. It burned seven hundred gallons of diesel fuel a day, which meant it could work for twenty consecutive days without returning to port. Another condition of safe operation was to keep the factory watertight. The factory raised the center of gravity of the boat but also increased its buoyancy as long as water did not infiltrate the space.

Olney's goal was to have the boat ready in time to begin fishing the summer of 1999. But by then, the market for sole had become more challenging. The price paid for sole had fallen. His first trip took him northwest of the Pribilofs, about the same place the boat eventually sank. It performed well on the open water, Olney said. He spent most of the summer on the boat, taking his son aboard as a deckhand. The *Arctic Rose* was never in perfect shape, and Olney did not expect her to be. He planned to make small improvements and repairs over time as money and opportunity allowed. To do everything all at once would be too expensive and would keep the boat from fishing. For example, Olney hoped to eventually replace the trawl winch, which reels in the net when it's full. Nonetheless, the boat was a far cry from its days as the *Tenacity*. Fishermen who knew the *Tenacity* well didn't even recognize the *Arctic Rose*. After that summer, satisfied that he had worked out the bugs, he hired a captain, an old friend from his days working the Arica. His name was Davey Rundall. A planned sixty-day trip was cut in half because of the boat's operational limitations. Olney lost much of her crew to attrition. John Porsche, the cook aboard the *Arctic Rose* that fall, remembered being nervous about the boat from the start.

"If you were me and you see a bunch of boats, and I hoped that was not my boat, and it was," Porsche said. "And I was pretty nervous because I would like to be on a bigger boat. I guess it seemed very small and I've heard some pretty good stories up there."

All the while, Olney continued to put money into improving the *Arctic Rose*. For the winter season of 2000, he hired another captain. Jim Kelly was among many East Coast fishermen who came to Alaska when it seemed that the Atlantic Ocean had run out of fish. He had owned and operated several trawlers in the Atlantic, most of them small by Alaskan standards. He came to Alaska for good in 1991. And for the next eight years, he would watch the company he worked for change owners three times. He thought about ending his fishing career in the fall of 1999, until he met Olney, who offered him a job as captain of his new boat.

The engine tended to overheat and lose power when towing, Kelly said of the *Arctic Rose*'s performance that season, making it hard to catch as many fish as quickly as other boats. Because she was not able to handle rough seas very well, Kelly said he tended to stay within striking distance of an island in the event he needed to run for shelter.

As a general rule, the boat stopped fishing if the winds exceeded forty knots and if the seas got bigger than fifteen to twenty feet. He would always lose three to four days of fishing to larger boats because of the weather. Kelly was especially aware of taking rough weather from the stern, which seemed to be the boat's weak spot.

"I recognized early on that it was going to be a challenge to walk the line between staying safe and staying profitable," he said.

If the boat had trouble taking weather from the stern, it seemed to perform well riding into the weather, never taking waves into the wheelhouse, impressive considering it was built so close to the bow.

Kelly began the season already in a hole. The first mate originally contracted to work that winter, John Winsberg, quit after one day before the boat ever left Dutch Harbor.

"I went up to the boat, and then when I got on the boat and looked around," Winsberg said, "it just, I don't know, I mean, it . . . the house looked weak to me, the factory was dirty. I stayed one night on the boat, and then I kind of made up a story, I had a family emergency, and took off, said no way. I saw it and I—it just—my intuition said no, this boat is not stable enough for fishing off the Bering Sea."

It was, Winsberg said, the first and only time he was persuaded by a gut feeling to leave a boat. As a result of Winsberg's sudden departure, Olney had to quickly find another first mate. In a panic, Kelly made a call to Tom LaPointe. The men knew each other only by reputation. He found LaPointe at home in the foothills of the northern Cascade Mountains in Washington State. LaPointe lived with his wife and young daughter in a small house on $3\frac{1}{2}$ acres in a town called Marblemount, the last town along Highway 20 that gets plowed in the winter. The couple moved there in 1990 so LaPointe could hike the nearby mountains and glaciers. Another transplant from the East Coast, LaPointe has done very little else for a living but fish. He started as a teenager, hauling lobster traps in Maine. He graduated to gill netters and trawlers on the East Coast, all the while hearing stories about the legendary fishing in Alaska. He gave college a try but dropped out of the University of Maine. When he was twenty-six, he and a friend decided to spend a year and all their money traveling across the country climbing mountains. They ended up in Seattle, sleeping in their car under the Alaskan Way Viaduct with about $50 left between them. As if they had planned it, they applied for fishing jobs aboard a factory trawler in Alaska. LaPointe's first job, in 1990, was aboard the *Ocean Rover*, one of about a dozen U.S. fishing vessels stripped and rebuilt in Norwegian shipyards as a way of taking advantage of a loophole in maritime law. As long as a boat contained a small percentage of U.S. steel (about 10 percent), it could be flagged as an American vessel and fish American waters. So Norwegian interests bought American boats, discarded everything but the keels, and built bigger and better boats on them. Consequently, deckhands like LaPointe learned the trade from a mostly Norwegian crew. The loophole was eventually closed. But until well into the 1990s, foreign companies were, in essence, allowed to fish as American entities, finding a way around the Magnuson Act and its two-hundred-mile exclusion of foreign vessels. LaPointe was hooked from the first trip.

"The first bag I saw was seventy tons," LaPointe said. "It just jazzed me. It was a blast. I loved it."

He met his wife, Jill, on a fishing boat. She was the foreman aboard a factory trawler named *Heather Ann*, and as a woman she was a rarity in the field. She worked through her seventh month of pregnancy. The marriage lasted, in part, because Jill came from a large Scandinavian fishing family. All her sisters are married to fishermen, so she was familiar with the life and the long absences. By the winter of 2000, LaPointe had reached a sort of breaking point with fishing, weary of its relentless pace. Conveniently, the owner of the last boat he had worked on sold his quota and the boat was mothballed. The owner was one of many who were essentially paid off by the government to stop fishing, a buyout designed to reduce the number of boats fishing off Alaska. LaPointe found himself home for nearly three uninterrupted months, the longest since he started fishing. To make some money, he helped build fishing nets in Seattle for $25 an hour. He climbed and hiked and hunted deer in the woods behind his house. He was looking forward to ski season, an indulgence he had almost forgotten. Money would be a little tight, but the leisure time gained seemed worth whatever dollars he would forsake. He had happily resigned himself to sitting out the season when Kelly called. It is an exceptional fisherman who can turn down a job, and LaPointe was no match to the task. Kelly called LaPointe on January 21 and just about begged him to get on the next plane to Dutch Harbor.

LaPointe first saw the *Arctic Rose* tied up at the Delta Western fuel dock on Captain's Bay. Used to working on much larger boats, he was taken aback by the size of the *Arctic Rose*. He could barely imagine how it could be a factory trawler and considered getting on the next plane back to Anchorage.

"Kelly had misrepresented the boat to some extent," LaPointe said. "I had never seen it. But if you back out or bail, word gets around. You may be able to get away with it once, but if you do it again . . ."

To him, the boat looked plain and cramped. The factory was in disarray, which is somewhat normal at the start of the season. He looked for leaking oil or hydraulic fluid but did not find any. The survival gear and flare kits appeared to be in good condition. He thought the boat could have used a paint job.

LaPointe was reassured to find two friends working as deckhands, Jim Valentine and Billy Tarbox, experienced fishermen whose skills and judgment he had great faith in. He would come to find that the rest of the crew did not inspire similar confidence. The number of crewmen who started the season would be cut nearly in half by April. Tarbox and Valentine were the first to quit, in late February, after just two trips. Expecting to make about $10,000 a month, the men made about $6,100 in that amount of time.

"I also had some safety concerns on board the boat," Valentine said. "I had gotten a real uneasy feeling when we first left Dutch and we made a few turns. The boat didn't seem really stable to me. When it would turn, it wouldn't right itself right away, you know, it would stay listed over for a little bit. And it was just a real queer feeling."

The boat seemed to ride well as long as it was pointed into the weather. It climbed up waves with surprising ease. But it seemed vulnerable from the rear, riding low in the stern. LaPointe also noticed that the boat tended to recover slowly when it rolled. It did not snap back to center, staying too long on edge. The two men tried to convince LaPointe to come with them and made a tempting argument. Even under optimal conditions, making money on the trip would be a challenge, as the price of sole with roe had fallen that winter by more than 40 percent in the Japanese market. With a small factory, fickle plate freezers, a sick engine, and a small net, the *Arctic Rose* didn't have much of a chance.

"Every day, I thought about leaving," LaPointe said, "but I'm not going to break my word ever to anybody. I'd get branded. But the thing that really determined how I operated was that I felt responsible for the crew."

One that would get smaller in short time. Before the season ended, Kelly fired the cook, the factory foreman, and several processors. The boat "pretty much did him in," LaPointe said. "He looked like Tom Hanks from that movie *Castaway*. I started to see the toll it was taking on him."

The departure of Valentine and Tarbox left LaPointe feeling vulnerable. He made sure more than a few people stayed up all night to keep an eye on the boat. The crew was in the habit of sometimes using a broom to prop open the overboard chute in the factory. The processors dumped unwanted fish and by-catch through this chute. LaPointe made sure that hatches stayed shut, and he kept the pumps working, clearing them of fish heads that could clog them. LaPointe said the outer door to the factory could be made weather tight, but the crew seldom closed it properly. They also never closed the weather-tight door connecting the factory to the ship's galley. From the factory, he said he could smell breakfast cooking. LaPointe remembers not sleeping much that winter. He worried about the engine or the factory or the hatches or the pumps. He did not feel the boat had the equipment to deal with a huge fire or a sudden flood of water. Production disintegrated, and the last six weeks of the season had ceased to be about catching a lot of fish and making money; it was simply about finishing the season. As a boost to morale, both LaPointe and Kelly worked in the factory.

"In a way, it was more relaxed," LaPointe said of the final weeks.

The engine suffered for much of the season, losing power suddenly and registering high exhaust temperatures. Afraid of losing the engine in the open sea, LaPointe and Kelly never pushed the throttle and watched the temperature gauges as if they were attached to a dying patient. The men drove the boat gently. If the net got caught on the bottom, the boat would simply stop—one advantage of an underpowered engine. If the seas got higher than fifteen feet, Kelly or LaPointe halted fishing. Any higher and LaPointe would have to brace himself in his chair with one foot wedged against the console. The *Arctic Rose* was an idiosyncratic boat. Her plate freezers were twitchy and prone to stalling. When men off-loaded the boat, the factory equipment had to be moved around to access the freezer hatch.

"I thought we could operate it safely if we were very conservative," LaPointe said.

The next time the boat was in Dutch Harbor, a mechanic advised Kelly against continuing to fish, telling him that doing so was to risk a catastrophic failure of the engine. Kelly was persuaded by the advice and relayed his thoughts to Olney. On April 17, 2000, after consulting with his crew, David Olney agreed to have them bring the boat back to Seattle, about one month earlier than planned.

"Dave's got a good reputation," LaPointe said. "Any time we had any safety concerns, if we needed to buy equipment or make upgrades, Dave Olney supported us 100 percent. He'd say, 'You don't even need to ask; if you need it, just buy it.' He's one of the better boat owners. But in the end, it's hard to dress up a pig."

When the boat reached the Inside Passage, LaPointe felt a huge weight lift from his shoulders, knowing that weeks of nervously regarding the seas and constantly studying the boat's gauges were over. "I felt like I had lost a hundred pounds," he said. "I knew there was a concrete end to this thing."

When his wife picked him up at Fishermen's Terminal, she told him, "If you ever go out on a boat like that again, you can find yourself a new wife."

7

The Former Crew

One week into the hearing, after listening to testimony from more than a dozen witnesses, the board seemed no closer to finding a cause for the sinking. The hearing had revealed no obvious malfunction, no catastrophic event, no single and fantastic explanation that would account for what, by all signs, had been a swift and monstrous end. What the board had assembled was something much less spectacular, even mundane, but important nonetheless. It had constructed a thorough history of the boat, one with consistent patterns. Its history did not suggest it was necessarily a dangerous boat, but it was one with chronic problems and challenges. It had never been lucrative and, financially, had failed all of its owners. Hiring experienced crew was a regular problem. It remained to debate whether it belonged in the Bering. But its size was certainly a handicap. During the first week, investigators heard mostly from former crew and experts familiar with the boat. The testimony was belabored at times, covering the minutiae of naval architecture and other technical details. Relatives of the crew who attended the hearing hoping for clear answers got few. They hoped that might change in the second week, when some of those who worked aboard the boat during its doomed season were scheduled to testify.

The board did pause to consider, during that first week, an intriguing theory suggesting weather might have had something to do with the sinking after all. On the sixth day of testimony, board member Robert Ford produced a weather chart showing precise weather conditions on the morning and in the particular area the

Arctic Rose sank. Up until then, severe weather had not been raised by witnesses as a possible factor in the sinking. When asked about the weather, witnesses suggested the opposite. The crew of the *Alaskan Rose*, only ten miles away from the *Arctic Rose*, reported moderate conditions. A storm was on its way but had not yet arrived when the boat sank. Prevailing weather conditions suggested ten-foot seas and thirty-knot winds, not exactly smooth, but normal for the Bering winter. But Ford, an investigator representing the National Transportation Safety Board, said there was some meteorological evidence that an isolated but formidable low-pressure front might have moved through the *Arctic Rose*'s fishing grounds about the time its beacon went off. The location of the front at that hour and the position first recorded by the beacon were almost an exact match. The weather chart was an important revelation in the construction of an explanation for the sinking. The leading edge of such a front, Ford said, could have suddenly amplified wave heights and wind speed to something more closely resembling storm conditions. And if weather conditions were shifting, as they appeared to be doing at the time, the boat could have been hit by waves and wind from different directions almost at once. Although the suggestion of a sudden squall was interesting, the weather chart was inconclusive. Ford said more consultation with meteorologists would be necessary.

The days of testimony took on a polite and predictable rhythm, like a school day with breaks between long lectures, and a lunch period, and regular gatherings outside the auditorium of witnesses and families of some of the crew. David Olney still sat in the front of the auditorium, seated between and guided by his lawyers. He continued to postpone his testimony, making it seem less and less likely that he would speak at all. Investigators knew Olney's decision was a legal precaution. His lawyers told the board they wanted Olney to receive immunity from criminal prosecution in exchange for his testimony. Immunity was not the Coast Guard's to give. That decision belonged to the Department of Justice, so such an agreement would take some time to engineer. The Coast Guard would make the request. In general, prosecutors obliged the request of the investigators in such cases. The Marine Board still held out hope that Olney might speak anyway once he had heard what the other witnesses said. Family members listening to the testimony viewed Olney's refusal to speak as evidence that he had something to hide. His recalcitrance gave some of them yet another reason to resent Olney.

On Tuesday, June 19, 2001, the seventh day of the hearing at the NOAA complex, the board listened to testimony from two of the boat's 2001 crew, Milosh Katurich and Nathan Miller, two men who by the grace of quitting midseason lived to return from the Bering. Katurich, chief engineer at the start of the season, was the first to testify. The boat rode best, he said, when the forward tank was full, the aft tanks were empty, and it was towing a net. He spoke dismissively about naval architects who sit in offices and calculate stability requirements. "These guys who write these books, they don't ride the boat," he said.

He expressed himself emphatically and gesticulated aggressively. He once accidentally knocked his microphone out of its stand. He was asked repeatedly about the condition and disposition of the propeller shaft, a significant mechanical problem at the start of the trip. Yes, it had overheated, he confirmed. Yes, it had to be repaired. Yes, he had installed temperature gauges on the bearings so that he could monitor them closely. But no, he was sure it was not the cause of the sinking. In the end, he stated only the obvious: "The boat is too small," he said. "I would pass a law. No boat less than a hundred and twenty-five feet . . . can fish farther than ten miles from shore. This boat had no business being out there."

Katurich had spent most of his time in the engine room, sitting on a stair step, using a flattened cardboard oil filter box as a cushion, throwing spent cigarette butts into a coffee can full of water. In bad weather, he said, rolling was less pronounced deep in the boat's bowels. And, he said, "I don't like to be surprised . . . if something gets busted and I'm not there."

During breaks in his testimony, Katurich puffed busily on ciga-rettes. He smoked two packs a day. He took medication for high blood pressure and had various heart problems. He had six uncles who died of heart failure in their seventies, "without medication," he says. "With medication I figure I can hit ninety-five."

Milosh Katurich's favorite roost, at the corner of Market Street and Ballard Avenue, used to be a funeral home and then later became a store that sold Bavarian-style cuckoo clocks and now is a forgiving and accommodating place for a road-worn immigrant who needs a job, could use some company, but will settle for a place to sit alone and smoke. There was a time his American dream seemed to have come true, when he had more cash than he knew what to do with. He bought an apartment and tipped like a millionaire. The sea was full of jobs back then for a man not particular about the company he kept. He once worked on a freighter that took Japanese sewing machines, guitars, and radios to South America and delivered fish meal and coffee back to Japan. When the ship stopped in Hawaii, he drank with abandon. His drink of choice was vodka. He could drink every night for two months straight, sometimes an entire fifth of vodka in one night, and go cold turkey once he went to work on a boat. He always maintained that wall of sobriety, suffering on one side so he could gorge on the other. But as he got older, his hangovers hit harder and lasted longer. He needed a boost and turned to cocaine.

"Abracadabra. In one second, your head is clear," he said, describing the feeling. "You wake up like thunder and you're ready to go."

So he medicated one vice with another, and eventually he was outdone. In September 1998, Katurich was arrested and charged with robbery, unlawful imprisonment, and possession of cocaine. He was using coke regularly by then. He said he accompanied a friend, a drug dealer, while he tried to collect on a drug debt from a junkie. Unable to pay the dealer, the junkie was prevented from leaving and threatened with physical harm. Katurich denied participating but admitted to being there. He was charged as an accessory.

In February 1999, he was convicted of all three charges and sentenced to sixteen months in prison. His Coast Guard–issued engineer's license expired while he was incarcerated. It must be renewed every five years in a relatively simple process consisting mostly of paperwork and a drug test. If an expired license is not renewed within a year, and Katurich's was not, an applicant must submit to extensive technical exams. While in prison, he also lost the one-bedroom condominium he had purchased in 1997 for $86,000.

The bank foreclosed on Katurich's mortgage. He got out of prison in November 1999, having served ten months of his sentence, and took a job cleaning boats for $7.50 an hour. Because he was on probation, he was required to stay within King County, which ruled out jobs at sea.

"I don't know how to live on land, but put me on a boat and I'm a tiger," Katurich said.

Katurich's probation ended in December 2000. On January 4, an employment agency Katurich had signed up with called him and told him the owner of a boat called the *Arctic Rose* was looking for an engineer and was willing to pay $250 a day. More important, because of her size, the *Arctic Rose* was not required to have a licensed engineer aboard. Engineers need to be licensed to work on boats weighing more than two hundred tons. The *Arctic Rose* weighed just under that, so Katurich was eligible for the job. On a Friday morning at 10:00 a.m., he met with David Olney and Dan Richmond, the previous engineer, on the deck of the *Arctic Rose*. After a tour of the boat, he took the job, starting first thing the next morning. He was offered a three-month contract but asked for a contract lasting two months, hoping to resume work aboard a Russian boat later that winter. He chose the guaranteed pay of $250 a day over the option of a 3 percent share of the profit. He wanted to keep his mind on his work and not worry about the fishing if it went bad.

"The boat was a piss pot, but it did not require a license," Katurich said. "I've never worked on a boat that small in my life. I thought, This is going to be a tough one."

Katurich joined in the preparation of the boat. He oversaw the welding of batteries, the rerouting of cooling-water pipes. He removed and overhauled the 750-horsepower engine, the same kind used in heavy construction equipment. It drove a five-inch propeller shaft. He replaced a shaft bearing and a generator. He guessed he would net about $7,000 from the job, a decent take. He was accustomed to more, but now his expectations were set low, giving him something in common with most of the men aboard.

The money the men from Mexico thought they could make was well beyond the dreams of their countrymen at home. Alejandro Ortiz Espino, twenty, painted houses in Mexico, where the best-paid workers pick coffee for about $30 a week. In one season fishing, he stood to earn a veritable lifetime's worth of a coffee picker's wages, as did Justino Opoll Romero, thirty-nine, who in Mexico packed tomatoes and sold chickens, earning about $15 a week. Katurich understood the Mexicans, understood their thirst for the new world and the sacrifices they made to reach it. He grew up in the village of Lisan in the state of Montenegro. Lisan is a town of fewer than two thousand, without so much as a shoe store or a pharmacy. The young Americans who lumbered around the fish factory, read their Bibles, or listened to their noisy music, Katurich was fairly sure, had never lived with this kind of austerity.

Few would have described Katurich as a lucky man when he boarded the *Arctic Rose*. He had no true love, had saved little money, and had lost his home, and his prospects were low. But on February 28, 2001, he got off the boat in Dutch Harbor. And for that one decision, he made himself, for a change, one very lucky man, although he must have felt very much the opposite as he slept on the floor of the airport, waiting for a flight to Anchorage. On that day, Seattle experienced a strong earthquake that closed its airport for several days. Katurich was separated from his checked luggage, in which he had unwisely placed his passport and other important documents. Unable to leave Dutch Harbor, he lost the job he planned to take with the Russian boat. He finally returned to Seattle a few days later and retrieved his luggage three weeks after that. Instead of working on the Sea of Okhotsk, Katurich returned to his usual haunt, in front of Tully's coffee shop. Katurich said he started his life as a shepherd and wants to end it that way, on a hillside with five goats, a gun, and a sheepdog with a spiked collar to ward off wolves, living in a cottage with an open fire and a kettle of soup over it. The script of his life, arbitrary as it is, kept alive the possibility of Katurich's wish.

Katurich's testimony about the boat's mechanical systems did not bolster the theory that the propeller shaft was behind the sinking. The problem seemed to have been solved long before the boat went down. If the fatal flaw was mechanical in nature, Katurich's recollection of events did not reveal it. Perhaps the flaw was not mechanical at all, but human. This was what the board hoped to determine, or disprove, by questioning Nathan Miller. The sequence of events that winter had, fortunately, allowed another crewman to get off that day. He too was not fond of the captain. That was about all Nathan Miller had in common with Katurich, who coolly described Miller as "not mentally balanced. There was something missing. It's like he took no pleasure in living."

Miller worked as a processor on the *Arctic Rose* for six weeks before quitting for a spot aboard a crab boat; clearly, it had been six weeks he had not enjoyed. His guarded personality became apparent almost immediately during his testimony, as he resisted answering even the most perfunctory questions, such as where he attended high school.

"Do I need to answer that?" he asked, looking at the board members.

Captain Morris, looking puzzled, didn't answer. He simply looked back at Miller, who relented an answer before any more was said.

Miller was something of a departure from the typical Bering Sea fisherman. He was, very much in the spirit of the phrase, clean-cut. An ardent Christian, he wore bookish glasses and cut his hair short in the fashion of a bond analyst or professor at a Bible college. He did not come from an economically imperiled background. He spoke with eloquence, and he fancied himself the literate type. After studying broadcasting and elementary education at Asbury College (a small Christian college whose students are expected to adhere to a pious lifestyle, abstaining from alcohol, tobacco, and premarital sex, and attending church regularly), Miller dropped out in 1997, his junior year, and headed off to a series of odd jobs in faraway places. He sought one adventure after another, fighting forest fires, fishing, traveling the world. The *Arctic Rose* had been his latest.

During his testimony, which lasted several hours, he criticized the way the boat was run and ravaged the character of the captain, Davey Rundall. Captain Morris knew that what Miller had to say would be difficult for the Rundalls to hear. As a courtesy, Morris told the Rundalls before Miller's testimony that they might want to leave the auditorium. The relevance of his testimony, at times salacious and uncomfortably frank, was not always obvious. In Miller's retelling, Rundall came off as cruel, or at least severe. What investigators hoped to gain from Miller was a sense of crew morale and whether or not it was bad enough to compromise the safe operation of the boat.

"He [Rundall] would perform crude impersonations and insulting impersonations of crew members," Miller testified, his disdain for the captain obvious, "whether it was their accent or the way that they worked or the part of the country that they were from. He referred to a lot of the guys as white trash and talked about the Mexicans and their responsibility to perform the more undesirable tasks . . . He vented his frustrations with the chief engineer while I was on the boat . . . just his unresponsiveness to his requests or demands to get things done on the boat.

"The only person that I ever saw him instructing or making any attempt to teach was Jeff Meincke, the combie, who worked both as a processor and deckhand as needed. But other than teaching Jeff some of the operation of the boat, and mending nets, no, I never saw him attempt to impart any skills or teach or advance anybody's knowledge of the boat."

Most of Miller's testimony reflected poorly on Rundall. Life on the boat, according to Miller, was miserable; spirits were always sagging. The primary target of Rundall's ire, Miller said, was the tall, friendly deckhand Eddie Haynes. Miller reported a rumor that circulated on the boat that Rundall, thinking Haynes to be feckless, intentionally slashed Haynes's rain suit.

The bunks in the crew staterooms, as Miller described them, would have been difficult to alight from. Narrow, crowded, and cluttered, the cabins afforded very little room to move around in. And conditions in the fish factory were sloppy. Waste water collected on the floor and sloshed around. Near the end of his testimony, Miller was asked whether he felt Rundall was a competent captain. Miller put aside his judgment of Rundall's personality and gave his endorsement of his captain.

"I had confidence in his ability to handle the boat and his ability to provide for our safety," Miller said. "I never questioned those. His skill on deck was very impressive. He was light on his feet and very quick with his hands and very proficient at handling the net and tears and obstacles and problems he might run into. There was the incident where we broke our net reel, where that broke down, and I saw him, again, lose his cool and make some bad decisions that affected all of us. But that was also one of my last days on the boat."

Of the details Miller provided, the most important seemed a small thing at the time. The crew was in the lazy habit of leaving the rear hatch of the processing deck tied open to let in fresh air and make exiting the room easier.

Miller's characterization of Olney was of an owner who either condoned or was oblivious to abusive behavior. Olney's lawyers called Miller earnest and sincere but naïve to the rigors of working on the Bering. They guessed he was also very upset, because two of the men who died, Shawn Bouchard and Jim Mills, had been good friends of his.

The two buddies from Montana arrived in Seattle in January and eagerly cruised the docks and offices of Fishermen's Terminal for jobs on a boat. They had tried this before, one summer in Homer, Alaska, with no luck. So they felt especially blessed to have picked up two spots on the *Arctic Rose*. Bouchard and Mills arrived late in the month, but because Jeremy Busby and Brandon Conrad both flunked drug tests, there were still positions left aboard the *Arctic Rose*. Once addicted to drugs themselves, Bouchard and Mills must have recognized the irony. And being born-again Christians, they might have seen it as a sign from God. If they needed any more reassurance, they soon saw it. From a short distance on the dock, they spotted Nathan Miller, whom they had met the previous summer in Montana, where Miller had found work fighting forest fires. A mutual friend had brought Miller to the Assembly of God church Bouchard and Mills attended in Harlowton. The men were elated at such a coincidence. None had previously discussed with one another the possibility of fishing in Alaska. It was pure serendipity. To three committed Christians, it had to be God's plan that put them together.

Among the three friends, Jim Mills was the most accustomed to hard labor. He once operated a ski lift in California and helped build a mountain Bible camp in Montana's Glacier National Park. He also took a job as a pipefitter in a platinum mine. His father died of leukemia when Jim was ten, an event his older brother, Chuck, said dissolved the family, leaving the two boys clinging to each other. With no emotional compass, Jim drifted into adulthood with no particular plans, and like Shawn, he devoted his energy to finding and taking drugs. On one camping trip, Chuck said, Jim dropped so much acid that he remained in a trance for three days.

"Then we prayed over him," said Chuck, who lives in Salt Lake City. "It was instant and very powerful, and real, like something you'd watch on TV that would make your skin crawl. It was impossible for anyone to deny it was the power of Christ."

Jim soon after devoted his time to church, and it would serve to answer all the questions he alone never found solutions to. In the summer of 2000, their addictions under some degree of control, the two set off on an adventure, driving Shawn's old Nissan pickup truck up the Alaska Highway to Homer, where they hoped to find jobs fishing. But they arrived too late and settled instead for work pouring cement and serving food at McDonald's. They slept in tents pitched on the spit dock. Spit rats, they were called. But in this new year, they were determined to get on a fishing boat, and it seemed, to these hopeful young men trying hard to redeem their lives, that their luck had turned in a big way.

Before Shawn left home, unbeknownst to his mother, he told his younger brother, Brad, "If something does happen to me, don't be down, you be dancing a jig and enjoying life. I'll save a seat in heaven for you."

Shawn wanted his mother's blessing, which she would not give. What little Joan knew about fishing, she was not comfortable with. Short of a blessing, Shawn settled for a stalemate. It was days after he left, while she was making the bed, that Joan heard God's voice as clearly as her own.

"I'm going to make a man of him," said the voice she heard.

From phone calls from her son in Alaska, it seemed true that God in fact was making a man out of her son, teaching him patience and responsibility and consistency, values that escaped so many boys. Shawn was once a very troubled young man, who had once attempted to kill himself and whose hopes had touched bottom two years earlier when a deputy knocked on the front door to inform his mother that Shawn had been arrested. Addicted to methamphetamines, he had broken into a veterinarian's office to steal whatever drugs he could find. They took him to jail thirty miles away. The news was a deep embarrassment for his family in such a small town. The family could afford to bail out Shawn, but he refused. He served a total of about seventy days and was sentenced to three years of probation and given a fine, which he paid in monthly installments. He enrolled in a drug treatment program in Butte. His recovery so impressed the prosecuting attorney that he wrote a letter to the family, saying how proud he was of Shawn and how rare it was for someone with such an addiction to recover.

Shawn got a job selling mobile phone service, saving his money to pay for tuition at missionary school. And when he saw an appropriate opportunity, he sold the promise of God's love on the streets, ministering on the spot to anyone who seemed in search of something. He looked for men who appeared to be in pain, many of them Native Americans with their own addictions. He gave away a number of his things, like his microwave oven. He did not lock the door to his apartment, and once someone robbed him. He told his mother he didn't really care, that "I did enough stealing while I was on drugs, and if they can use the stuff, let them have it." The arithmetic seemed fair.

"This was not just a fishing trip to them," said John Bouchard, Shawn's father. "This was their mission."

Her fears about fishing unabated, Joan once tried to talk Shawn into grabbing Jim and walking off that boat.

"Mom, I signed a contract and I want to do it right this time," he told her. The Montana code, she remembered. A handshake is a handshake. He was proud of the work, too. He was looking forward to the next time his father or grandfather talked about how hard they had to work in the "old days." Now he had stories that would top them all.

After Shawn died, Joan and her second husband, Mark Branger, along with Shawn's brother, Brad, drove to Seattle to fetch his car, which he had put in storage. Joan retrieved the beige Honda CRX that Shawn, all six feet six, 240 pounds of him, somehow managed to pack himself into. In it he had left a bag of dirty clothes, one of them a fleece sweatshirt Joan had bought him for Christmas. Sizes that fit him were hard to find. The sweatshirt, she said, still smelled very much of Shawn, and she didn't know if that was something beautiful or just plain cruel.

In general, the fathers of the dead crew members seemed better able to absorb their losses, while the mothers angrily resisted them. Like Kathy Meincke, Joan Branger felt horribly swindled out of her greatest love.

"I'm not able to handle this," she said. "I didn't know how dangerous it was. I had no idea that a boat could just sink like that. You could say that's really stupid, but . . . You can't imagine the pain that you feel. You can wake up and think it's going to be a good day. But then you're driving home and a song comes on the radio, and it just hit me. I just want to get rid of this feeling.

"At one time I thought a boat from Russia had come and picked them up, and if I never saw them again but they were happy, it would be okay. How stupid am I. But you wouldn't believe what goes through your mind. Maybe when some of these questions get answered, I'll be at peace with it."

The only thought that brought her a second of comfort was that he had died with his best friend and after he had become "a true Christian."

Miller's stories gave those who wanted one a new villain in Rundall, whose responsibility the boat ultimately was. What few could have imagined was Rundall's own sad family history.

David Rundall the elder was born in Seward, Alaska. His father was a civilian supply officer in Dutch Harbor when it was bombed during World War II. After the war, the elder David's parents separated, his mother moving to Vashon Island (near Seattle) with him, and his half-brother, Sherwood, staying in Alaska with his father. David was shuttled back and forth between Vashon Island and Juneau. By the time he was in fifth grade, David had attended about a dozen grade schools, four in one year. His last school year in Juneau was the eighth grade. A new movie came into town every two weeks.

Otherwise, the only entertainment was to watch cruise ships smash into the dock. He decided he wanted to live with his mother, left, and never saw his father again. Four years later, his father died while transiting by ferry between Juneau and Ketchikan. Death by drowning, a coincidence the elder Rundall would remember forty years later when his son died the same way.

Davey Rundall was born in 1966, one of two sons, until, in the summer of 1970, the Rundalls took in three brothers sent by a foster care agency. They were the young boys of an alcoholic mother and two fathers. Their Aleutian village of Unga, on the Alaskan Peninsula near Sand Point, doesn't exist anymore. Unable to build a working harbor, inhabitants abandoned the place many years ago. The oldest boy, Steven, was eight, only months older than Lou Anne's own son, John. Norm, the middle brother, was six. Jimmy was four. Young as they were, it seemed a small miracle to the Rundalls that they had survived even that long. To keep them still and quiet, their mother had let the boys drink until they passed out. She had let Steven drive her car. She had once left the boys with a baby-sitter and did not come back for three days. Sometimes she just left them alone. When Steven went to a neighbor's home to borrow food, the neighbor got suspicious. The state took the boys from their mother and shuffled them through several foster homes before matching them with the Rundalls. It was supposed to be temporary, just for a few months until their mother got on her feet. A caseworker helped her find an apartment close to the Rundalls and buy furniture. She took parenting classes. She was supposed to take back her sons. But the summer ended and the Rundalls kept her sons. The foster care agency wanted to split up the three brothers and send them to separate homes. But the Rundalls offered to keep them all.

"We thought they deserved a chance to grow up together," said the elder David Rundall. "That's the main reason we got them. Maybe they would have been adopted by rich people if we hadn't meddled."

Baby brother Jimmy's blinding instinct was to find his mother. That first summer with the Rundalls, he drove them crazy with panic when he ran away to the nearby Kmart. Another time he walked farther away, to a different mall.

"I wanted my mom for some reason, I didn't know why," Jimmy said. "I was bound and determined, though. I guess they never understood that. I didn't say anything. I blacked a lot of things out."

Their mother, Pat, was encouraged to visit regularly. That way, she could learn to become a good mother, little by little. She said she would come to visit on Saturday. So her boys sat out by the door, waiting on the porch for hours, and she never showed up. After that, the Rundalls decided not to announce her visits to the boys, so if she didn't show, they wouldn't know she had broken a promise again. When she did visit, she spent all her time talking to David and Lou Anne instead of playing with her sons. One day she said she was leaving for California. She didn't come back for two years. When she did, the boys were so happy she had returned, they didn't even think about whether or not to forgive her. They couldn't remember what it was like to live with her, but all they wanted to do was be with her. They believed every unhappy feeling in their lives would be solved if they could just live with their mother again. The boys did not know their fathers.

While they were all growing up, the mix of boys worked exceptionally well, with no one taking sides across bloodlines. On August 12 of every year, one day after Davey's birthday but one day before John's, all five boys were consecutive ages. For all intents and purposes, they were real brothers who built and shifted alliances the way brothers do. They erected a playhouse out of scrap wood in the corner of the yard and would tear pieces off of it when they got mad at one another. They joined the Boy Scouts together, played on the same football and baseball teams, and defended one another in fights with other boys.

Steven was the most troubled of the three brothers. A caseworker who took a particular interest in him when he was young put him through a battery of medical tests. Scans showed he had abnormal brain patterns, the possible result of fetal alcohol syndrome. So Steven received disability benefits at an early age. He spent his Social Security stipend on drugs and alcohol. He smoked pot and stayed out until very late at night.

At sixteen, he dropped out of Chief Sealth High so he could run away and live with his mother. He forced her to take him in. He just showed up at her home in Queen Anne, a neighborhood across the bay, and moved in with her and her boyfriend.

"Shortly after Steve ran away, I thought I could do the same," Jimmy said. "The idea was to move in with my mom, force her to take you, she'd have to, and she did take me for a while, until it was impossible.

"We constantly made a beeline. It was a lovey-dovey baby thing, I guess. Steven would often say, 'I wonder what my mother is doing now?' I would walk over there to Queen Anne ten times a year, just to walk over there."

Adulthood was a mystery to Steven, a land for which he had no map. As he got older, he hopped railcars and occasionally cooked in greasy spoons or helped his uncle Bob weld at his metal shop. Disability checks kept Steven going. He needed a permanent address to receive them, so he'd use a hotel, which took half his money for granting him the privilege of using the address. The checks would arrive on the third of every month, about $600. Sometimes he took advances on the check from Jimmy. But he could never keep up and seemed always to be about $300 in the hole. Steven adored Jimmy, even as he manipulated him with guilt and begging, reminding him that when they were young, Steven had saved Jimmy's life, rescuing him from drowning. He threatened to kill himself when he thought that would get him anywhere.

In 1991, Norman got Steven a job aboard a fishing boat in Alaska, a factory trawler called the *Northern Victor* based in Dutch Harbor. Norm was a crane operator. He got Steven a job as a processor. Steven ended up quitting. They offered to let him cook instead, but he refused. It was his last job. He stayed for a time at Norman's apartment near the Ballard locks, using his brother's phone to dial 900 numbers. He stuck Norm with a $2,000 phone bill and went back to the rails, riding trains between Denver and Salt Lake City.

In the summer of 1994, Pat killed herself. She had never threatened to kill herself before. By then, she was married. She and her husband lived in a tidy apartment in Ballard. She worked off and on as a bookkeeper. She did have some health problems, living with severe neck pain after a car accident. She shot herself in the apartment with her husband's .22-caliber pistol.

David last saw Steven in 1995, in Salt Lake City. Once overweight, Steven had withered to skin and bones. He was the tallest of his brothers at five feet six and weighed less than one hundred pounds. He lived in a mission for homeless men. His mother's death broke him. He threw away a red pocket Bible given to him by the mission. He had nothing to say to God anymore. He descended into a deep depression, medicating on intravenous drugs. He moved into an alcohol treatment center. He asked for a weekend pass. Before he left, he took off a crystal pendant that meant a lot to him and gave it to another patient. Then he got a room at a motel. He used the bedsheets to hang himself. The Rundalls got the call from the Salt Lake City Police Department. Norm insisted on paying for the cremation.

The boys are of Russian, Norwegian, and Aleut descent. And from their Aleut genes, they inherited the programmed memory of oppression and learned hopelessness. It is as if the Aleuts possess a suicide gene. Alcohol stokes the tendency. The murder and suicide rate among people of Aleut descent is unfathomable. The overall mortality rate for Alaskan natives is three to four times higher than the national average. Alcoholism is high, as is the rate of fetal alcohol syndrome. The reasons are known and obvious. Since contact with Europeans, native families have been in constant upheaval. Theirs is a history of cultural death, political deprivation, psychological maiming, and a near complete loss of spiritual values. Those wounds manifest themselves in many ways: unemployment, incarceration, substance abuse, infant mortality, birth defects, murder, low school test scores, shorter life expectancy, heart disease, suicide, and broken homes.

Young native men between the ages of twenty and twenty-four are especially vulnerable, accounting for more than 80 percent of native suicide victims. Only car accidents kill more young native men than suicide. In the late 1980s, the suicide rate for young native men was thirty times the national average. While many causes of death among Alaskan natives are declining, a few have remained constant or are increasing, among them cancer, alcohol-related deaths, and suicide. In a recent report by the U.S. Department of Health and Human Services, experts estimated the yearly rate of suicide among Alaska natives to be the highest in the country, generally between forty and fifty per one hundred thousand, or five to six times the national average. The disparity swells among Alaskan native teenagers, whose suicide rate is eight times higher than the suicide rate for all American teens. Put another way, an Alaskan native teen is more than twice as likely to kill him- or herself as the average American teen is likely to die in a car accident. But as dramatic as the statistics are, they could not have predicted what happened to Pat's sons, nor could they account for the family's deadly history.

The boys' maternal grandfather, the family always suspected, probably killed their grandmother before killing himself. Pat's brother Dick was the next to kill himself. He was an alcoholic. The family called him Drunkle Dickie. He gave himself an insulin overdose in a motel. Uncle Bob somehow quit drinking, but his son Andy couldn't. Andy, an alcoholic, killed himself, too.

Of the five boys in the Rundall house, Norman was the odd brother out, the one who didn't naturally pair off with another. He spent a lot of time alone. He found odd things soothing. Occasionally, the family would hear a steady banging coming from upstairs. It would be Norman rocking back and forth, tapping his head against the wall. Norm was the quietest one and also the one with the most volatile and unpredictable temper. The boys could be just sitting at the table, eating cereal, when one of them would make some noise and Norm would blow up. Once he came leaping out of the kitchen in a boiling rage. John was sitting in the living room, holding hands with a date. And Norm went straight over to him and punched John in the face. Norm never said why.

Norman was the last of the boys to try to run away to his mom. He was in high school by then and somehow managed to get his diploma from Inglemoor High School in the nearby suburb of Bothell, where he lived for a time with a different foster family. He was the least inclined of the boys to leave the Rundalls and got the most years under their roof. They think that might be why he got as far as he did. When he was a kid, he even talked about wanting to become a lawyer. The boys laughed at him. They felt bad about it later, teasing him for whatever little bit of pride, ambition, and hope he had. There was a time when Norman's prospects looked good. He enlisted in the navy in May 1986. In 1991, he served in the first Gulf War, guarding Kuwaiti oil tankers before the American offensive began. He said he planned to make a career of the navy. But he quit in 1994 and went to work for AT&T aboard a ship called the *Global Sentinel*, which installed undersea optical cable in the North Pacific Ocean near Japan and between the Hawaiian islands. He worked as an apprentice, painting the ship's doors and keeping the ropes perfectly coiled. Between trips, the ship docked at Seattle's Harbor Island, near the shipyard that, off and on, employed Mike Olney. Norman kept an apartment near the Ballard locks, which he lived in for about ten months in two years. It seemed the perfect bachelor job. He got along well with his co-workers. The only pitfall was that he had up to two months off in Seattle between trips and he used the idle time to drink too much.

Comfortable at sea, Norman tried to pick up fishing jobs in between trips on the *Global Sentinel*. He found work with Western Pioneer, a company that operated small boats that supplied villages in Alaska's bush. He worked for AT&T for three years, until Harbor Island was designated a Superfund site by the Environmental Protection Agency. He seemed to change in those years after leaving the navy. His already volatile temper got worse. He picked fights with family members. In a tantrum, he drove his car up and down Davey's lawn. He once drove raving mad down a street, bouncing his truck off parked cars. When he finally quit working for AT&T, he ran off the ship screaming and crying. His family figured he had a nervous breakdown. He checked into the VA hospital south of Tacoma, the Madigan Army Medical Center.

As part of his treatment and recovery, they assigned him to live in a group home near the hospital, putting him in charge of the patients he lived with. He was supposed to make sure they didn't break rules, like sneaking liquor into the house or stealing other people's food. He found out he couldn't take the pressure of the responsibility.

In the summer of 2000, the Rundalls took him in. He was clinically depressed. He was also probably suffering from the latent effects of fetal alcohol syndrome. He got in touch with a girl named Gina, someone he was in love with when he was in high school. She worked nearby in Seattle and was glad to hear from him, and he thought maybe they could get together again. He lived for the e-mails she would send. When they arrived, he was ecstatic. When she didn't write, he would fall into a spell and lock himself in the bedroom all day. Eventually, he heard she was getting married to someone else.

The Rundalls could no longer cope with Norman's depression. Not long after the *Arctic Rose* sank, he had himself voluntarily committed to an outpatient program at Harborview Hospital. When he wanted to leave, they had him involuntarily committed. The hospital later put him on a program that allowed him to live on his own. He never told the Rundalls. In November 2001, he went to live by himself in the Star Motel on Fourth Avenue, one of the city's industrial blocks south of its sports stadiums. The Rundalls assumed he was living in some kind of group home. He had stopped calling, stopped answering his mobile phone. They hoped that wherever he was, he wasn't alone.

When news of his mother's death arrived in 1994, Jimmy had been diagnosed with Crohn's disease, a chronic inflammation of the digestive tract. It made working on a boat difficult. He was fishing in Alaska at the time, his weight down to 117 pounds. He doesn't remember who told him that his mother had shot herself. Jimmy hated his mother's husband, Bud. With him in the picture, he thought he would never have the chance to have a relationship with her. None of the boys did. He was just waiting for him to get fed up and leave her and didn't understand why he never did. When they were together, Jimmy said, all he did was hit her and curse and get drunk and spoil any occasion the boys ever had to spend time with their mother. She never did understand what her sons needed from her.

There was a time when Jimmy loved Bud. Starving for someone to lead him and love him, he looked up to Bud. Bud took the boys to the carnival and bought them candy, and it felt like love. Jimmy once moved in with Bud and his mother when he was thirteen and thought it was perfect. And within a week, Jimmy said, Bud beat the hell out of him. His response was to get into every kind of trouble he could get into. In and out of a juvenile detention center, he finally settled in with another foster family in Bothell instead of returning to the Rundalls. He never got past the seventh grade, but he earned his general equivalency diploma (GED).

He worked construction. He cooked. He fished for salmon in Bristol Bay with his uncle Bob. The boat and the gill-net permit belonged to Bob. Some seasons they made $30,000 in two weeks. Jimmy reunited with his high school girlfriend Cheryl, the girl he sneaked into his room, the girl he skipped school with, and they had a child in 1988, a daughter named Whitney. Cheryl and Jimmy got married in 1990. One year later, they split up. Jimmy couldn't count on salmon fishing anymore. The yields and the prices kept dropping. So he got a job as a housekeeper for a disabled man. Cheryl remarried and moved to Renton. Her new husband is a good provider, Jimmy said. Whitney makes straight As. She's smart "for some reason," Jimmy said. She attends a private school in Issaquah, an upscale suburb east of Seattle. Jimmy hasn't talked to her since 1997, even though she always asks what her father is doing, when she can see him, when she can talk to him.

"Yeah, I should call her," Jimmy said, knowing he won't.

On November 29, 2001, eight months after Davey died, Norm slashed his wrists and died in the Star Motel. The same week, he was finally approved to receive Social Security income for having a documented mental disability. At the next reunion of all the Boy Scouts, John was approached by a kid in his old troop. He asked how "all your brothers" were doing, and John had to tell him that three of them were dead. It was an awkward moment. Only he and Jimmy were left. He didn't say that Jimmy could have been on the boat, too.

Jimmy knew the *Arctic Rose*. He fished with Davey during the 2000 season, setting the gear. He planned to go again in 2001. But he was using drugs and knew he wouldn't pass the drug test, so he didn't bother trying. He didn't want to embarrass Davey. He was looking forward to working with his brother and his new friends Angel Mendez and Aaron Broderick. Davey, Jimmy said, was always a little worried on that boat. He always kept his survival suit close at hand.

Jimmy said he didn't go to the bathroom without it and took it to the wheelhouse with him. He even slept with it. He did not let the suit out of his sight. No, Jimmy was not surprised when they told him that when they found Davey, he was wearing his boots and his survival suit.

Jennifer Eichelberger, the fisheries observer who disembarked just before the boat's final trip, was one of the last witnesses to answer questions, well into the second week of the hearing. She became Rundall's redeemer.

Eichelberger's memory of crew morale was the opposite of Miller's. Her testimony went a long way to restoring Rundall's reputation. She recounted how the crew participated in a safety drill four days into her three-week assignment aboard the boat. She said she found Rundall engaging, confident, and competent. She said she never observed him abusing his crew. He made conservative judgments when it came to the weather, she said, always making sure to avoid rough seas. Morale aboard the boat, she said, was quite good, especially in light of the poor fishing. The men complained about their idle time more than about one another, she said. She recalled moments of levity and camaraderie.

"The guys seemed to get along pretty well," she said. "There was some teasing, nothing out of the ordinary, they were all just typical guys. I didn't detect any problems."

The safety drill, she said, "seemed like it was much more extensive than drills I typically see on fishing vessels." Eichelberger said the drill took place in inclement weather, during a steady sleet. The crew paid attention, she said, taking turns throwing the life ring and putting on survival suits. Angel Mendez translated for the Mexican men.

Eichelberger reported little out of the ordinary from her time on the boat. She also felt it was small, that its size made for an especially rough ride. But she never felt in grave danger. She recounted a few interesting details about the trip, situations that seemed odd if not uncomfortable, awkward if not dangerous. Sometimes, after a particularly good tow, the net was so full of fish that it would not fit on the rear deck and had to be hoisted on top of the factory roof, clearly not what it was designed for. She also remembered an instance, late at night, in which an excessive amount of water was allowed to accumulate on the factory floor. Someone had left the water running. She notified the engineer on duty, G. W. Kandris, who shut off the valve. Eichelberger corroborated testimony of former crew members, saying that she also remembered the weather-tight doors in the factory being tied or propped open.

Near the end of her testimony, investigators asked Eichelberger what she thought might have happened to the boat. She replied, "I have no idea what happened."

8

Dutch Harbor

The stone dust of the Aleutian Islands is released every spring from beneath a steely lid of ice. The drench of constant squalls turns the dust into a gray mud, and within days it seems to cover everything man-made in the Aleutian community of Dutch Harbor and Unalaska. The pale gray mud travels on boot heels, pant cuffs, and the bodies of pickup trucks and eventually gets inside buildings, on seat cushions, desktops, and telephones, until everything seems colored a shade of gray. Winter is white. Summer is green. But spring is the season of gray, the color of the mud and the color of the horizon, blurred by the low clouds in permanent residence, so thick that planes arriving from Anchorage often turn around and fly back rather than land.

Life in Dutch Harbor is like living in a black-and-white movie, residents say. Just twenty years ago, had you arrived in Dutch you would have seen only gravel roads, cars and scrap metal discarded by the road, and chuckholes that could swallow half a Toyota. Vehicles lasted little more than one season before needing to be junked or repaired. Until 1980, the port of Dutch Harbor and the town of Unalaska were separated by a narrow, shallow strait only a few hundred yards across. The community was, in fact, two separate islands, Amaknak and Unalaska, the name shared by the city. Dutch Harbor, widely used to refer to the entire community, is officially the name of the city's port. (Locals call their home Unalaska.) But to those just passing through, and that is most people, the place is Dutch Harbor. The port, and its fishing industry, is the reason anyone is here. Fishing is the warmth and light and motion that come out of the ice and the dark. Fishing brings in the jets and the container ships, and the people who accept death as a function of life.

"Death, here, is kind of a constant companion, I guess because of the remoteness and the weather," said Dave Stanton, a former fisherman who now works as a supply agent in Dutch Harbor. "Everything here is a struggle. That's why I want to leave."

His job is to receive and store supplies for fishing boats, everything from propellers to coffee filters. The *Arctic Rose* was among his clients. He counted Davey Rundall as a friend, "a pretty driven person, driven to excel, a hard, hard charger," Stanton said of him. "Most skippers or a lot of them are similar to David. It goes with the nature of the job. There are a lot of unmanageable people to manage, bad weather, mechanical problems, a lot to stay on top of."

Stanton and Rundall were neighbors, too, in Hilo, Hawaii, where Stanton and his wife, Connie, who charts the weather at Dutch Harbor's airport, own a home. Extended visits to the tropics and satellite television have helped the couple tolerate the past fifteen winters in Dutch Harbor. They live in an old cottage with a large wood-burning stove, a small garden, and windows looking out on to Iliuliuk Bay.

"It takes a tough person to live here," Stanton said. "It takes a different kind of person because you live about at the limit of everything."

The shoreline is narrow and rocky, the terrain more suited to birds and sea mammals. Flat land is scarce, and what little there is gets used. Dockside cranes and massive tanks full of diesel fuel are the tallest structures. Bald eagles as big as Irish setters are as common a sight as pigeons are in southern cities. In the treeless Aleutians, eagles are forced to roost on abandoned trucks or on unused crab pots, stacked twenty and thirty feet high by the sides of roads and docks when boats aren't working.

Recently paved, the main road here is barely two miles long and runs from the airport to the public utilities building. Several gravel roads loop off of it; others meander off into the mountains, quickly becoming undrivable. The only stoplight in the town is not really a stoplight; it turns red twice a day when the morning and afternoon jet nearly skims the road as it lands on the impossibly short runway. To span the strait and join the islands, the town built a bridge with a steel frame and a wood deck. It is simply called "the bridge to the other side."

The prebridge years were the time of the king crab boom, when men who fished for them could become rich, when most of the life in town was lived aboard processing vessels anchored in the harbor. Once the crab boom ended in 1981, millions of dollars in revenue disappeared overnight and crab boat owners scrambled to convert their vessels for trawling. Snow crab replaced king crab as the preferred crop. Pollock would not emerge as a force until the mid- to late 1980s. When it did, its powers were transformative.

The population of the community known as Dutch Harbor has always been difficult to calculate because of the transient nature of its inhabitants. As a Russian colony, no more than a few hundred people ever lived here. As recently as 1970, the population was only 178. The population changed very little over the decades except during the years of World War II, when up to 60,000 navy and army personnel were stationed in Dutch Harbor. The end of the war and departure of the military left the place nearly empty of people but full of abandoned vehicles, broken buildings, scrap metal, industrial waste, and other trash. The 1980 census showed a population of 1,322, the growth the result of the king crab fishery. The 1990 census reported 3,089 residents as the pollock fishery began its ascent. The number exceeded 4,000 in 1993 and has since leveled off, with the largest concentration of people in the Aleutian Islands, where only five towns are inhabited. These 4,000 approximate a floating population, a number that is constantly being spent and replenished. These are not the same 4,000. One person leaves, another arrives. Few stay very long, although more are doing so. It is one of the most diverse communities in America, with a remarkably even mix of races and nationalities. The population over the last thirty years has also grown older, owing to the relative lack of families raising children. Men generally outnumber women two to one in Unalaska. More than half the residents hold commercial fishing licenses. In that time, the amount of seafood landed at Dutch Harbor has increased tenfold as the per pound value of that seafood has been halved twice. That is because instead of king crab, pollock is now what is mostly taken from the Bering.

The end of the crab boom also marked the start of Dutch Harbor as a true town. Pollock could be fished year-round. And the income the fish generated was reliable and steady. Permanent jobs were created, and with them came a need for a more permanent population. Work was less focused on a single season. The town needed a larger service industry. Former processors and deckhands have opened restaurants or become clerks in city offices. Fishing now happens almost every month of the year, with only short respites in parts of May, June, and December.

The city taxed the offshore fleet and the shore plants, taking a cut of all the fish brought into Dutch Harbor. The city of Unalaska can now count on annual tax revenues of $20 million, generous for a town of only four thousand people. In recent years, the city has built a new school, library, community center, play field, senior apartment complex, museum, and City Hall and paved several miles of road, all paid for indirectly by the seafood industry, with cash not bonds. The new structures are painted in pleasing taupes and vibrant greens and reds to counteract the pallid landscape around them. Once housed in a trailer and World War II–era huts, City Hall is now a handsome two-story clapboard structure with windowed offices for all its employees, who can all walk to the city's gym to play racquetball, jog on its indoor track, or learn to tap-dance. Next to the City Hall parking lot is a skateboard park where boys practice their maneuvers on a half-pipe. The city also built a new mooring for the Coast Guard so that its high-endurance cutters may dock for long periods of time. The hope is that the Coast Guard will become a larger presence in the town. Only a few Coast Guard personnel are stationed permanently in Dutch Harbor, which is considered a hardship posting. They are not allowed to bring their families. With more Coast Guard might come certain amenities like a full-time doctor or dentist. Pregnant women still have to fly to Anchorage to give birth. Even a root canal requires a flight to Anchorage. Specialists visit Dutch Harbor periodically.

The city would still like to pave more roads, build a larger small-boat harbor, and add moorage space for the fishing fleet. But its greatest wish would be to add another two thousand feet to the airport runway so that more jets could land. Transportation to and from the island is the single largest factor limiting its growth. Apart from a monthly ferry or a fishing boat, the only way to get to Dutch Harbor is on a modified Boeing 737 jet operated by Alaska Airlines. About a third of the seats in the plane have been removed, creating a cargo hold in the front of the jet. The airline had to get a waiver from the Federal Aviation Administration to land on the 3,900-foot runway. Normally, 737s need at least 5,000 feet of runway to take off and land. Because of the shorter runway, the jets do not fly full and never fly at night. Two flights are scheduled per day, although weather often halts air traffic for up to four days. Lengthening the runway would require a feat of engineering since flat land is as scarce in the Aleutians as it is in Manhattan. There is plenty of open space, but most of it is mountainside. To extend the runway, builders would have to reach into the ocean and construct a jetty. The city estimates it would cost $150 million to lengthen the runway.

"It's probably not in the cards, even though we're the number one fishing port in North America," said Frank Kelty, the longtime mayor of Unalaska and now the city's natural resource analyst.

The city is also limited by the amount of electricity it can generate. All of it comes from low-sulfur diesel plants. The possibility of wind-generated electricity was studied, but it was determined that the Aleutian winds were too violent to be harnessed. So choices here are driven by necessity. The local bowling alley went out of business. No one has attempted to open a movie theater, although movies are sometimes shown for free at the school. There is enough money, but not enough people with enough discretionary time to spend. Nor is it entirely family friendly—there is no day care center—although it is becoming more so. Few are here to have fun or invest in a life. In most ways, life here is still all about business. And the only business in town is fishing. One way or another, almost everyone in the town is fed by the fishing industry whether they are municipal employees, longshoremen, or short-order cooks.

City planners have paved, plumbed, and excavated Unalaska from outpost to respectable town, a bloom on the tundra. But the burst of activity is probably not the beginning of anything much greater. These are not the seeds of a metropolis. Dutch Harbor is not the twenty-first-century example of old Damascus or London. It is still more moon colony than boomtown. Because of Dutch Harbor's remoteness, its inhospitable climate, its limits to growth, and the expense of procuring materials and labor in the Aleutians, the heart of the industry will probably always be based in Seattle.

The greatest impact of the sinking of the *Arctic Rose* was felt in Seattle. The pipeline of fishermen from Alaska to Ballard spread the word before stories appeared in the local newspapers. News of the disaster also quickly made the rounds in Dutch Harbor, where, as horrible as everyone agreed it was, it was digested without great emotion. The crews of factory boats like the *Arctic Rose* that trade out of Dutch Harbor spend very little time in its streets and among its people.

"They come in and they're gone," Stanton said.

Time spent in the town is time and money lost or opportunities for drinking binges, hangovers, and trouble. So time in port is left for the essentials, fuel, water, food, phone calls. To the people of Dutch Harbor, the names of the fifteen dead men were unfamiliar.

"The reaction was relatively detached," said Jeff Richardson, editor of the one-man local newspaper. "The feeling was not, 'These were some of our brothers.' I don't think there was a sense that this was a local event."

Richardson is part of a small, well-paid, professional class of teachers, nurses, city executives, and plant managers who never experienced Dutch Harbor's reputation as a Wild West colony of saloons and knife fights. There are bars, but they do not dominate the culture. Even a strip club didn't last in Dutch. Called Mermaids, it opened and closed in the same year, as residents objected to its placement so close to the school, rated among the best funded in the nation. Compared with the oil industry towns in the north like Barrow or Bethel, Unalaska is a cosmopolitan, progressive technocracy.

Dutch Harbor does have a place for its honored dead. Seamen lost to the Bering are remembered at Dutch Harbor's Memorial Park with a granite monument at the foot of a hilly graveyard overlooking Iliuliuk Bay. Some of the graves are more than a hundred years old, mottled, symbolic markers for nineteenth-century seamen from Russia, Ireland, Brooklyn, and Boston. The headstones, whose inscriptions are mostly unreadable, are clustered in the tops and creases of bulging earth, arranged haphazardly as if they were men who fell on a battlefield. The crosses are mostly those of the Orthodox Church, some painted white by caretakers, others left to the weather.

There is very little to mark the passing of the first people who arrived. The last few hundred years are a relative blip in their history but changed the course of their destiny forever. For thousands of years, they imported nothing yet thrived on only what they could scrape off the rocks and pull from the ocean.

The indigenous people of the Aleutian Islands are thought to have arrived by the land bridge thousands of years ago, settling in numbers as high as twenty-five thousand along the archipelago, a two-thousand-mile necklace across the breast of the Bering. The Aleuts were the most rugged of all native Alaskans, dependent on the treacherous seas around them for life. Examination of the preserved human tissue of early native Aleuts showed they possessed the same carbon composition as seals, their bodies similarly adapted to the climate. They ate fish, sea mammals, and seabird eggs but had very little fruit or vegetables. Yet the arteries of tribal elders were discovered, upon autopsy, to be as clear and healthy as those of a teenager. They called themselves Unangan, "the People of the Passes." They were the first people of Alaska, the ancestors of what we know as Eskimos. Aleut artifacts have been found dating back nine thousand years, while the oldest artifacts found in the rest of the Arctic are four thousand years old. The early people were successful, on the verge of civilization. Almost every kilometer of coastline in the Aleutians has evidence of a former village.

The Aleuts made the most of what they hunted, finding a use for every part of a sea mammal. They also made use of any driftwood that found its way to their shores, as the islands supported no trees.

Driftwood became the frames for their kayaks. They were covered with seal and sea lion gut, making them nearly transparent. From these light, agile craft, Aleut hunters harpooned more seals and sea lions. The Aleuts had few peers when it came to fishing and hunting at sea. They could harpoon an otter or a seal from a boat a hundred feet away. After killing a large mammal, like a sea lion, a hunter filled its stomach with air so that it floated, then towed the huge carcass to shore. The Aleuts also fabricated parkas out of seal gut, the membrane light, waterproof, and very durable. An experienced hunter could paddle twelve to eighteen hours without rest. Traveling at speeds approaching eight knots, a hunter could venture one hundred miles out to sea, using the wind, tide rips, direction of ocean swells, and flight of birds as directional cues. To the Aleut, the terrain of the sea was full of detail, every current and ripple unique.

Families lived communally in bunkers, built partly into hillsides. They were framed with whalebone and driftwood, sheathed with sod. Entrance was gained through a porthole in the ceiling. A notched log served as a ladder. As many as forty families might have lived in these bunkers, some of which were almost two hundred feet long.

Had the Russians not arrived two hundred years ago and hijacked the Aleut culture, scientists believe, it would now be quite sophisticated.

"They were about to make that big cultural jump," said archeologist Richard A. Knecht, director of the recently created Museum of the Aleutians in Unalaska. "It tends to happen when you reach a point in the population growth when all of a sudden technology and art race forward."

The decisive expedition, Vitus Bering's final voyage, was called the Great Northern Expedition. Once reports of the massive herds of sea mammals made their way back to Russia, the fur traders called *promyshlenniki* quickly came. They had eager customers in China and England who were willing to pay a high price for otter fur, which was among the densest of all furs. It did not take much hunting to make a trip highly profitable. The *promyshlenniki* were cowboys of their day, generally uneducated, rugged, fearless, independent, defying interference from the government, focused on the success of their enterprise. They are like most who have come to Alaska. The *promyshlenniki* were concerned primarily with otter pelts, hunting them as if they reproduced like fish. In fact, they produced maybe one pup per year and were quickly hunted to near extinction. The otters still have not recovered.

The damage to the otter population, started hundreds of years ago, is reflected in the decimated kelp forests of the Aleutians. Without the otters to eat sea urchins—because their metabolism is so high, otters eat about a third of their body weight in fish and shellfish every day—urchins have overrun the forests, eating all the kelp, attaching themselves to everything like a spiny plague. The otters that numbered in the millions were swiftly reduced to about one thousand by the end of the nineteenth century. The population rebounded to about seventy-five thousand within eighty years. But a recent count estimated a population of only a few thousand in the Aleutian archipelago. The further reduction was eventually attributed to killer whales, which had recently begun feeding on otters and other sea mammals, species they previously ignored. It seems humans are still driving otters out of existence—if not directly, then indirectly.

The fur traders did not blend peaceably with the Aleuts, killing the disagreeable ones, raping women, committing atrocities that, for the most part, went unpunished and unreported. Efforts at justice by the Russian government might have been made in the form of warnings or reprimands. But they were hardly enforceable in a place so remote and far away. The fur traders passed diseases like tuberculosis and syphilis to the Aleuts and introduced alcohol, which soon became a scourge. It was a story repeated in many places in the world. The Aleuts could not defend themselves, not against disease or assault. Armed with arrows and spears, they could not drive off the Russians and their guns, although some tried to fight with limited success, attacking some hunting camps. The Russians retaliated with overwhelming force, making it clear that winning the battle was impossible for the Aleuts. Once subdued, the Aleuts were made virtual slaves. The Russians forced the Aleut men to hunt otter for them, holding their families as ransom. The Aleuts were valued for their hunting skills and their agile kayaks. The brutal recruitment of

Aleuts was justified, in its day, as the gift of civilization to a backward and savage people. World opinion never intruded on the slavery or on the hunting to extinction of the manateelike sea cow or the near extinction of the otter, the whale, or the walrus. Only decades later would economic necessity force social change.

By the time the British navigator James Cook reached and charted the Aleutians in 1778, the Aleuts were used to the taxes of European men and to obliging, out of custom and defeat, their sexual impulses. Aleut women easily traded sex with Cook and his men in exchange for nothing more than tobacco. The Aleut men stood by agreeably, quite used to it already. And the British happily presumed the behavior was a quirk of the native culture. They were glad for it, even as they looked down upon them for it. At the end of the eighteenth century, a population originally estimated at twelve thousand to fifteen thousand Aleuts or Unangans had fallen to a few thousand.

By then, the Russians were not the only ones wanting to make money off the region's furs. The Spanish, English, and Americans coveted the area's resources At that time, there was much more commercial interest in the Bering region, despite its remote location, than there was in California. As a result, the Russians formed a fur-trading monopoly called the Russian American Company, which for all intents and purposes would serve as the de facto government for Russia's American territories. The company was led by a governor appointed by Russian rulers. What we know as Alaska was born not as a colony or state per se, but as a corporation. By 1830, profits had become slim. The cost of provisions and transportation had always been high. And now the otter population was substantially depleted. Sentiment in Russia to sell the territory and the holdings of the company was building. Alaska's purchase by the United States would become the legacy of William Henry Seward, secretary of state to both Andrew Johnson and Abraham Lincoln, to whom he lost a bid for the presidency.

Born and educated in upstate New York, Seward was the state's governor from 1839 to 1843. As a U.S. senator from 1849 to 1861, he took a firm position against slavery. As secretary of state, he pushed a policy of American geographic expansion. He tried but failed to persuade Congress to approve the purchase of several Caribbean islands and the annexation of Hawaii. But in 1867, Seward successfully brokered the purchase of Alaska from the Russians for $7.2 million. Most of the Aleutian Islands were included in the deal. But the Commander Islands to the west were kept by Russia. At the time, the sale was seen as holding more political than economic value. (Deemed imprudent by public opinion, the purchase was called Seward's Folly, Seward's Icebox, and Walrussia.) The true motivation was the obvious wealth of minerals and fur. Even today, Alaska's value to its country is its extractive resources, wood, oil, fish. The hunting of otters initiated by the Russians was finished by the Americans with frightening efficiency, culling an estimated population of millions down to a few thousand, the otters an allegory for the people who first hunted them.

Like the otters, the once thriving Aleuts barely survived into the twentieth century. Half of them, about five hundred, lived in the village of Unalaska, which by then had become the closest thing the Aleutians had to a city. Methodists and Russian Orthodox Christians had a church and orphanage there. The U.S. Bering fleet was based there. Life for the surviving Aleuts resembled that of their ancestors in a few ways. Some still made kayaks and clothing out of gut and fished the waters with great skill. They subsisted on what they could catch, occasionally sold fox pelts, and picked up work offered by the various American ventures that came through. Almost all had succumbed to the indoctrination of the Russian Orthodox Church and were devout servants. They were compelled to buy consecrated candles at an unreasonable markup but did so obligingly. To this day, Aleuts are closely tied to the Russian church.

The port of Dutch Harbor came into prominence when gold was discovered in Nome in 1898. Within a year, the land around Nome was completely staked off, except for the beaches, which were also found to hold large stores of gold. The rush lasted about ten years. During the Alaskan gold rush, Dutch Harbor served as a coaling station for ships making the transit from Seattle to Nome, then a thriving city of 20,000, now a town of 3,500. Prospectors spent winters in Dutch Harbor so they could be in Nome at the start of spring. The gold rush gave birth, in Dutch, to a small industry building flat-bottomed riverboats the miners needed in Nome. If they didn't buy the boats in Dutch Harbor, they would have to sail them from Seattle, a dangerous and foolish journey.

Back then, government stood in the form of the U.S. Revenue Cutter Service, the precursor to the U.S. Coast Guard. Unalaska was its headquarters. The vessels of the Cutter Service carried judges, doctors, and scientists. They rescued mariners and acted as federal custom agents.

The fur trade continued well into the twentieth century. Arctic blue fox replaced the nearly extinct otter as prey. Found naturally in the western Aleutians, the foxes were captured, released, and allowed to breed on other islands. In 1913, a trapper could lease an entire island for $25 a year. Trappers camped all winter on many of the islands, breeding and hunting foxes until the 1940s, when at last the foxes could not breed quickly enough to satisfy the metabolism of the hunt. The fox population had been spent.

Industrial fishing did not yet exist in the early 1900s, although it was approximated by a Bering Sea whaling industry based in Akutan Island forty-five miles to the east. President Taft, in the final days of his term, signed an order setting aside all of the Aleutian Islands as a wildlife reserve. But then, as now, commercial interests took sway, and under the administration of the next president, Woodrow Wilson, Taft's order was amended to allow whaling. After depleting the Atlantic and the Pacific oceans, whalers traveled to the Bering.

The American whaling industry peaked in the mid-1800s. Companies from New England had sailed as far as the South Pacific in search of whales and their precious oil. The method of hunting whales with harpoons and teams of men in small boats remained unchanged for decades. By the turn of the century, however, what little whaling was still being done, as it was in the Bering, was made more efficient by using explosive harpoons. The ships that hunted whales were the earliest catcher-processors. Whales were dissected aboard them. They were hunted for their oil, rendered out of the blubber and flesh. The rest of the carcass was turned into fertilizer. Whaling demanded a lot of capital to purchase equipment and secure a crew for work so far away from the offices where the deals were struck. There was little fear back then that the hunt would drive whales to extinction. The whalers of Akutan rendered their catch onshore and employed men from a mix of nations. Even then, the life drew men from around the world. Aleuts, Japanese, Scots, and Norwegians worked side by side, for the most part happily. From journals kept by some of the whalers, we know that fights broke out over the same subjects, over how much money was being made, about the quality of the food. To pass the time and deter boredom, men made games out of routine experiences, like growing their facial hair. In every group of men, there was always one who acted as the scapegoat, one who hated the captain, the oddball, the suspicious one, the shy one. And so it was for the crew of the *Arctic Rose*. So much of what was true long ago remains true today of the Bering fisherman's life.

In the 1930s, herring became the first Bering fish crop processed in bulk. The small fish were salted and put in barrels for transportation to the mainland and abroad. Soon, Dutch Harbor would prove its worth to the military.

In 1939, the total military presence in Alaska amounted to three hundred soldiers, most of whom lived in Chilkoot Barracks in the southeast. The navy had a radio station in Dutch Harbor, with thoughts of developing a seaplane base there. But when Pearl Harbor was bombed and the United States entered the war, the army quickly turned Dutch Harbor into a full-scale military installation with artillery nests, an airfield, barracks, and a weather station. In June 1942, the Japanese attacked Dutch Harbor as an attempt to divert American naval forces away from the South Pacific, where the two nations' navies would wage the pivotal battle of Midway. Two days of bombing killed and wounded more than one hundred in Dutch Harbor. American fighters, launched from a secret air base disguised as a cannery, engaged the Japanese in dogfights. American bombers went looking for the Japanese carrier fleet presumed to be nearby. But most of those planes were shot down or got lost in the Aleutian fog. The bombing and ensuing battle was a small one, amounting to relatively few losses for both sides. As a diversion, the bombing of Dutch Harbor was ineffective. A much bloodier battle lay ahead.

The only foreign occupation of the Americas during World War II took place with little notice on the western Aleutian islands of Attu and Kiska, where as many as 7,500 Japanese troops lived and maintained antiaircraft batteries, a radar station, fighter floatplanes, and midget submarines. The Japanese even built a hospital and sanitation system. To thwart the Japanese presence, the Americans, from their air base on Umnak Island, dropped more than twenty-six thousand bombs on the Japanese and destroyed or harassed Japanese supply vessels and troopships headed for the Aleutians. Eventually, the Japanese military abandoned their troops in the Aleutians. The carrier group assigned to support them was needed in the greater war. Now isolated and vulnerable, the Japanese-controlled islands were ripe for an American invasion.

About 2,500 Japanese troops remained when the Americans retook Attu in a lopsided battle, one of the few fought on American soil during World War II. More than thirty major U.S. ships and 12,000 troops were involved in the invasion of Attu on May 11, 1943. They landed on opposite ends of the island, pushing the vastly outnumbered Japanese occupying force up to a ridge, where the soldiers' only hope was the arrival of reinforcements. None ever arrived. After eighteen days of fighting, the surviving 750 or so Japanese soldiers led a final charge down from the ridge and were easily defeated as the battle for Attu ended. Almost 3,000 soldiers died, the vast majority Japanese. Many committed suicide with hand grenades rather than be captured. Only twenty-eight Japanese soldiers were taken prisoner. Nonetheless, it was as costly a battle for the Americans as the battle of Iwo Jima.

The taking of Kiska was far easier. Near the end of July, using the cover of thick fog, Japanese warships evacuated 5,100 troops in less than an hour. Unwilling to believe the Japanese had given up without a fight, U.S. forces went through with their plans to invade the abandoned Kiska two weeks later. Not a single Japanese soldier remained. But hundreds of U.S. soldiers were killed by friendly fire, booby traps, and land mines. After retaking Attu and Kiska, the

Americans put the Japanese air bases to use, launching bombing raids on Japan from the islands.

The natives paid a price in the war, too. Some Aleuts were taken prisoner by the Japanese. Others were relocated by the Americans to southeast Alaska during the war, where the land of thick forests was foreign to them. And many suffered from malnutrition in the relocation camps. Their villages in the Aleutians were dissolved and never reconstituted. Even once the war was over, they had no homes to go back to.

Apart from the battle for Attu, a posting to Dutch Harbor meant more boredom than danger for American soldiers. Most of the war years were uneventful. To fight the monotony of the gray days, soldiers turned to their own version of moonshine, nicknamed "the Aleutian solution," a concoction made from raisins fermented in a fire extinguisher for two weeks. Soldiers also drank cough medicine, aftershave, or vanilla extract.

Modern Dutch Harbor comes with many more diversions, comforts, and pastimes, provided they can be loaded onto a container ship or transmitted by satellite. The port is so busy, it has two cranes to off-load ships. For its isolation, the town is impressively connected to the rest of the world, to its entertainment, its news, its fast food. It all comes, however, with a substantial markup. A gallon of milk costs $5, same for a Whopper with cheese. Its supermarkets, as large as any in suburban America, stock all manner of international delicacies for its global workforce. You can buy wasabi, masa flour, chorizo, and lemongrass. You could find Filipino groceries more easily in Dutch Harbor than in the middle of most American cities. Its few restaurants cover all the necessary cuisines, serving tamales, sushi, kimchee stew, and Vietnamese pho. If someone will buy it, a store here will find a way to stock it. What you cannot buy here is also telling, high heel shoes for one, neckties for another, both of which are impractical and therefore useless in the Aleutians. However, the store shelves do allow for daydreams, secret wishes, and longed-for vacations, so you will find tropical print sport shirts hanging next to the rain suits.

In Dutch Harbor, the employer of the most people is the UniSea Corporation, which operates the biggest fish-processing plant in

Alaska. At any given time, about one thousand people live and work at UniSea's plant complex on the back side of Iliuliuk Harbor, where fishing boats arrive to pump mostly pollock from their fish holds into the plant's holding tanks, filled with refrigerated seawater.

For the duration of their contracts, the people who work at UniSea lack for nothing. Room and board, airfare from Anchorage, and laundry services are all provided. About the only thing the company won't do is clean your room. The UniSea dormitory has a full-time cafeteria, weight room, lounge with a projection TV, commissary, and game room. Employees bunk three to four per room and work every day during their five-month contracts, earning a little more than $7.15 an hour, much of which employees can save, as almost all their living expenses are paid for. The workforce comes from far away, the Philippines and even Ethiopia. Alaska's fishing industry seems immune to recession. One of UniSea's employers used to work at a hotel in Honolulu, another assembled circuit boards for Cisco Systems in California. Both found greener pastures here in the Aleutians, after the Japanese recession curbed tourism in Hawaii and after technology spending slowed to a trickle.

UniSea is owned by Japanese but run and managed by Americans. The complex is self-contained and self-sufficient. Electricity comes from UniSea's own diesel generators. The company runs its own medical clinic and upscale (by Unalaska standards) hotel, the three-story Grand Aleutian a few hundred yards away. The only real hotel in Unalaska, it is famous among Coast Guard personnel for its Wednesday night seafood buffet.

The buildings of the plant are clad in ice blue corrugated metal. The company's offices are clean and brightly lit, with cream-colored walls, mauve carpeting, and stained-oak furniture, setting a cheerful and efficient mood against the icy squalls outside. UniSea processes crab, halibut, and cod, but its major product is pollock.

UniSea ships its pollock directly to Europe and Asia and to distributors in Washington State. Asia is its largest market, Europe its fastest growing. The U.S. market is static. The same long-liners and trawlers, dozens of them, have had contracts for years with UniSea to catch fish and deliver it to the plant. They are strictly catcher vessels, which do not process or freeze the fish. They generally stay close to shore in order to get back to the plant quickly, usually within twenty-four to thirty-six hours of catching the fish. They cannot hold as many fish as the processors but don't need to since they unload frequently.

Pollock are first sorted by size, with the smallest being turned into surimi. Machines behead the fish, eviscerate them, and remove the backbones. The flesh is minced, washed, and then spun dry much like laundry. The larger fish are turned into fillet blocks. Machines also skin and fillet the fish, leaving to humans the task of inspecting the flesh for worms, bones, or bruises. Only perfect fillets will be frozen into blocks. A conveyor belt, lighted from below, aids the inspection process. Illuminated this way, pollock flesh is beautifully translucent. Almost none of the fish is wasted. The roe of female fish can be eaten. The milt, or sperm, from the males is sold for use in the manufacture of cosmetics and gourmet chocolate. Oil is extracted from pollock livers. Any waste is converted to fish meal or bone meal. But the true prize is the fillets, which are put into shallow pans and frozen for two hours to minus thirteen degrees Fahrenheit. The pans are sent through an X-ray machine to detect stray bones and then through a metal detector before the fillets are packaged and stored in a giant freezer the size of an indoor tennis court.

To appreciate what the crewmen of the *Arctic Rose* were asked to do, consider that they had to perform essentially the same work done in UniSea's warehouse-size plant but on the backs of tumbling waves.

As the Marine Board hearing in Seattle came to an end, the planned testimony of David Olney was postponed indefinitely. On Friday, June 22, 2001, his attorneys told the board he would not testify unless he received in advance a guarantee that his testimony would not be used against him in any criminal investigation. Olney buried his face in his hands and wept as his attorneys spoke. Olney, his lawyers said, wanted to testify and was reluctant to ask for immunity and remain silent because of the impression it would create. But in the end, he listened to his attorneys. After the 1990 sinking of the factory trawler *Aleutian Enterprise*, in which eight crewmen and one fisheries

observer died, the chief executive and several employees of Arctic
Alaska Fisheries, as well as the owner of the boat, were indicted on
negligence and conspiracy charges by a federal grand jury. Six were
convicted, including the boat's captain. At the time, Arctic Alaska
was the largest fish-processing company in the nation.

Olney's testimony was important to the board. But they did not
expect to find the answers to their biggest questions in David Olney's
head. For those answers, the investigators planned to visit the boat
itself, which they hoped could be found somewhere on the floor of the
Bering Sea. Before the conclusion of the hearing in Seattle, Captain
Ronald Morris announced that the board planned to send a robot
submersible to the ocean bottom to find the *Arctic Rose*. The expedition would depart from Dutch Harbor, in the best scenario, sometime
in July. The money to pay for the mission, about $200,000, had been
approved by Coast Guard headquarters. The technology was available.
The board needed only to find a sonar operator, a pilot for the
submersible, and a ship to transport the team to the last known
location of the *Arctic Rose*.

Through the lenses of a videocamera mounted on the submersible,
the investigators hoped for a peek at something, perhaps a hole,
perhaps a much smaller clue, something that would tell them what
happened in the last hours. They could not look into the minds of the
dead. So the boat would have to do.

9

The Last Voyage of the *Arctic Rose*

On the evening that some would judge later as his reckoning, G. W. Kandris put away his tools, washed his hands, and announced his intentions for the rest of the night. It was the kind of thing Kandris often said. Usually, it was little more than enthusiasm and bravado and a bit of the aftershave talking, the fragrant vapors going to his head, spent tucked under the hoods of cars all day. The toiling of the day turned to electricity at night. And this was a special night.

"I feel like getting into some trouble," he said with a smile. "It's New Year's Eve."

His kind of fun often meant something got broken or someone got hurt. His kind of fun was lean on imagination and ambition and was not intended to be constructive. He worked hard enough at his job and took pride in it. He was good at it, no one challenged that. He had had few head starts in life. The top of his head often brushed against the low ceiling of his expectations. This was the charitable way to explain him. So with clean hair and clean pants, but with a little bit of the devil in him, he shot off into the night that would change his life forever.

He attended a New Year's Eve party hosted by a friend in Puyallup. An argument started. As usual, it was over nothing, talking too loud or singing too much. Whatever it was, it led to an insult. And that was the spark. Police were called to the house at about 2:00 a.m., responding to a fight involving a gun. When officers arrived, they found Kandris, bleeding and injured, locked in combat with another man. Kandris resisted arrest and had to be strapped to a stretcher so he could be taken to the hospital. Later that night, after feigning unconsciousness, Kandris fled the hospital still wearing his examination gown.

Fearing arrest, he looked for a way out of town. A friend told him about a fishing boat called the *Arctic Rose*. It needed more crew and was leaving Seattle for Alaska in a few days. Kandris passed his drug test and was hired on the spot. A few days before the *Arctic Rose* left her mooring along the west wall, where the crew fixed and prepared the boat, Kandris and a few others got drunk in a bar called the Highliner a short walk away. As near as anyone can tell, that was his last drink. So as the *Arctic Rose* prepared for what would be her final voyage, she had aboard her a fugitive among the crew, an unintended omen.

The *Arctic Rose* left Fishermen's Terminal on January 13. Davey Rundall was the captain, and the acting first mate was deck boss Angel Mendez. Milosh Katurich was the engineer, Mike Olney his assistant. Eddie Haynes was a deckhand. Nathan Miller, Jim Mills, Shawn Bouchard, and the men from Mexico known as Robert Foreman, Michael Neureiter, and David Whitton were processors. Aaron Broderick was the factory foreman, Jimmie Conrad his assistant. Jeff Meincke, the youngest aboard, was assigned to work in the factory and on deck, even though he had never been to sea before.

Within twelve hours of the departure, Katurich noticed one of the shaft bearings overheating. By the next morning, one of the bearings had melted. The boat had put in a full day of travel and reached Vancouver Island. From there, Rundall turned the boat around and returned to Seattle to have the propeller shaft pulled out. While repairs were made, the crew was given some time off. The boat left again on January 18 for a nine-day transit to Dutch Harbor.

At roughly the halfway point, five hundred miles south of Kodiak, the boat encountered rough weather. Those at sea for the first time, and they were many, were initiated to the unique agony of seasickness. Those who have experienced it have said death is preferable. The greenhorns vomited relentlessly. The others made fun of them, showing little sympathy. Katurich said the rear deck of the boat sounded like a seal rookery. Wind gusts rocked the boat constantly, once throwing Katurich from one side of the engine room to the other. The incident provided an occasion for Katurich's first run-in with Rundall, with whom he argued about the boat's course. Katurich said the two eventually compromised, and Rundall took a slightly less aggressive path to Dutch. Katurich and Mike Olney rotated shifts in the engine room, with Katurich working from noon to midnight. The bombastic Katurich was so loud, you could hear him from the bridge, talking in the engine room. Not having full faith in Mike Olney's abilities, Katurich felt the need to watch over him. Katurich kept his mattress on the floor and the door to his berth open at all times in case an emergency arose. Mike Olney was not the most ambitious or gifted man, but he had an accommodating and pleasing nature. Because David owned the boat, many assumed he was the accomplished one and Mike the fallible kid brother who rode on the coattails of his prosperous older sibling.

Mike did not care for fishing, and he could not figure out what was noble about it. If he could be a stockbroker, if he had had that kind of education, he'd rather do that. But what his life equipped him to do was make parts for ships, valves and conduits and coils and joints, and it translated well enough to being the engineer on a fishing boat when the tide went out on work at the shipyard.

"I can't say he enjoyed fishing," said Sue Olney, his wife and the mother of his two sons. "It's not like he couldn't wait to get out there. He did it for a living, to support his kids . . . Now David has been doing it since he was sixteen, that's his calling. Mike kind of followed David into fishing. But Mike, he was a machinist. He wasn't in love with the sea."

When he first tried fishing, about ten years earlier, Mike was part of a crew waiting out a storm, his fishing boat lashed to four others as a precaution. To pass the time, Mike and some of the men from the other boats convened at a table for a card game. After the game, Mike went back to his own ship, leaping from one deck to another. At that moment, a swell stretched the loose knit of boats. Mike missed his landing, hitting the side of the boat and falling into the ocean. He grabbed at whatever he could, the end of a loose rope. No one knew he had fallen overboard. Unable to hoist himself, he waited in the freezing water for several minutes, thinking he would die, before someone noticed. The incident filled him with caution but did not deter him entirely. Another layoff at the shipyard coaxed him to sea again. But he had a psychological layer of security. He did not work for just anybody, he worked for his brother.

"He trusted Dave," Sue Olney said. "Some skippers you didn't trust because they're more interested in money than safety. I worried when Mike fished with other skippers, but when he was with Dave, I felt more comfortable. And so did he.

"He would tell me about the danger, how the sea can change so fast. When he was gone, out there, I'd always pray, 'Please, let him come home safe.' I worried, but I always knew he was with a skipper that would take care of everyone."

The crew arrived in Dutch Harbor on January 27. David Olney was there to meet them, as was a roe technician sent by Olney's Japanese buyers, an elderly man in his sixties, a retired Japanese trawl captain who spoke no English. Japanese companies generally insist that technicians accompany non-Japanese fishing crews to guarantee the quality of the roe.

Ahead of time, Katurich had requested the purchase of $1,400 worth of instruments in Dutch Harbor to monitor the temperatures of the shaft bearings. Olney had easily agreed.

"He is a fair man," Katurich said. "I never had a problem with him. He was decent. He never bitched at you. He was always very calm even when there was no fish."

Katurich oversaw the installation of temperature gauges in Dutch Harbor. A mechanic put rubbing compound on the shaft to grind down the bearing, which was made of a softer material than the shaft and designed to reduce friction. The compound seemed to work. Further testing revealed normal temperatures. The overheating of the boat's propeller shaft stopped once the boat started fishing.

As one problem was solved, another arose. Just days into the fishing season, Olney had to replace a member of the crew. The boat's cook told Olney his grandmother was very sick and that he wanted to go home before she died. Many fishermen have lied to get out of a contract, but Olney took him at his word. He burned or overcooked most of what he made, anyway. He let cooked pasta sit out and dry so that it resembled barbed wire. He was disorganized, unnecessarily using every pot, pan, and dish in the kitchen, and he allowed bottles and plates to slide and break. His ineptness in the kitchen probably went unnoticed during the transit north because most of the crew were too seasick to care about eating. Olney scrambled to hire a new cook. Leafing through résumés, he found Ken Kivlin's.

Kivlin got a call from Olney while sitting in the kitchen of the home he shared near Bremerton, Washington, with his son, John, and his daughter-in-law, Michelle. She heard him tell Olney reluctantly, "Well, I'm not sure I'd be completely available." He mentioned his trip to Florida. Then he listened more and asked Michelle for a pen. After he hung up, he got out a calculator and began working the hypothetical numbers. He had a gleam in his eye as he added up his potential earnings. From what Olney told him, he figured he stood to make between $10,000 and $15,000 for a few months' work. The boat was already under way. He made a spur-of-the-moment decision to fly to Dutch Harbor and join the crew. The *Arctic Rose* was his third job on a fishing boat. He knew it was a much smaller boat and mentioned it to John and Michelle. They expressed their reservations and their worry about its size but stopped short of trying to talk him out of going.

"It was completely a monetary decision," John said. "He said he didn't really want to do this. But they made it sound like he'd clean up. It was just too good an offer . . . When we got his paychecks . . . it was just so tragic. He only made a couple thousand dollars."

Before Kivlin left, he drove Michelle to a doctor's appointment. She was pregnant for the second time, and it was shaping up to be a difficult pregnancy. She knew if she asked her father-in-law to stay, if she said she needed him to get through the coming months, that he would do it, that he would feel too guilty to leave. For a few minutes, she considered using her pregnancy as leverage.

"Now I wish I had hit him up to stay here, but at the time it seemed too self-indulgent," Michelle said. "I would have needed to say one word and he would have stayed."

When Kivlin came aboard in early February, the quality of the

meals served on the *Arctic Rose* improved dramatically. He knew
twenty different ways to cook seafood and was in a mood to show off.
His crew feasted happily off his enthusiasm and his recipes for
poached salmon, steamed crab, baked halibut. By law, a crew is
not allowed to keep by-catch like halibut and crab. The catch is to be
tossed overboard, dead or alive. Usually it is dead. Onboard observers
make sure this policy is followed. But smaller boats like the *Arctic Rose*
are not required to have full-time observers. And when no one is
watching and the crew is given a choice between tossing a dead but
perfectly delicious halibut overboard or giving it to the cook, the
choice is easy. Observers assume that fishing crews eat by-catch when
they are not on board to police them. And most observers are not
bothered by the practice.

"There wasn't anything he couldn't cook," Olney said. "It didn't
matter if one of the Mexicans wanted a taco or burrito. There was
nothing he wouldn't make. If somebody wanted something, in the
next couple days it was on the table."

Kivlin posed a fatherly presence in the galley, curbing arguments
before they broke out and smothering everyone with food. Most
fishing boat cooks barely qualify for the title. Some have short-order
experience. Some are just injured processors demoted to the kitchen.
Almost none are gourmet chefs like Kivlin.

He had an unusual background for a chef. Born in 1946 in
Willimantic, Connecticut, Kivlin was the middle of three children
and the only boy. He started cooking at about age twelve when his
mother died of leukemia. After high school, with the Vietnam War
under way, he enlisted in the navy to avoid being drafted into the
infantry. His tactic produced the opposite result. Instead of being
assigned to a ship, he was made a medic attached to a platoon of
marines on the front line. (Because the U.S. Marine Corps does not
have its own medics, it gets them from the navy.) Of all his friends
drafted into the war, Kivlin was the only one to see combat. In 1966,
while he tended to an injured soldier, a land mine exploded nearby.
With shrapnel embedded in his foot, he saved the injured man and
moved him to safety. Kivlin was awarded a purple heart and, for his
efforts to save the soldier, a bronze star for bravery. The shrapnel

wound got him out of combat duty. He stayed in the navy, working as an X-ray technician. After the war, he got married. His son, John, was born in 1969 in Maryland while his father was at a naval training center. "I was a celebration of him making it through Vietnam," John said.

His parents' marriage lasted only two years. She was an alcoholic, John said, and drifted away after the divorce. John was raised single-handedly by his father. Ken Kivlin served in several hospitals and hospital ships in Scotland and Spain. Although permanently docked, the hospital ships counted as required sea duty for Ken, who needed to be land-bound to care for John. When Ken was discharged in 1988, he had achieved the rank of senior chief, about as high as an enlisted man can ascend.

In 1998, Ken enrolled in a cooking school in Portland, Oregon. After mastering the basics, he attended a culinary school in Ireland to learn the finer techniques of baking breads and pastries. His first job as a chef was at an upscale lodge in Colorado, where he concentrated on preparing various kinds of meat, including exotic game. In the kitchen, he was meticulous and sometimes inflexible with those he worked with, perhaps because of his years in the military with its structure and regimen.

His family suspected his perfectionist tendencies became an obstacle to getting jobs. If he didn't have regular work, he'd still find ways to cook, taking low-paying jobs in hospital kitchens or volunteering to cook for children in summer camp. He felt good about the people he was cooking for, despite the pay. Occasionally, he'd put in for jobs on passenger ships or help cater special events. He wasn't too concerned about employment. He made enough to travel, to keep his options open and spend time with John, Michelle, and his granddaughter, Emma. He had a bedroom in the basement of their house. In return for boarding, he bought groceries and cooked gourmet meals.

He still had a thirst for faraway places and long voyages. He first cooked in Alaska in 1999, aboard two large fishing vessels. It was indelicate work under less than ideal conditions, but he liked the challenge of working with limited ingredients and of pleasing the tastes of a diverse crew. He quit one job over differences with the owner. Kivlin had his own ideas of what a boat's menu should contain and how clean the galley ought to be kept and what supplies he needed to keep it that way. The owner wasn't willing to spend the extra money, Ken told John, so he quit. The next year, 2000, Ken found what seemed to be the perfect job, cooking at a remote fishing lodge on Kodiak from May through September. It allowed him to spend the holidays with his family and the winter traveling and visiting friends. He chose the Kodiak job over one that would have sent him to the Bahamas to cook at a resort.

The lodge catered to small groups of people who wanted an exotic fishing vacation in the wilds of Alaska. Guides took out groups of three to five fishermen. Kivlin cooked for no more than twenty people a day. He was the only person in the kitchen and was given full control over the menu. The arrangement suited his temperament and personality. The lodge's owner, who lived in Portland, Oregon, became a friend. Considering him quite a find, he allowed Kivlin to try out any dish that struck his fancy. He had never before employed a chef of Kivlin's caliber, probably because no one so accomplished cared to spend months in such an isolated place, accessible only by seaplane or boat. Kivlin had planned to resume working at the lodge in May 2001 and had decided to spend the preceding winter in Florida visiting friends. He had no mortgage to pay and few responsibilities beyond his own happiness. His one financial aspiration was to buy some land near Bremerton. With that in mind, even as he made his plans for Florida, he applied for jobs on fishing vessels, leaving résumés with seafood companies in Seattle. That was how he came to the attention of David Olney. Kivlin had a little less than forty-eight hours to get to Dutch Harbor. He packed a few cookbooks, sweaters, a warm jacket, and his laptop computer, which contained his recipes and menus and digital photographs of his granddaughter, Emma.

David Olney felt confident in the crew he joined in Dutch Harbor. He trusted the experience of the few who had it and the diligence and enthusiasm of those who didn't. He had his best men where it counted, on the bridge and in the engine room. The deck boss, Angel Mendez, was on his second season aboard the boat. Most of his previous work had been on a shrimp boat. He started trawling in the summer of 2000, after coming into Olney's office and applying for a job. Aaron Broderick, the factory foreman, and his assistant foreman, Jimmie Conrad, also got their jobs by walking through the door. Both applied about the same time in 2000 and started out as processors. Like Mendez, they were on their sophomore campaigns, which made them veterans on this boat. Olney especially liked Broderick's personality. He caught on quickly, worked hard. That season, he replaced Rafael Olivares as factory foreman because he had won Olney's respect.

"He was a likable guy," Olney said. "He knew what he had to do . . . I really liked Aaron. Most of the crew got along well with him. He kept a good friendship with the guys, which is not easy to do when you're the foreman."

Olney liked Jimmie, too, liked his attention to details, his ability to keep the mood in the factory buoyed with his sense of humor. But Olney didn't care much for Jimmie's taste in music.

"I don't know what you'd call it," Olney said, "Like a combination of rap and heavy metal. I'd rather listen to a grinder cutting steel."

The crew had little time to warm up to the realities of Bering Sea fishing. Nothing about the beginning of the season was easy. From the start, mechanical problems arose, catches were paltry, and the weather was punishing. After the boat's first trip, deckhand Jeff Meincke wrote this letter to his girlfriend:

Dear Jessica,
The weather has been shitty. Last night we were in 40 foot swells with 70 knot winds. Pretty nasty. As soon as we did our second haul back, bringing in the nets & gear, the owner split for an inlet and dropped anchor. I had to help pull a crab pot out of the net. It sucked because of the weather. We had to put on life jackets just to go out on deck. Don't worry, I'm being careful. The last thing I want to do is die before I get to see you again . . . Think of how it will be when I get home. I miss you more with every day I can't touch you or kiss you. It'll work out don't worry because I still want you more than ever. Well goodbye for now my little princess. Love, Jeff your lonely fisherman.

Although he was hired as a processor, Kandris took the initiative early on to spend his spare time in the engine room, gleaning knowledge from Katurich. Kandris was familiar with the kinds of tools used aboard, since they were not dissimilar to those used in an auto shop. Katurich found him a good listener, a quick study. He appeared very much in his element. It took little time for Kandris to learn how to weld, to understand the ship's electrical system, to make simple repairs like changing out generators or fixing the freezers. Before long, maintaining the relatively simple machinery in the factory also became part of his responsibilities. He was a sponge of mechanical knowledge. On land he invited trouble, but on the boat he was a marvel, a master, and constantly in motion.

"He never wanted to be sitting around," Olney said.

Anatomically, Kandris was also suited to the physical tasks aboard the boat, as he was thin and agile. He could squeeze behind awkwardly placed posts and fit comfortably in most of the ship's tiny spaces.

"He was like a mongoose," Katurich said.

Kandris's first substantial contribution was to help repair the hydraulic system for one of the freezers. Plate freezers work partly by mechanical compression. The refrigerated plates compress the trays of fish, squeezing out excess water. The compression is powered by hydraulics. And on one occasion, a metal hydraulic ram snapped. Katurich supervised the repair. Kandris, deft with his hands and comfortable with the guts of any machine, reached the broken part and positioned it properly for repair. Haynes welded it back into working order.

In those early weeks, the men settled into the tasks they were best suited to. In the factory, the Montana boys, big and strong but not so handy with knives, did most of the stacking and lifting of frozen fish.

Another problem in February was the main net. Olney had purchased, to start the season, a large net of 150 feet. He quickly learned that his modest boat couldn't tow a net that long in heavy weather or against the current. He made adjustments, dragging the net higher in the water and adjusting the width of the trawl doors to change the width of the opening in the net. In calm weather, the net worked fine. But the tide and the wind presented problems. In rough weather, the only option was to pick up the net and tow in the opposite direction, with the wind at their back. The improvement was nominal. The boat's net reel broke on the first trip off the slime banks, near Unimak island, causing the crew to return to port early. Eventually, Olney figured he had to order a smaller net. Between the first and second trips, the Montana boys helped install a new winch in the blowing snow without complaining. The rest of the crew was changing the oil.

"You haven't been really cold until you've been to Montana," Bouchard told Olney.

On its second trip, the crew fished the north side of Bristol Bay. That trip, too, was cut short a few days because Jeff left a mending hook in the net. The hook damaged the net reel when the net was spooled up for storage, breaking a reel bearing. The crew spent four days in Dutch Harbor waiting for parts. Bouchard used the break to convince some of the crew to attend a church service in Dutch.

"For a bunch of fishermen, that's pretty good," Olney said. "I think six guys went with them. I know he got the guys to listen to grace once at the table. I never noticed he was irritating anybody. He definitely let you know he believed in God."

Making matters worse, the fish did not school up as they usually did. Tows lasting up to four hours often yielded little or no fish. The empty net made for rough towing, as a full net acts to calm a boat's ride. Instead of making four or six trips by the end of February, the crew had made only two. Each time, the boat's freezer hold was not more than 60 percent full, this during prime roe season when head-and-gut boats are supposed to make most of their money for the year.

The crew trawled day and night to help make up for the slow start. The middle of the night was left to Jimmie, Jeff, and Nathan, who sorted the fish and emptied the freezers, a process called "breaking the freezers." They put the frozen fish into bags and moved the full bags into the freezer hold. The night crew worked from 6:00 p.m. to 10:00 a.m. The only other men up in the middle of the night were Mike Olney, the assistant engineer, and Rundall, who was officially the captain but took the bridge at night so David Olney could work during the day.

While Olney was aboard, Rundall generally slept between 2:00 and 10:00 p.m. At about 5:00 p.m., Olney and Katurich discussed the day's events and problems. Olney's assignment on the trip was the net, his official title trawl master. He knew the most about the new nets. He baby-sat the gear and kept it working. Olney never planned to stay with the crew very long. He just wanted to make sure the new nets worked properly before returning to the office in Seattle. But because of all the problems with the net, Olney spent more time at sea than he had anticipated. While he was aboard, for three trips, the boat's fish hold was never more than two thirds full. When the boat returned to Dutch Harbor, it was because it was out of fuel, not because it was full of fish. The men would sell what fish they had caught, trade videos with crews of other boats, take on fuel, and be on their way again.

Of all the men aboard, Eddie Haynes had perhaps the most difficult time adjusting. Nathan Miller testified at the hearing that he had become a preferred target of Rundall, who took out his frustration on Haynes. Although this view of events was not uniformly corroborated, it was no secret that Rundall was not exactly easygoing or good at hiding his frustration. And it was no secret that he did not find the affable Haynes the most able deckhand. So if there was an easy and acquiescent target among the crew, it was Haynes. He was an excellent welder, but his talents were not of sufficient use enough of the time. On deck, he was slow and awkward and not very robust. He tired easily. He absorbed the verbal abuse, mild and otherwise. Despite years living life on and off the road, his hide was not so tough. The weather got to him. So did the requisite cruelty of fishing. He told his mother on the phone how it disturbed him that so much sea life went to waste, the starfish, the octopus.

"They're so delicate and smart," he said of octopus to his mother. To her, he said nothing of his unhappiness on the boat.

He did not seem to fit in with any of the men. He had few to joke with, to talk with, and was especially unhappy. He was too old to be part of the clique of Pierce County boys or to shoot the breeze with the boys from Montana. The men from Mexico were friendly enough but bound together by their inability to speak English. The man closest to him in age was Mike Olney, who worked nights and slept days. That left Katurich, in whom Haynes found an unlikely sympathetic ear.

"This is not a job for me, Chief," Haynes told Katurich. "When you leave, I'm going with you."

Haynes was peculiar in some ways. He drank odd concoctions made with ginseng and ate oysters packed in oil, all of which he brought with him on the trip. His expressions were large and exaggerated. He absorbed teasing and had an easy laugh. And he told stories no one knew what to make of, like the one about the hundreds of acres of land near the Spokane River he had inherited from his father. It was worth $1 million, he said, but failed to explain why, then, he would need to take a job fishing. Whatever his eccentricities or shortcomings, they probably would have been forgiven, ignored, or invisible had the fishing been good.

No matter where the crew of the *Arctic Rose* cast her nets that winter, the fish were scarce. Olney and Rundall tried new spots, fishing in areas they weren't accustomed to. Unfamiliar waters meant tearing a lot of nets on rocks.

The Mexicans were the most eager to help repair the net. It was a chance to get out of the factory and busy themselves with something new. They stayed out on the rear deck the longest, helping the deckhands put the gear back together again. They impressed everyone with their work ethic. Olney was not sorry he hired them. Although their given names did not seem to match them, Robert, Michael, and David all had Social Security cards and what appeared to be legitimate documents.

"They had legal identification that had their names and Social Security numbers," Olney said. "Their green cards looked good. So we hired them. From an employer's standpoint you have to consider discrimination regulations. You can't exactly tell them, 'Hey, you don't look like a Mike.' If they're qualified, unless their documents are false, you can't discriminate against them just because they appear to be Hispanic and don't have Hispanic names."

Justino Opoll Romero, the man who called himself Michael

Neureiter, was the quietest and spoke the least English. He smiled often and said little. He never complained about fixing gear or cleaning the factory. Romero patiently held the net straight so it would be easier to sew. Sewing is nearly an art. The men had to match the weave, knot for knot, and make sure they maintained the net's taper. Everything had to be lined up straight. Loose ends had to be tied off before the two points were sewn together. Olney, Rundall, and Mendez were the most experienced net menders and tried to teach the other deckhands.

The crew, on its third trip, had mixed luck. Another storm kept the *Arctic Rose* from fishing, forcing attention on one of her biggest weaknesses, her inability to make money when the weather got rough. Jeff wrote letters to Jessica on consecutive days, February 21 and February 22.

Hi Honey,

Not much going on these past couple days, just the usual routine. I guess it's getting easier in some aspects of the whole work thing. It's still really long exhausting hours. My body is keeping up okay. I wake up in the mornings with cramps in my shoulders down to my fingers but they usually work out once the labor starts. Our foreman isn't doing a very good job unfortunately. You remember Aaron from the hotel. Well he's the former. It's probably hard for him because we are friends. He's in charge of day shift and Jimmie is in charge of our 3 man crew. It sucks because Aaron expects us to pick up day shift's slack even though there are 10 of them. But there's not much we can do about it. Last night was kinda exciting. We got hit by a good sized storm, windier than fuck and some good sized waves. I got hit pretty hard bringing the net. My boots filled with water, through my rain gear. But we tucked tail and ran as soon as the net came up. Now we're anchored in a harbor close to some remote island. Don't worry about the weather. If it gets bad, we have to wear life jackets. I know that's not much, but I'm not really worried about it. I'll come home safely. Well gotta go. Need my beauty sleep. As always I miss you lots. Nighty night. Love, Jeff.

On Febuary 25, while on her third trip, the *Arctic Rose* was boarded at sea by a Coast Guard inspection team from the cutter *Storis*. Such inspections are routine and intended to keep captains and owners honest. They are unannounced so fishermen cannot prepare for them. The team from the *Storis* checked for violations of safety and fishing regulations, making sure the crew did not keep any illegal by-catch. Shortly before the team boarded, Meincke had helped throw overboard an illegal halibut weighing 250 pounds, a gaffe hook stuck in its mouth. A few hours later, the crew would ensnare the same halibut, still wearing the hook, which provided the men with a good laugh.

Fishing boats are classified as uninspected vessels. Unlike passenger ships and cargo vessels, fishing boats are not subject to mandatory inspections when they are tied up at the dock. The Coast Guard can inspect a fishing boat at the dock only if the captain consents to an inspection. Usually, only the captains of well-run boats submit to inspections at the dock. But on the open sea, the Coast Guard can inspect a fishing boat at any time with or without the captain's consent. Still, of the approximately one hundred thousand fishing vessels in the U.S. fleet, the Coast Guard estimates it is able to inspect only about 7 percent. The policy almost ensures that dangerous or noncompliant boats will never get inspected, unless it happens by chance at sea. If the Coast Guard had its way, it would have the authority to inspect all fishing boats whenever it wanted. But such a change in regulations is not likely to happen because the fishing industry and its lobbyists are highly opposed to a mandatory inspection policy. The four-person team from the *Storis* spent an hour aboard the *Arctic Rose*, finding nothing dangerous or out of the ordinary, and allowed the crew to resume fishing.

"The only thing I remember," said Petty Officer Michael Ingrassia, "was the ladder going into the engine room was a vertical trunk ladder and on my way down I slipped and fell off the ladder about the second rung from the bottom because it was greasy. I came back up and reported that. Other than that, we didn't find anything wrong."

The inspection, said Ingrassia, was just one of hundreds he has done and did not stand out in any way.

Nathan Miller's recollection of the first month aboard the *Arctic Rose* was far different from that of David Olney, who remembered the lousy fishing, but none of the emotional torment or constant peril Miller described in his testimony. Miller never seemed upset or unhappy, Olney said, and attributed his description of the voyage to his grief at losing his friends and the shock of working at sea for the first time in his life.

"I remember seeing all three of them," Olney said, "Nathan, Shawn, and James up on bow, soaking in the weather, like they were on a new adventure, catching the sea spray."

Nonetheless, Miller's memory of the season provided an eye-opening view of life aboard the *Arctic Rose* in those first weeks and more than a few clues into what might have sunk her. He made no secret of his dislike for Rundall and Broderick, the men who supervised him. He was among those laughed at, he said, when he got violently ill during the tough transit to Dutch Harbor. He remembered food spilling from cupboards and the refrigerator. The galley and the staterooms were a constant mess, he said. The men were given a safety briefing on the way to Dutch. They were called into the galley and instructed on how to put on a survival suit. Each man had to practice putting one on and was timed to make sure he could do it quickly.

During the transit, the men suffered from rug burns from being thrown out of their bunks so often. On one occasion, Miller said, a row of men were thrown from the galley bench. For that reason, some preferred to eat on the floor of the hallway, their backs and feet wedged against the walls. More experienced seamen like Katurich took wide stances wherever they stood, and the greenhorns soon copied them. Miller frequently visited the bridge to ask about the weather, a bit too frequently, he guessed, as he got the impression his visits started to annoy Olney.

"I asked him if he had heard the weather report," Miller said, "and he said that he didn't listen to the weather, that the weather was going to come, that there was nothing we could do to change it, and that we were there to fish."

Miller reported waking up to bilge alarms almost every night and being told by Broderick not to worry about them. Miller doubted that the men, stacked as they were in cramped bunks, would be able to exit the stateroom in a hurry.

"I mean, if we took our time and coordinated our efforts and talked with each other and had an order to do it, we could," he said. "We did when we woke up for our shift or when we woke up in port. And then we took our turns getting out and getting our gear on and moving through the door."

The men stored their gear either on their bunks or in one of a few available storage compartments. That meant that many of the men threw their gear on the floor of the stateroom while they slept. Bouchard and Mills, in particular, always put their gear on the floor when they slept. The men were also in the habit of throwing their gear in the hallway when they slept because it smelled so much of fish and the messy work of the day, and they didn't want to sleep with the odor at their feet. Next to the engine room was a break room, where the men changed into and out of rain gear. It was not large enough to hold all of the clothing, just the rain gear and boots. And when people were in the room changing, it was difficult to open the door to the engine room. It was Kivlin who usually made sure the hall stayed clear.

"He was very deliberate about the way that he maintained that space," Miller said, "and that impressed me at the time because he was the first person that I had seen, really, to take charge of an area of the boat."

But as the season went on and the men bought more supplies and their belongings accumulated, housekeeping became more and more difficult. Eventually, any diligence they had about tidiness wore off. The obvious difficulties of exiting the boat quickly gave rise to gallows humor.

"If the weather was real rough or we had a lot of water," Miller said, "somebody would make the comment, 'Oh, this is it, we're going down, how do we get out of here if we go down,' and everyone would laugh. That was the joke."

There was a forward hatch that opened to the deck, in the engineer's quarters just below the anchor. But, said Miller, most of the crew probably didn't know it was there. And even if they had, they would have needed tools to open it, he said. Quick access to the survival suits, kept on the port side of the top deck, would have been difficult from the staterooms, he said, and would have required crossing the cluttered factory and climbing a narrow ladder. He said tools were kept in the same box as the suits, a cutting torch, a pipe wrench, mallets, extra fishing line, and several metal bars.

"Once up there, you would have had to open the box," he said, "and it seems to me, and I've thought and thought about it . . . that it was secured with a piece of line, that it was tied shut. And then they were packed in there, all of them in one place. And it took me jumping up and down on them to get them all to fit in there. And then there were tools stored on top of them. I didn't know where the life raft was. The exits weren't marked. There wasn't an emergency procedure indicated. My thought at the time was, If this was a construction site and OSHA [the Occupational Safety and Health Administration] was coming, we would be shut down, and especially with the hatches being tied open."

The hatches in question led from the factory to the rear or aft deck and to the mudroom and galley. Those factory hatches would prove crucial to figuring out how the boat sank. Every compartment of the boat was cramped, Miller said, particularly the factory.

"We were literally elbow to elbow in the factory," he said. "You were assigned your position by the factory foreman, and in a lot of cases that's where you stood for the duration of the shift. It was hard to move around."

The factory had no windows. One's sense of time vanished inside. The length of a trip, usually two or three weeks, was hard to measure. And it was only when the men returned to port and called someone that they realized exactly how many days they had spent at sea. The only sense of the weather outside came from the roll of the boat, which sometimes threw fish off the conveyor belts, and the breeze that came through a small hole near the floor. Miller described it as a five-inch drain hole, at floor level, on the port side of the factory, covered by a plastic cap. In calm seas, the men removed the cap with a pipe wrench to drain the water that collected on the factory floor. In rough weather, however, more water came in than drained out, Miller said. The hole was merely a backup. Sump pumps were the primary method of keeping water from collecting in the factory. These pumps failed several times, Miller said, and had to be replaced at least once. During one incident, water reached such a depth in the factory, about ten inches, that the bottom two plates of the freezer were submerged. Investigators considered this another important clue.

Miller described the fishing as erratic. Most days were bad, although he remembered a few successes.

"There were nights that we had an overflowing truck and it was such a good bag, so slippery, that Jimmy and Jeff and I were able to go up on the sorting belt up there on the incline belt and do nothing but sort and go through an entire truck in as little as two hours and have all of our by-catch over the side, all of our target fish in their bins bleeding, or waiting for the day crew.

"And there were nights that ran so efficiently that we had the truck empty, we had all of our bins full, and we had our incline conveyor . . . and the gutting belt completely full of fish. We overflowed them to make room. There were nights that it went that well.

"There were other nights where we spent the entire night just in the truck with shovels trying to get the mud and starfish and everything over . . . On nights that we caught really muddy or sticky bags, there were a couple of times we spent the whole night just trying to get the fish out of the truck. And where we would either pull up big rocks or big loads of starfish or real muddy bags. And that was our night, just getting the truck ready for the next bag."

If clearing the truck of mud and junk fish took a long time, Miller said, the crew would tow the net longer than Olney wanted to because there was no place to put the catch. The truck could not hold a lot of fish, and the factory could not process an unusually large amount of fish. That meant it was important to keep the truck empty. The night crew, only three people, was not able to do any processing. All they could do was sort, bag fish, and stack the bags. A good day of fishing meant a night spent breaking freezers. A bad day of fishing meant a night spent mostly sorting fish for the day crew.

The physical rigors of the work took a toll, as Miller reported hearing men crying or screaming in their sleep because of the pain in their wrists caused by the repetitive motion of cutting fish all day. After a few weeks, Miller got off the processing line and, like his friends from Montana, shifted to breaking freezers and stacking fish bags in the hold. He took every opportunity he could to get out on deck, to help dump fish into the truck or sort them. Occasionally, Mike Olney would ask Miller to help him with repairs in the engine room. Olney first asked Jimmie Conrad if Miller could be spared. Miller appreciated the break, which he saw as another opportunity to get out of the factory and learn something new. He and Mike Olney got along, and Miller found the work in the engine room interesting.

"I might grease some bearings or check on the shaft bearings," Miller said.

He and Mike Olney also took care of routine repairs in the factory. While Katurich maintained the machinery in the engine room, Olney was handed the responsibility of overseeing repairs in the factory. Many parts for the processing equipment were custom-made and relatively fragile, so repairs were frequently needed. Replacement parts often had to be fabricated on board. Mike Olney, as a former machinist at a shipyard, was suited for these tasks.

Men usually took their breaks on the small aft deck of the boat. Seawater, splashing onto the deck, often collected there in large amounts. That amount of water did not easily or quickly drain out of the scuppers, small openings in the side walls designed to keep the deck clear of water. Cold water shot up pant legs and sometimes knocked a man off his feet. This detail, of deep water on the aft deck, also provided investigators with an important clue.

The night shift started in earnest at about 8:30. Miller, along with Jimmie and Jeff, would typically finish dinner about then. They dressed in rain gear and went out on deck as the boat slowed to reel in its final haul of the day. Two of the men would secure the trawl doors. As the net came up, one of the men would attach it to a winch as the others released it from the net reel. The net was raised above the deck and its contents released into the truck. Then the sorting would begin. On one such occasion, Miller reported what he considered to be an attempt by Rundall to threaten Jeff Meincke's life:

"Jimmie and Jeff and I were hauling the bag. Jimmie was running the aft gilson winch. The captain had shouted for Jeff to wire up, and there was a delay, and Hawaii Dave (Rundall) jumped into the truck and rushed Jeff . . . I don't know, it was rough weather that night and there were a lot of other things going on."

Miller said he saw Rundall grab Meincke by the collar. He looked as if he were going to throw Meincke overboard. Miller moved to intercede but was stopped by Jimmie Conrad. Miller later asked Meincke about the incident.

"He didn't want to talk about it," Miller said.

After three trips, Miller no longer wished to work on the *Arctic Rose*. While in port, he attended church and afterward ate lunch with some men he met there. He stayed longer than he was supposed to, a passive way of inviting the end of his employment.

"I expected to get in trouble for it," he said.

He was reprimanded when he returned. Miller was offered an opportunity to quit and join the crew of a crab boat, the *Shishaldin*, a slightly larger boat with a crew of six. He jumped at the chance. He complained one last time to Rundall, telling him communication in the factory was terrible, and also suggested his friend Jim Mills be promoted to assistant engineer. Rundall took neither the assertion nor the recommendation very seriously.

"I talked to my friends before I left, and I was worried about them," Miller said, "but they were all more worried about me leaving for the crabbing boat because it was a more dangerous fishery."

David Olney also departed after the third trip, leaving Rundall in charge. The new first mate, Kerry Egan, joined the crew in Dutch Harbor. Olney didn't know Egan very well, though he had talked to him over the radio before, trading information about fish while trawling the same waters. The two met for the first time on the docks of Dutch Harbor. Egan came well recommended by Rundall, who had worked with Egan aboard the *Beagle*, Rundall as captain, Egan as first mate. Anything Olney had ever heard about Egan was positive. Also joining the crew was a fisheries observer, a woman, they soon found out, named Jennifer Eichelberger.

The second person to leave the *Arctic Rose* was Katurich, who asked to be let out of his contract early. It was due to end in a few weeks anyway. Olney agreed and promoted his brother to chief engineer. Kandris became the new assistant engineer. Other men were also growing weary of their assignments but had resigned themselves to finishing the season. Ken Kivlin phoned his son from Dutch Harbor, telling him he didn't plan to take any more jobs on fishing boats. Kivlin's voice was faint against the noise of machinery in the background. He mentioned bickering among the crew, the seasickness he never quite conquered, and, regretfully, his growing realization that he was probably going to make a lot less than he had hoped. He told of breakdowns with equipment and empty trawl nets. Those weeks aboard a small boat seemed to have shaken him, made him more intimate with the risks of working at sea, even if he was always belowdecks. John expected his father to say he was quitting and coming home, but he never did.

Eddie Haynes had also become disillusioned about fishing. Earlier in the season, he told Katurich he planned to quit when Katurich left the boat. But for some reason, Haynes later changed his mind.

"I wish I could afford to leave with you, Chief," Haynes said. "This boat's not worth a shit."

Haynes was asleep when, at 6:00 a.m., on February 28, Katurich left the boat and found a ride to the Dutch Harbor airport. He made it a policy not to make enemies or friends on boats. He did not want to wake up Haynes, the shipmate most resembling a friend. So Katurich left without saying good-bye.

10

A View of the Wreck

Near the point of the horned tip of Texas, in the town of Los Fresnos—the butterfly and marsh-grass suburb to the broken-glass, thieving, fishing town of Port Isabel—the young widow Benita Mendez lives in a white, gabled, prefabricated home laid on a concrete slab, all of it paid for by a large insurance settlement. Even in death, Angel managed to take care of his Benita. The road to the widow's home on North Indian Lake Drive is pressed dirt. Angel put her here, safe, blanketed by the fragrance of blossoms, the songs of birds, and the hum of insects.

Benita, or Bennie, parks her blue Dodge Durango, also purchased with insurance money, under the carport by the front door. The windows have plastic green shutters that do not open or close. There is a wind chime and a birdhouse. The neighborhood of trailer homes is a former citrus grove and now a bird sanctuary designated by the state of Texas, an officially protected refuge for the birds who do well in the swampy heat and inhabit the tall grass and the flowering trees. The lot is small, with a little bit of room for a clothesline, cactus, shrubs, a bank of gladiolus, and a small orange tree. Bennie answers the door shyly and is quiet when she speaks; she appears bound to the place, like the birds, to the small ponds and the low branches.

The community is called Indian Lake, and some years ago it became a separate city, able to elect its own officials and levy its own taxes, much to the suspicion of some residents. The sewer and the paving are slow to come. Hard rain kicks up the exposed dirt so that what little asphalt there is often gets covered by mud. Indian Lake started as a large estate and orchard. Its owner began leasing space on the land to retirees with recreational vehicles. The RV resort grew and became more profitable than the oranges, and the land was gradually sold off, bit by bit. A lot now goes for about $20,000. Most residents live there full-time, a mix of young Hispanic families and retired gringos, Lopezes living next to Klumpfelters. There was tension at first, as there always is when change comes. Some white couples welcomed the brown families that moved in. Others wondered out loud why they didn't live in neighborhoods with other Mexicans. The question was condescending; the answer was obvious. They wanted something better, a place with safe streets, pretty views, and quiet nights, the same thing everyone wants when they finally earn enough money to be in a position to better their lives.

Angel Mendez and his wife, Benita, moved here in 1993, after buying a small lot for less than $10,000. They were eager to put a comfortable distance between them and Port Isabel, where they met, twenty miles to the east. Port Isabel smelled of the toil of the Gulf, and the petty crime sometimes grew violent. Indian Lake was their sanctuary.

As a young man, Angel Mendez did as many before him had done, wading, paddling, striding across the Rio Grande in darkness to breach the border and get into the United States for work and a chance to make a powerful income. He ended up in Port Isabel, which at times has been a prosperous port for shrimpers prospecting for the pink herds found in great numbers in the Gulf. It is work done with nets and hands. Fishermen bear permanent sores from rope burn. Eventually, the insides of their hands turn as hard as iron. In the good days, when buyers paid $7 a pound for caught shrimp and diesel fuel cost fifty cents a gallon, profits were good. Large plants called "head houses" employed hundreds who pulled the heads off shrimp. A quick worker could make $70 a day. Now shrimp prices have plummeted to less than half what they used to be and fuel costs twice as much. The head houses have closed down, no longer able to pay what the work is worth. Shrimping has become the domain of the most robust and desperate. The uninsured boats are covered with flaking paint. The crews of shrimp boats are almost all Mexican men, some with temporary work permits, some illegal. The captains are Americans. At night, they probably drive cabs or guard office buildings to make ends meet. The rate of theft in Port Isabel is high. Televisions and stereos are stolen, pawned, purchased, and stolen again, a cyclical harvest sometimes more profitable than the shrimp. The port reflects the struggle. The docks are sand and gravel and broken concrete, strewn with discarded tires and trucks, their cabs missing doors and rusted from the inside out. This was where Angel and Bennie met, where they both took work in a foreign country with dreams of living in a place like the one Bennie now has.

In the widow's home, there are three framed photographs of Angel on the walls. The most outstanding was taken in 1993, in Massachusetts. Angel is wearing a sweater, and his hair is neatly groomed. He looks urbane, debonair, his expression somewhere between pride and contempt with his lot in life, hauling shrimp out of the Gulf and scallops off Massachusetts. In other photographs, he wears work shirts, jerseys with sports team logos on them, baseball hats. But here he is dressed in a black turtleneck, standing in front of his large, older-model American car, his long black hair combed back straight. He had never been so far from his home, so far from Mexico. The feeling must have been mighty. And in the photo, he looked it. He had come a long way.

He was born May 5, 1964, on his family's farm in the mountains of Veracruz, Mexico, called Rancho La Soledad, near the town of Misantla. His father was Eusebio Mendez, his mother, Maria Rosas, and Angel was the seventh of eight kids, six of them girls. The family lived in a small house with two bedrooms, shared by many children. The modest farm was planted with sugarcane and banana and lemon trees. As a boy, he was expected to work on the farm, picking fruit and cutting the cane fields. By the time he was a teenager, he no longer attended school. He dreamed of something else at least once in his boyhood. He put on a cowboy hat, holsters, and a western shirt, and his parents took his photograph.

Of all the kids, he thought and worried the most about money. When he was eleven or twelve, he took off for Mexico City to find work. He washed cars and waited tables, driven by the desire to start a cattle ranch one day and take care of his *mamacita*. He stole into the

United States for the first time in 1986, fording the river with an uncle and hitching a ride to Port Isabel, where he found work on a shrimp boat. Before control of the border tightened, men took chances returning to Mexico and reentering the United States. Angel did this several times to visit his family. Sometimes he would get caught and be sent back, and he would try again after a few days. It was the necessary risk and inconvenience of illegal transit. A few years after he first entered the United States he received a green card. He caught shrimp and sent home money, enough to eventually help his family build a new pink stucco home. It was made of cinder block and had a modern bathroom.

Bennie also came from a farming family, one worse off than Angel's. They grew corn and pumpkins in the state of San Luis Potosi. She was the fifth of seven children, six of them girls, and did not advance past the sixth grade in school. Her mother died when Bennie was eight, and she did not get along well with her stepmother. So she was glad when her aunt in Port Isabel sent for her in 1984, when she was fourteen. The aunt needed help caring for her diabetic husband. She arranged for a friend to help young Bennie cross the river at night. They made the journey with few problems. Once she arrived, Bennie was encouraged to enroll in school in the United States but she didn't want to. She looked after her uncle and earned money cleaning apartments and hotels in South Padre Island, the tourist resort nearby. Angel and Bennie met in 1987. Her aunt ran a boardinghouse near the docks, and Angel was one of her tenants. He was twenty-two, she was eighteen. They started talking because Angel wanted to introduce her to one of his friends. She was interested only in Angel but entertained his proposition in order to talk to him. They married in 1988, a year later. From that day forward, Bennie never had to work again. In 1989, Angel helped Bennie get her green card.

They had a little girl once. She would be sixteen today, had she lived. The little girl they named Cristal died during the night when she was three. She stopped breathing in her own bed. They think she might have thrown up some food and suffocated on it. They tried to have more children, but Bennie never got pregnant. Angel had a daughter from a previous relationship, a girl named Mariela who lives in Jalapa. He last saw her in 1999, for one day. Angel and Mariela's mother had an unforgiving relationship. She blamed him for money he didn't send and money he did send, which was never enough. And after 1999, she did not allow Angel to see Mariela.

When earning a living from the Gulf became too difficult, Angel looked north. He spent one winter, in 1993, in Massachusetts. From 1994 to 1999, he worked on a shrimp boat out of Coos Bay on the southern coast of Oregon. Without the little girl, he and Bennie had only each other. So Angel insisted Bennie live with him in Oregon during fishing season. The couple lived in an apartment building with other fishermen and their families in Charleston, Oregon. He fished all week but would be home all weekend. While Angel was gone, Bennie went to nearby casinos with the wives of other fishermen. Bennie, unsure of her English, kept steady company with the slot machines. By then, Angel had grown confident in his English. Both came to love Oregon, so cool and damp and unlike their homes in Texas and Mexico. Just as northerners wish for the sun and the heat, Bennie and Angel longed for and luxuriated in the coolness so rare in the south.

One month, Bennie visited Angel on the boat as he and the crew prepared for a trip. She fell asleep on one of the bunks, and the captain suggested to Angel that they let her sleep and get under way. She would be forced to finish the trip. They could put her to work, and if she liked it, she could join the crew and they could be together all the time. Angel thought it was a good idea. Once she got over her surprise, Bennie did, too. She was assigned to cook and clean, but she immediately grew seasick and could not stop vomiting. Unable to adjust, she spent a miserable month battling nausea and not getting much work done. She tried again six months later and this time lasted only one week. Her fishing days were done.

Bennie says that she sometimes feels the desire to go back to Oregon, to where she and Angel spent all those winters beneath the tall, sweet-smelling pines. Sometimes the desire is so strong, it feels like need.

"I think I might find him there," she says.

Angel earned more money shrimping off Oregon. But like most

fishermen, he didn't save his money very well. He lavished himself
and Bennie with trips to San Francisco and Las Vegas. They stayed in
nice hotels and ate well. She did not want him to fish farther north, so
when Angel first got the chance to fish in Alaska, he did not tell her
until the day before he was to leave. The money, he explained, would
be much better. He did his best to convince her, but she could not be
moved past her anger. In July 1999, he took his first trip aboard the
Alaskan Rose. It would be seven months before she would see him
again, although he called every few weeks. She flew to Seattle to meet
him, and this time he won her blessing. The money he earned was
good. The last time she saw Angel was on January 6, 2001, before he
left Texas for the last time. He had been promoted to deck boss of the
owner's smaller boat, the *Arctic Rose*.

The sad windfall paid to Benita after Angel's death built and
delivered a comfortable home. The new modular home arrived on a
truck bed. It has three bedrooms, a vaulted ceiling, oak moldings,
new appliances, cheerful wallpaper, plush carpeting, and central air-
conditioning. The living room is furnished with a bright green sofa
and two matching wing chairs. The drapes are also green. There is a
stereo and television and a menagerie of animal figurines—marlin,
dogs, swans—set in an oak entertainment center nearly the height of
the wall. The home is thoughtfully decorated by the hands of someone
with time to consider every detail, window valances, picture frames,
gilded mirrors, clocks, and silk pansies in porcelain vases. But with all
the ornaments and loveliness, her life has no sense to it, she says.

"I feel alone. I feel hard on the inside. I feel very alone. And I have
nothing to look forward to."

She is still a young woman. Already she has lost a mother, a
daughter, and now her husband.

"I think in my life, I am destined to be alone," she says.

Her cousin Juanita, who lives in Wisconsin with her family, has
invited her to come up there. She has a sister in Matamoros she could
live with. She has no particular reason to stay in Indian Lake. She has
no particular routine, no job, no design for her life. She has only a
certain feeling.

"I want to stay here, because I feel like Angel is here," she says.

And then she weeps. Because Angel, she knows, is nowhere near here. She lost him somewhere so far away, she can scarcely imagine it. The Bering Sea. He last spoke to her from that place he called Dutch Harbor. It too has roads of pressed earth, although it is not any kind of earth she has known, hard, coarse, the color of shale. From there you cannot go much farther.

On the night of July 15, 2001, Coast Guard investigators departed Dutch Harbor on a unique expedition, one they hoped would take them to the *Arctic Rose*. They planned a course to the last known location of the boat, its coordinates given by the emergency beacon the night she sank. Once there, investigators planned to use side-scan sonar to locate the wreck on the ocean floor. Then a robot submersible would be lowered into the water to find what was left of the boat. It was only the twelfth time the Coast Guard has used a remote-operated vehicle (ROV) during an investigation. Before the boat left, Captain Morris purchased a wreath in Dutch Harbor.

The man who brokered the mission was Rick Hansen. His company, Maritime Consultants, specialized in marine salvage. Hansen didn't own the vessels or equipment needed for such projects. What Hansen did was arrange funding, lease the equipment, hire specialists, manage the logistics. He started the one-man business only a few years earlier in an attempt to recover Alaskan gold from a sunken steamship, a quest that had yet to end in success. He recently took on a partner, a fisherman named Steve Toomey, whom he met at a convention in Houston in 2000. Toomey was looking for something he could do with his fishing boat *Exito* when it wasn't fishing in Alaska, and treasure hunting seemed as good an idea as any. Toomey started fishing when he was eighteen. His first job was cooking on a salmon boat that supplied a cannery on Prince William Sound. With a partner, Toomey bought his first boat at age twenty-two, borrowing for a down payment and lying on the loan application. The boat eventually caught fire and burned to a total loss.

Hansen, fifty-five, was an entrepreneur and dilettante. In the early days of cellular phones, he sold them out of his car at the Washington State Fair in Puyallup. The phones worked only in one county and cost thousands of dollars, but he sold them. He started several businesses from scratch, a charter bus service, a phone-messaging service. He also developed property, buying several blocks of downtown Puyallup, a former timber and farming town that is now a suburb of Tacoma. A member of Puyallup's city council, he owned an auto dealership and a boathouse in Tacoma out of which he was trying to start a boat storage business. Like many in the Seattle area, Hansen had been following news of the *Arctic Rose* in the newspapers.

A friend of Toomey's, John van Amerongen, covered the hearings in Seattle. When Captain Morris raised the possibility of investigators examining the wreck, van Amerongen approached Morris and told him about Toomey and the salvage work he did. He and Hansen were invited to put in a bid for the board's proposed expedition. Toomey offered to use his boat, the *Exito*, a combination trawler and crab boat. He had finished snow crab season and had spent a couple of months, with Hansen, searching off the Washington coast for an 1800s sidewheel paddleboat that sank with gold from Alaska aboard while on its way to San Francisco.

The mission, expected to cost about $200,000, was organized quickly. Only one month after Morris proposed the idea, the board was nearly on its way to the wreck. A submersible pilot was hired. Equipment was leased and arrangements made to have it shipped up to Dutch Harbor. The trip had to be made during the short Bering summer, when weather conditions are relatively mild. If the board did not locate the *Arctic Rose* by the end of August, it would have to wait another year to try again. The board's choice of a platform vessel was the *Ocean Explorer*, a 155-foot trawler owned by Trident Seafoods and often hired by the National Marine Fisheries Service to do marine trawl surveys, analyzing the impact of trawling on the ocean bottom. The week it was used to find the *Arctic Rose*, it had just finished a one-month assignment for NMFS. The crew who worked the trawl survey stayed on for the ROV mission. Morris chose the *Ocean Explorer* because it essentially came ready for the mission, with all the people and almost all of the necessary equipment. Only the submersible needed to be added. Morris called it "a turnkey operation." The cost of chartering the boat ran about $6,300 a day plus fuel.

The ROV arrived by air freight July 15 on a relatively calm, clear day. Nineteen people were on the *Ocean Explorer*, including a representative from the *Arctic Rose*'s insurance carrier. The sonar technician, Richard Dentzman, was from a company that developed the sonar software, Triton Elics International. He was joined on the trip by three more technicians from the Naval Underseas Warfare Center.

The trip to the site of the wreck would take about forty-eight hours. The men played cribbage, watched movies, told stories. A reporter working for the Associated Press and a cameraman from CNN made the trip. The crew was small: the captain, first mate, two deckhands, and the cook. All were interested in the mission and, like everyone, took turns speculating on the cause of the sinking. The men were anxious, both excited and nervous about what they were going to find and see. The wreck, all the men understood, was also the grave of many of the crew. Toomey was a fisherman himself and over the years had heard of many boats sinking. He knew men who died. But he had never before looked for a wreck. It crossed his mind that he might see a body. And he didn't want to.

The voyage was relatively smooth. The *Ocean Explorer* gently breasted six-foot seas. Hansen spent most of the two-day journey in his berth, battling nausea. He was not much of a seaman, despite his business. Mostly he wrote business plans, raised money, talked to lawyers. So he enjoyed getting out from behind his desk. While running the bus company, he learned to rebuild engines. He learned how to rewire phones after starting his answering service.

The *Ocean Explorer* arrived at its intended destination at 10:00 p.m., July 17, in the half-light of an Alaskan summer evening. The captain turned on the fish sonar, used to locate schools of fish, fixing on the spot where Rundall's body was found. The investigators charted a grid five hundred meters wide. The boat was not difficult to find. It was almost exactly where the EPIRB had indicated it was. They made one pass picking up a strong image of the boat, telling them they were in the right area. The crew went to bed and waited for the morning. At daybreak, the sonar technicians used a more precise device, a side-scan sonar vehicle, to spot the wreck. The body of the Klein 5000 sonar vehicle looks similar to a missile, guided by fins and a large

mounted wing. Pitch, roll, heading, speed, depth, and distance from
the bottom are all measured and relayed back to the operator on his
computer screen. It took only a few hours for sonar operators to locate
the boat in about four hundred feet of water. The first image of the
wreck showed it to be sitting almost straight up on the bottom.

Hansen had one big concern, that the boat the Coast Guard was
using for the mission did not have dynamic positioning or the ability
to hold a fixed position on the surface of the water regardless of drift or
current. The ideal vessel would have thrusters at four corners of the
hull, controlled by a computer that adjusted them automatically.
Since the *Ocean Explorer* had only its main propeller and anchor to
regulate its position on the surface, success depended on calm weather
and gentle currents. So far, the weather did not present a problem.

Although initial reports of weather conditions on the day the *Arctic
Rose* sank were of relatively calm seas, investigators were chewing on a
theory that the boat might have encountered an isolated squall.
Another vessel, the *Crazy Anne*, ninety miles west of the *Arctic Rose*
that night, reported northeast winds of forty knots and seas of
eighteen feet. Robert Hopkins, a meteorologist for the National
Weather Service in Anchorage, a forecaster in Alaska since 1978,
said an occluded front might have passed the *Arctic Rose* at the time of
the sinking, creating maximum sustained winds of forty-five knots for
as long as six hours and wave heights of up to twenty-four feet. An
occluded front is created when storms weaken and a cold front
overtakes a warm front, lifting the warmer air. An occluded front
creates erratic weather, and conditions can be very different in
locations as few as ten miles apart.

As the investigators prepared to send down the robot submersible,
the crew noticed a thick bank of fog surrounding the boat. But
somehow the sky above them remained clear. The conditions seemed
the work of a divine force, Morris and the others thought, as if the sky
had opened up just for the occasion. A gray whale breached in the
distance, coming up twice, seeming to look right at the boat. With
everyone present on deck, Morris led an informal ceremony before the
operation began.

"We're gathered together today to remember the crew members of the fishing vessel *Arctic Rose* . . .," Morris began. He read off the names of the crew. "Let us also remember their families and friends who grieve for their lives."

Then he read a passage from the Bible.

"We pray that the memory of the crew of the *Arctic Rose* be in our hearts and minds and guide and protect all who work and travel in the seas and the waterways here in Alaska."

The wreath Captain Morris had purchased was made of nineteen red and yellow roses. Together, the three Coast Guard investigators held it in their hands before dropping it over the rail of the *Ocean Explorer*.

At about 9:00 a.m., a crane lowered the submersible into the water. Its power supply and systems were checked before it was released. Hansen was in the control room with the ROV pilot, Jamie Sherwood. Toomey stayed on deck. The submersible had horizontal and vertical thrusters. This particular model, the Phantom HD2, is a workhorse in the oil industry and costs about $80,000. Most are used for repair work on oil rigs. The machine is relatively small, and most of it is built into a rectangular steel frame about the size of a large-screen television. The submersible, operated by joystick, reached the ocean bottom in about thirty minutes.

Clouds of silt, illuminated by the ROV's headlights, obscured the view transmitted above to a small video monitor. The ROV quickly approached a dark-colored hull. A loose tarp hung over the rail, partly covering the letter *R* on the name of the boat. But there was no mistaking it. She was the *Arctic Rose*. The first glimpse of the hull showed it was intact. There was no obvious damage, no gaping holes. The ROV rose for a view of the wheelhouse, painted white, its windows darkened like the eyes of the dead. The ship, as the sonar showed, was almost perfectly upright. It appeared to have hit the bottom stern first. No one expected to find so much debris trailing off the boat, most of it fishing line. The ROV moved toward the stern. Both trawl doors were not in their normal storage locations and could not be found. But the boat's net was spooled around the net reel, the open end aboard the boat and secured. That meant the boat clearly was not fishing at the time it sank. As the ROV made its way back to the bow, on the other side of the boat, one of its thrusters sucked in a stray fishing line.

The image of a mangle of rope, colored orange and blue, filled the monitor. The ROV's umbilical cable could also be seen on the screen. The vehicle was stuck. In a desperate measure, the crew pulled the ROV's main cable in hopes of setting it free. The cable tore from the ROV, and the crew lost all transmissions. A fishing line crippled the main propeller, breaking a seal around the propeller shaft. Water breached the machine's electrical system, rendering it useless. It was now a doomed craft, just like the one it was sent down to find. As a disappointment, the loss of the ROV was hard to get over.

"We looked at it like we screwed up," Toomey said. "We didn't complete our job. If I say I'm going to do something, I'd like to get it done. We did have some success. We found the *Arctic Rose*, but we didn't find an answer to bring home to the families of crew members."

The ROV had been in the water less than two hours before its mission ended. It was able to record only images of one side of the hull, the wheelhouse windows, and the top of the wheelhouse. One image alone had spooked Toomey. As the ROV passed the wheelhouse, he thought he saw a gloved hand. It seemed to flutter, perhaps in the ripple caused by the ROV. He told himself it was just a glove, that it contained nothing. It eased his mind only a little bit.

"I saw a glove, let's just leave it at that," he said.

The board had no choice but to end the trip and return to Dutch Harbor. The two-day transit seemed longer because of the silence. When the boat arrived in Dutch Harbor, Morris knew he and the others needed to see the *Arctic Rose* again. He immediately called Coast Guard headquarters to request funding for another mission before the summer ended. Hansen quickly agreed to broker the second trip. By July 20, the Coast Guard had approved a second expedition. And on July 24, investigators played video from the abbreviated first trip for nineteen family members in Seattle.

In August, the same team of people readied themselves for a second attempt to record video of the wreck. This time Sherwood, the ROV pilot, used his own submersible, transporting it in a van from his home in Toronto to Tacoma. His van broke down in eastern Washington, delaying his arrival in Tacoma by a day. The shippers in Tacoma didn't like the way the ROV was packed, so they waited another day to recrate it. By then, the ship it was supposed to be transported on had left port. So the ROV was put on a truck and driven to Anchorage. The truck made the journey in two days, beating the ship there. It was then put on a freighter and sent to Dutch Harbor.

The second ROV was far bigger and came with more equipment, including its own winch, one thousand feet of cable, and various boxes of electronics. Worth $300,000, about four times as much as the smaller ROV, it was six feet long and weighed one thousand pounds. It had two cameras, one for close-up images and another for wide-angle images. Four 150-watt halogen lamps lit its view. It had a clawlike arm to manipulate objects, and it was armed with a cutting tool in the event there was time to try to recover the first ROV.

The team was scheduled to leave Dutch Harbor August 18, but its departure was delayed several days because of bad weather. Finally, on August 24, the team put the ROV into the water. The crew did not need to relocate the boat, because it had recorded the precise position of the wreck from the first trip. They sent the second ROV straight to the *Arctic Rose*. Looking at the boat through a remote camera was not like looking at it with your eyes. At very close range, which the mission required, the camera showed only a few square feet of the vessel at a time. Examining a large section of it took hours. The water was dark and murky. But this time, the ROV was able to completely encircle the wreck and record images from all angles. Morris and the others were startled by what appeared to be a large hole in the hull. Thinking they might have discovered the answer they were looking for, the investigators asked for a closer look, which revealed the hole was merely a patch of the hull where the paint had worn away. The submersible arm touched solid steel, confirming there was no hole.

The clue investigators did find was far more subtle, an open hatch. It presented itself as a dark gap, an opening along the top edge of the door, slim proof that it was not locked tight. Beyond the gap was a sliver of white, something from inside the factory. A section of wall, perhaps. If the door was closed, this white line would not be visible. The hatch was a weatherproof door that led from the fish factory to the rear deck, a hatch that was supposed to be kept locked according to the boat's stability book. The image from the ROV clearly showed the hatch was not locked when the boat sank. But the ROV's camera was not able to capture images of the entire door or a view of the door from the front or side. What investigators did not know was whether the door was tied open, left open, or opened after the boat started to sink by crew fleeing the boat. Images of the hull showed that the overboard discharge chute on the starboard side was partially open. Investigators saw, too, that the boat's rudder appeared to be bent. The damage could have been caused by the boat hitting the ocean bottom. But more important, the first glimpse of the rudder revealed that it had been turned hard to port, likely the last desperate maneuver by first mate Kerry Egan. The rudder's severe position implied the boat had suddenly listed to starboard, causing Egan to react by turning hard to port.

Viewing the boat was a tedious process, especially near the stern where the boat had settled into the sea bottom. Whenever the ROV got close to the bottom, its propulsion system kicked up a blinding cloud of silt and sediment that completely obscured the view transmitted by the camera. Investigators had to wait, often up to ten minutes, until the slow gravity of the sea allowed the sediment to settle. Just as silt made it difficult to get a prolonged look at the boat near the bottom, near the top of the boat fishing line caused problems. The more time the ROV spent looking at the boat from above, the more it risked getting tangled in fishing line. Overall, the survey was slow and tortured. But eventually the investigators confirmed that the boat's trawl gear, mud lines, and wires had shifted to the starboard side, consistent with a list to the starboard side.

The fishing lines trailing the boat again proved an impediment to the expedition. After a few hours in the water, the ROV's cable became snagged on part of the wreck, and soon it too became entangled in line. Afraid of losing another submersible, the crew retrieved the ROV. The crew recalled the vehicle five times during the day to make sure it would not get stuck. Three times, line had to be pulled from the boat's propellers. The last time was the closest the crew came to losing the ROV. Every available man tugged furiously on the umbilical cable, finally freeing the craft. A clump of fishing twine had become stuck in its thrusters. By then the weather was worsening. The ROV had been unable to provide views of the pilothouse or much of the top deck. Additionally, investigators wanted to see the box the survival suits were stored in. But this was the most hazardous area in which to operate the ROV because of all the loose line. Morris decided he had enough footage. The crew was exhausted, having put in a full day of work from morning to about midnight. Morris called an end to the mission, and with the weather at its stern, the *Ocean Explorer* made its way back to Dutch Harbor. About one week later, Jim Robertson's second child, James Bragg Robertson IV, was born.

Now equipped with hours of video of the wreck, investigators had many more answers and more than a few questions. That fall, they showed some of the video to Tom LaPointe, the former first mate of the *Arctic Rose*.

He noticed bunches of loose twine, used for repairs to the net. He said lots of it was stored in a plywood bin on the wheelhouse deck. He also found it significant that the boat settled at the bottom in an upright position and that the net was secured. He remembered that the boat was heavy in the stern; in other words, the boat typically rode with its stern low in the water. He also remembered how many times the factory workers had left open the hatch from the factory to the freezer hold below despite being warned not to. It was an easy detail to overlook, he said, and would not constitute a deadly mistake under normal circumstances. Shown the footage of the rear hatch, LaPointe agreed that it appeared to be open at the time of the sinking. And like the investigators, he considered it a bad sign. He surmised a sleeping crewman needing to relieve himself might have walked through the factory, exited through the hatch to get to the rear deck, urinated off the boat, and returned to his bunk without securing the hatch.

"It appears to be open, and I think that's where the water came from," LaPointe said. "I think the water came in from the stern, got into the factory, and then got in the freezer hold. And I don't believe it would have taken a whole lot of time if it was uncontrolled and undetected, and again, I don't think there would have been a lot of people awake at the time.

"And these people have no conception or concern with typical basic seamanship. They're food processors . . . it's just another job in a factory, except this factory happens to float.

"It's not a big boat. It could be a very quick thing if it wasn't stopped in an incipient stage. It's like a fire. If you let it burn for thirty seconds, you can snuff it out. If you let it burn for three minutes, it's a big fire . . . The deeper that boat gets in the water because of flooding, the faster the water comes in. It accelerates as it occurs."

LaPointe, after viewing the video, also wondered if the flooding or a sudden shift of the cargo caused the boat to list to the starboard side, putting the overboard chute on that side of the factory below the waterline. That was another way seawater could have quickly entered the factory. The board presented to LaPointe its working weather theory, that an occluded front might have kicked up the weather at the time of the sinking and created rough conditions. The conditions the board described, LaPointe said, were "more than moderate" but not troubling, that the boat sometimes fished in thirty-to-forty-knot winds, that it frequently jogged in similar conditions. In other words, the weather would not by itself have alarmed the captain or crew or caused anyone to take extraordinary precautions. Egan would have stuck to his routine. The crew, accustomed to the rolling and bucking of the waves, would have continued sleeping.

At that time of the night, about 3:00 a.m., Jeff Meincke and Jimmie Conrad, who worked the night shift, might have been awake if there was fish to sort or stack. The two of them might have been in the factory or could have been deep belowdecks, in the freezer hold. If the previous day's catch was paltry, leaving little to process and freeze, the men might have been eating or dozing in the galley. But conversations indicated there was plenty of fish to process. Other than the first mate, the only other person sure to be up at that hour would have been the night engineer, G.W. Kandris, one month on the job, the fugitive who just a few months ago was an auto mechanic and might still be, had he not started a brawl on New

Year's Eve. Sometimes he fought, or so it seemed, because he was bored.

Kandris was born October 6, 1974. He hated his name, Geilund Wain, which has been spelled a variety of ways in various court documents from which his life can be charted, so he went by his initials, G. W. He grew up in Tacoma, the only child of a young teen mother named Karla Mae Kandris. He didn't know his father very well and rarely spoke of him with his friends, although he got a tattoo on the inside of his forearm as a way of honoring his father. The tattoo was of a cartoon worm wearing a necktie, glasses, and hat, a sort of bookworm. He told friends his father made dentures for a living but that he had died.

As a juvenile, Kandris was convicted of four crimes, all of them relatively minor property offenses. In March 1988, at age thirteen, he and Elmer Malatorre, a friend, walked by Lakewood Towing's fenced impound lot in Tacoma and threw rocks at cars. The boys dented several cars and broke windshields, causing $800 in damage. The court convicted Kandris of malicious mischief and sentenced him to a curfew, requiring him to be at school or at home and to break off all contact with Elmer. In March 1989, he brought a stolen and disassembled Yamaha motorcycle to school for shop class. In March 1990, he shoplifted $50 worth of remote-control car parts from a toy store near Tacoma. One month later, he was caught shoplifting disposable lighters and meat snacks from a Thriftway store. An employee saw him stuff the items, worth $12.80, into his jacket pocket.

As an adult, he was convicted of similar offenses, burglary, possession of stolen property, and drug possession. These crimes, like those of his youth, were not serious. Starting in 1995, he spent time in and out of jail. When he was twenty, he served five months for possession of stolen property, his only felony conviction. He was charged with drug possession in December 1996 and served three days. In March 1997, he pleaded guilty to burglary. He was sentenced to ten months in jail and one year of probation. He was convicted of third-degree attempted assault, a gross misdemeanor, in December 1999, and sentenced to 180 days in jail. The original charge was classified as a felony. He had to undergo evaluation for alcoholism and was ordered to cut off all contact with his victim.

Kandris's behavior on the last night of 2000 was not uncharacteristic. He drank excessively. He mouthed off. He grew belligerent. He got into a fight. He enjoyed fighting. He was good at it. Which is to say he could take punishment like few people. He was once knocked down by an automobile, only to get up and dust off his pants. In the early morning hours of January 1, 2001, Kandris was attending a New Year's Eve party at the home of a friend, Ross Ferguson, who lived in a duplex in Puyallup. According to arrest reports and witness statements, police were called to the house after 2:00 a.m. because of reports of a fight involving a gun. Officers arrived to find Kandris rolling in the street, locked in a clench with Adam Alicea, a car nearby with its doors open and a barbell lying by the street curb. A man named Cory Newingham, whom Kandris worked with, shouted obscenities at Kandris while telling officers he had hit his girlfriend with the barbell. Kandris had Alicea in a bear hug, refusing to let go unless Alicea stopped hitting him. Police ordered Kandris to let go.

According to Newingham, he and Kandris had argued and gotten into a fight in the garage. Inside the garage was a keg of beer in a garbage can full of ice. Kandris put Newingham in a headlock and began punching him in the face. The fight had moved just outside of the garage. Others pulled off Kandris, who then reached for the barbell and swung it wildly, hitting two guests, Jillian Hunotte and Tim Lanning, in the head. While Hunotte had only a deep bruise, Lanning's wound was more serious. He was treated for a three-inch laceration at the scene but refused transportation to the hospital, signing a release. Sometime during the scuffle, someone fired a gun into the ground, apparently as a warning shot. Police never found the shell casing.

Kandris tried to flee in a car but was pulled out by Alicea, whom witnesses say Kandris also struck with the barbell. Police arrived soon after that. They also arrested Newingham, who continued to yell obscenities at Kandris, for disorderly conduct. When they booked him into jail, police discovered he had a driver's license in someone else's name and charged him with possessing fictitious identification.

Kandris, police said, behaved erratically and displayed wild mood swings while appearing to be under the influence of alcohol or drugs or both. They treated him for minor wounds and placed him in an ambulance, where he took a swing at a paramedic and spat at a police officer, yelling that they weren't protecting his girlfriend, Tanya Raymond. Police strapped him to the stretcher. Kandris was taken to Good Samaritan Hospital. Police told the hospital staff they wanted to take him to jail once he was ready to be released. Kandris appeared unconscious to police, refusing to say anything. Sometime that night, he fled the hospital in a gown while waiting for X-rays.

The police had arrested him that night on suspicion of assault. They were not formal charges. Those would have to be brought forward by the county prosecutor. Kandris's case was assigned to a detective, to determine if he would be formally charged and re-arrested. By their actions, the police did not consider the evidence at hand to convey a serious crime. For instance, they did not attempt to capture Kandris. Instead, they merely called him at home, leaving messages on his answering machine. In the larger scheme of things, Kandris was just a drunk partygoer who got into a fight. But in Kandris's mind, he was a fugitive from the law, a wanted man with a criminal record. He certainly had a criminal record. Not understanding the details of law very well, Kandris assumed he was about to receive his third strike in a state that had passed a three strikes law. But Washington's three strikes law applies to only serious, violent crimes. None of his prior convictions would have qualified.

The police were not sure if they had a serious crime because they did not know if they had victims. As near as the police could tell, none of Kandris's alleged victims had serious injuries except for Lanning. His mother phoned the police, telling them that as a result of being hit in the head with the barbell, Lanning had to have surgery to remove a blood clot from his brain. She told them she and her son would come to the police station on February 16 and give a statement. The day came and neither showed up. Meanwhile, Newingham kept calling police and asking when they were going to arrest Kandris. Lanning's injury was central to the case, but the police could not reach him. Finally, the police spoke to him on April 5 and asked him again if he would file another witness statement. Lanning said he was unsure what to do because he believed Kandris was dead. He had heard rumors he had left town to work on a fishing boat and a few days ago read in the local paper that a man of the same name was among the crew of the *Arctic Rose*'s and presumed dead. On April 12, police spoke with someone from the *Arctic Rose*'s insurer, the Polaris Group. An employee confirmed that the man the police were looking for had indeed died at sea. The next day, the police closed the case.

Tanya Raymond was nine years younger than Kandris. They met through mutual friends at a Go-Kart racetrack. They dated, off and on, for about two years and shared an apartment in Tacoma. She said he went up to fish to "make a better life for himself and his son," which was less true when he started and more true by the time the boat sank. He had two sons, one six, the other two. "He said he was doing this to make a better life for us," Tanya said. "He had all kinds of plans when he got back."

To Tanya, in phone calls, Kandris bragged he was becoming fluent in Spanish and complained about his chapped lips and the weather, but in a way that suggested he was proud to have endured it. Although he did not live far from the ocean, he had not seen much of it in his life and was struck by its beauty. He was not earning as much money as he made repairing cars in Tacoma, but he didn't seem to mind. Something about helping run the boat had tapped into a great sense of purpose for G.W., and it became at least as important as the money.

"When he went on the boat," Tanya said, "he started talking about marriage, about us moving out of the state, to California or someplace south, someplace warmer."

And on February 15, 2001, from a pay phone on a dock in Dutch Harbor, he proposed.

"I was really surprised," Tanya said. "It wasn't too romantic. He just popped out and asked. We cried for a long time. He said, 'I guess you said yes.' And then we cried some more."

What she didn't know was that another girlfriend whom he had been involved with for several years had become pregnant with his child. It's not clear that Kandris ever knew. His daughter was born four months after he died. She was named Karma Rose.

11

The Last Days

By November 2001, the Marine Board had interviewed almost everyone associated with the *Arctic Rose* and her final trip to sea. It had consulted experts in weather, naval architecture, and wave formation; investigators talked to people who repaired the boat, worked on the boat, managed the boat, modified the boat; and on two trips to the site of the sinking, the team had recorded hours of video footage of the wreck, footage that at least ruled out the possibility of several catastrophic events. A very plausible scenario, in which the boat rapidly flooded and sank, began to present itself.

The country had also experienced its most deadly act of terrorism, the attacks on New York and Washington on September 11. The Coast Guard suddenly had to share in the huge responsibility of homeland security. Consequently, the investigation lost at least two months of time as Commander Bingaman and Captain Morris's full attention was given to port security and the threat of another attack. The event had a strange effect on the families of the crew, whose relatively small disaster had now been eclipsed by one much larger and profound. It seemed to them that their problems were no longer important, their losses forgotten, sacrificed to the smaller history of unintended catastrophe.

The investigation had already cost about $500,000, equivalent to the amount budgeted each year for marine safety in all of Alaska. Typically, fishing casualty investigations are given a budget of $5,000. The money for the *Arctic Rose* investigation came out of the Coast Guard's national budget, now taxed by the burden of guarding harbors and inspecting freighters. Shortly before September 11, Morris left open the possibility of another, third trip to the wreck, to either shoot more detailed video or perhaps send down a manned submersible or even human divers. After the attack, that option disappeared.

"We were basically told that was it," said Robertson.

The board had heard from everyone except the boat's owner, David Olney, who still declined to speak to investigators without a guarantee from federal prosecutors that his testimony could not be used against him in any criminal action. By November, he received those assurances and agreed to answer questions posed by the board. On November 28, before he began answering questions, Olney, wearing a black sweater over a blue shirt, read a statement he had prepared: "I welcome and am grateful for the opportunity to speak publicly for the first time about the loss of the *Arctic Rose* and her crew. They were quality men, all of them . . . Every one of them touched me in ways I will always remember."

He stopped and buried his face in his hands. The board members were visibly affected by the show of emotion.

"My friends and crew members of the *Arctic Rose* will never be forgotten and always live in my heart. Thank you."

Olney testified over two days, mostly going over his memory of events that had already been recounted by others. He said that after purchasing the boat, he had removed its stabilizer poles, or wings, and that the modification improved the ride. He verified changes he made to the mechanical systems, changes that affected the boat's weight and how that weight was distributed. He also confirmed the addition of twenty-five thousand pounds of ballast to the bottom of the vessel, weight that was not accounted for in the stability book. He admitted to operating the *Arctic Rose* outside the guidelines recommended by the stability report, produced by naval architects, because, he said, she handled poorly when the guidelines were followed.

He was asked about the rear door to the factory. Olney said crew members were instructed to keep the door closed but were allowed to keep it open when it got too warm in the factory. Hiring crew, he said, was sometimes difficult. Five of the men aboard, he said, got their jobs because others had flunked drug tests. The information Olney provided did not deepen the investigators' understanding of the sinking, but his answers reinforced information the board, for the most part, already had. At times, he wept as he answered. In the end, he said, he had no idea what caused the boat to sink so quickly.

"We never got a silver bullet from his testimony," Robertson said. "But what we got eliminated other theories on why the vessel sank."

About two months later, in February 2002, Olney went to sea aboard the *Alaskan Rose* to help the crew with the season's most important harvest, pregnant rock sole.

Olney last saw his doomed crew on March 1, the day he left Dutch Harbor. Milosh Katurich and Nathan Miller had also left the boat for other jobs, while Kerry Egan joined the crew to help run the bridge with Davey Rundall. Olney did not hire any others to make up for the loss of Katurich and Miller. One more person got on the boat that day, the only woman to work aboard the ship, Jennifer Eichelberger, the fisheries observer who would spend three weeks on the *Arctic Rose*.

She was unimpressed at her first sight of the *Arctic Rose*. She thought it small and filthy. Because of the modifications made to the boat, it also looked "screwed up" to Eichelberger. The factory was built behind the wheelhouse, so the two rooms looked like one long, continuous structure.

"It had a little bitty deck," she said. "It was weird looking. I didn't know what to make of it. I couldn't figure out how they would dump the bag. It was the weirdest setup I'd ever seen."

She could not imagine the technique sometimes used by the crew, winching the net onto the top of the factory roof, releasing its contents into a sort of movable truck bed and then raising the bed and sliding the fish into the factory. She thought of all the boats given unflattering nicknames by observers. The *Alliance* was called the *Appliance*. The *Pacific Pride* was called the *Pacific Nightmare*. The *Arctic Rose* looked ripe for a nickname. By then, Meincke had come up with his own, the *Savage Rose*.

"I knew it was going to be a tough assignment," she said. "It was probably not good living conditions. I didn't expect the boat to be clean or the food to be good. I had little choice. I had no grounds on which to refuse it. Observers are not qualified to evaluate seaworthiness. I'm not an engineer.

"The *Unimak* was tied up behind it when I first went on it. I talked to a guy named Mike, a deckhand I know. I went to say hi. He said, 'Hey, what are you doing now?' and I nodded at the *Arctic Rose*. I remember Mike's reaction was, 'You got to be fucking kidding me.' He couldn't believe I was going to get on it, let alone work on it."

Rather than interpret his reaction as alarm, Eichelberger took it as the pride fishermen commonly exhibit in their own boat, which sometimes takes the form of insulting another boat. She saw it as boat snobbery, not as any real fear he had for the *Arctic Rose*'s seaworthiness. Eichelberger jumped over the boat's rail from the dock onto the boat. The top of the factory was greasy. Someone had just repaired a hydraulic leak. She saw oil everywhere. But a lot of boats were like that. The interior, she was pleased to find, was clean.

She met David Olney briefly before he went to the airport. Rundall gave her a tour of the boat. She learned where the life raft, emergency beacon, first-aid kit, and flares were kept. She was quickly instructed on what to do during an emergency, how to tell one kind of alarm from another, which path to take in case of an emergency. She was shown her workstation and the main bathroom. The workstation was cramped and unkempt. The bathroom was worse, a grand mess. She was told she could use the captain's bathroom since the crew's bathroom would not afford her much privacy. She toured the factory and met the foreman, Aaron Broderick. Then she was shown to her sleeping quarters, which she would share with the cook, Ken Kivlin. It was a considerable luxury: The others slept six to a room, stacked on top of one another. Before departing, she went back to the Unalaska library to send e-mail.

Eichelberger, then thirty-one, grew up on a farm in western Illinois just outside a town called Versailles in Brown County, where about seven thousand people live. She was the middle of three children, the only girl. Her family still owns the farm, leasing most of it to other farmers. Her older brother is a guard in the nearby state prison, one of the county's biggest employers. A large food distributor called Dot Foods is another; it employs her mother. While growing up, her family farmed eight hundred acres of corn and soy. They raised cattle and chickens. To make ends meet, her father flew cargo planes between airports in Chicago, St. Louis, and Kansas City. He also piloted charter flights for the Texas A&M football coaching staff when coaches made recruiting visits and gave flying lessons at the College Station, Texas, airport. Before he flew for a living, he piloted his own Cessna, using it to take the family on vacations. Orphaned at age eight, Eichelberger's father was adopted by a strict religious family, from whom he ran away at age sixteen. He dropped out of high school and joined the navy. There, he learned to fly while servicing planes as a jet mechanic. Once out of the navy, he worked as a carpenter, mechanic, plumber, and electrician. He never hired anyone to fix or build anything at home.

Eichelberger also left home at an early age, although under better circumstances. At fifteen, she enrolled in a publicly funded boarding school near Chicago called the Illinois Math and Science Academy (IMSA). As a child, Jen was always told she was one of the smart kids. She went to science camp and archeology camp and was in her school's gifted program, solving word puzzles and logic problems. Admission to the academy was highly selective. Jen was one of two hundred students chosen statewide the year she entered. She begged her parents to let her go. She lasted two years. Her grades were poor, her attitude worse. She was nearly forced out. Nonetheless, the experience broadened her horizons and stoked her ambitions. Her classmates were aspiring doctors and scientists who had goals far above those of her classmates back at home. Jen did not elaborate on her failures at boarding school but said they were social, not academic in nature.

"Picture taking the kid from every small school who would have been valedictorian," she said. "It was the geek school. We were the go-getters, but when we got to IMSA we lost our identities as the smartest kid. We had no footing, and we fell into our own social groups. I fell into the burnout crowd, I wanted to be one of the bad kids. I listened to heavy metal, tended to get in trouble a lot, and I was really creative about it. I wasn't focused on school. I was out of my element, I was beyond being challenged. I got bad grades, and I was shocked to find out I'm not as smart as I thought I was. I guess everything that happened to me at IMSA happens to kids at college. I got that out of the way when I was in high school."

At about that time, she also experienced a shocking personal loss. Her father died when the cargo plane he was flying lost an engine on takeoff and crashed. Jen was seventeen. The family suddenly faced financial constraints. They lived off of her father's workmen's compensation benefits and his Social Security paycheck. An attempt to file a lawsuit against the cargo company failed.

Jen left the academy and spent her senior year at Brown County High School. There, she found no courses left for her to take. The most advanced math class taught was trigonometry, which she had already taken and passed. So while she waited to turn eighteen so she could earn her GED, she went to high school in the morning to take physical education and health and drove to junior college forty miles away in the afternoon. She graduated early, in January, and started classes at Western Illinois University. She graduated from college in 1992 at age twenty. From there she went to graduate school at the University of Alabama, Birmingham, studying molecular genetics. She did well and moved quickly along a carefully, almost hastily, designed academic track. She earned a fellowship and the opportunity to pursue a doctorate degree in molecular genetics. Ahead of her were several years of research and writing. And that's when she quit.

"I was unhappy," she said. "I was doing the wrong thing. I went through school so fast, I just took the next logical step instead of doing what I wanted."

In 1994, she started over, returning to Western Illinois to get a master's degree in biology, since she realized her real interests were in conservation and natural resources. Because her bachelor's degree was in psychology, she needed the master's degree to begin fieldwork as a biologist. For her graduate thesis, she chose to study the plague of zebra mussels in the Mississippi River. Accidentally introduced to the river by ships transiting from Eastern Europe, the small mussels attached themselves to larger native mussels, covering the river bottom like giant mats. The zebra mussels had no natural predators in the Mississippi as they did in their native habitat. Within two years, Eichelberger earned her master's degree and met her current boyfriend, Dennis, another graduate student at Western Illinois.

In 1996, they both moved to Florida, he to attend Florida State, she to work for the Florida Department of Environmental Protection. That's where she met a former fisheries observer from Alaska and first entertained the thought of working in the fishing industry. In March 1998, she went to Anchorage to train. She accepted her first assignment in April aboard the factory trawler *Defender*, intending to do it just once, maybe twice.

"I never anticipated it as a long-term job," she said. "I just thought that it would be neat experience. It was like getting paid to see Alaska and to see it in a way most tourists don't. I had never been on the ocean. Most observers do it once or twice and never come back. The attrition rate has got to be 80 or 90 percent."

An assignment aboard a head-and-gut boat is one of the most difficult for an observer. You work alone and must follow a random schedule of sampling so the fishermen do not know when you will inspect their catch. Keeping to a regular pattern of sleep is difficult, almost impossible. And because the catch is so diverse, sampling takes a long time. The minimum amount of fish that must be sampled at one time is 300 kilograms, or 660 pounds. The potential for animosity between crew and observer is high because the crew's quota is based on by-catch, which is monitored by the observer. The captain might get mad if, for instance, he thinks an observer is putting too much halibut in his or her sample basket. Captains have been known to spy on observers, placing cameras near sampling stations. The wheelhouse can sometimes be a touchy, tense place for an observer. Halibut is the nemesis of the head-and-gut trawler. It swims the same waters as sole and invariably gets into the same nets.

"Head-and-gut boat captains sometimes play games with you," Eichelberger said. "They'll say, 'I've worked real hard, who are you doing this for?' or, 'No one cares about what you do, no one uses your information.' They try to break you down, get you to slack, convince you that all the other observers don't do their jobs. I only encounter that on head-and-gut boats." But aboard the *Arctic Rose*, she encountered none of this kind of resistance.

Just how Alaskan Observers doles out assignments is a mystery to those who get them. Observers are assigned to boats by a coordinator, a former observer herself, who works in the company's office near the campus of Seattle Pacific University. Favoritism does not seem to play a role.

"I'm one of Pam's favorites," Eichelberger said of the coordinator, "and I've done as many flatfish boats as any observer I know. I get one after another after another. It's a matter of logistics and boat schedules. Her job is really hard. As an observer, you have to accept your assignments. You have to be prepared for a change on short notice, and you have to be willing to go where they need you to go. They tell you that up front. It doesn't even out. There are people who have done nothing but long-liners. I've done one. Some have done nothing but factory trawlers. Some do nothing but flatfish."

Eichelberger has worked on land and on factory trawlers, but for reasons beyond her ken, she usually gets assigned to a head-and-gut boat. To some degree, observers are encouraged to become proficient in the work of a certain kind of boat, which would explain why observers often get assigned the same type of vessel. An observer with added experience becomes a lead observer. Eichelberger is lead certified for factory trawlers, which includes head-and-gut boats.

With Eichelberger aboard, the *Arctic Rose* departed on its first trip of March, one long voyage west, past Adak Island in the western Aleutians in search of cod. She had at least a few days to acclimate since it would take that long to reach fishing grounds. She was exhausted, having worked overnight from midnight to noon at the plant earlier that day. She slept a lot during the first twenty-four hours of the trip. The weather was bad. She noticed the boat tended to roll farther than she expected. It was that same uncomfortable roll that former crew members had noticed.

"I always had this feeling it could go over any time," Eichelberger said. "If we got into severe weather, it did this back-and-forth thing, or even when we were just fishing in marginal weather."

She likened the boat to a rubber duck in a bathtub. It made her especially seasick. She had not been to sea in a long time. Now she was throwing up every twenty minutes. She tried to conceal her nausea while talking to Rundall. She excused herself periodically to vomit and tried to smile when she returned so Rundall would not know she was sick. But he quickly caught on and asked her, "Are you puking?" Each time, it struck her suddenly, with no more than several seconds of warning.

"You just wish you were dead; there's nothing worse," she said.

The *Arctic Rose* had two computers, at different helm stations, both with a satellite connection, but only one was capable of reliably managing the kind of work required of it. Rundall used the better computer to plot his fishing plan and track his haul. It contained electronic sea charts and was hooked up to the boat's GPS. Jen needed it to enter and send her sorting data. And since, legally, fishermen are required to provide observers with unobstructed access to a computer to transmit data, she and Rundall had to figure out a way to share the computer, which was in front of the captain's chair, the primary steering station for the boat. The second, spare computer next to the steering station had antiquated software that did not provide the tools and programs Eichelberger needed to enter her fish data.

To solve the dilemma, Jen entered data into the main computer and stored it on a disk, using the spare computer only to send the data. Meanwhile, Rundall used the spare to communicate with Olney and to send e-mail. At first, Rundall told Eichelberger to enter all her data at night when the first mate was on the bridge. When she objected to the arrangement, Rundall agreed to let her enter data during the day as long as he wasn't towing. The compromise seemed to work. And after both got past their negative presumptions of each other, they got along better than they'd expected. She found Rundall acerbic at times, but also likable, sharp, and offbeat. She was impressed to find out he had held his marriage together for many years, a feat for any fisherman.

"He was quirky," she said. "When he picked on you, he was testing the waters. If you took it in good fun, everything was okay. I thought he was pretty funny. He'd always finish sentences with 'Right?'"

He was not looking for an answer, just some reassurance that you were following him and still paying attention. He told funny stories with an identifiable style, repeating key words and names often.

"Joy Jackson, right," he once said about an observer he worked with. "Oh yeah, Joy Jackson. So she'd always want to be on deck. Joooy Jackson. Right. I was a deckhand then, and Joy, she didn't want to be in the factory, she had to be on deck. We'd tease her, play jokes, leave empty bottles of Joy dish soap in her bag. Yeah, that was Joy Jackson. Right. Joy Jackson."

Rundall spoke quickly and changed topics abruptly. He knew a little about a lot of things. He was well-read, full of opinions. For Eichelberger, sitting with Rundall on the bridge of the *Arctic Rose* was a bit like being a guest on a radio talk show. Rundall, like everyone, seemed to be trying to make the best of the season that remained.

When the crewmen reached their intended fishing grounds, the weather did not allow them to fish. Instead, they fled to the shelter of an island and, on March 5, practiced safety drills in driving rain and sleet. Rundall set off the ship's alarm, timing his crew's response, how many seconds passed before they reached the top deck. Everyone took the drill seriously. Rundall drove home the point that the boat had only one life raft, located on top of the wheelhouse. Rundall talked about getting into survival suits, but because it was raining, the crew didn't practice. They had all done it at least once before. Rundall did make the crew take turns throwing the life ring. Eichelberger was impressed. She thought it was one of the most thorough safety drills she had ever seen on a factory boat, lasting about twenty minutes. Most captains simply go through the motions, she said. But Rundall hammered in the details and spoke with conviction.

After the drill, the weather worsened to near hurricane conditions. Visibility was reduced to three miles, with forty-foot seas and sixty-mile-per-hour winds. Unable to fish, the men grew more frustrated. Five days into the trip, the *Arctic Rose* had yet to catch any fish. On March 5, Jeff wrote to Jessica:

Hi Girlie,

Day 5 and no fish. The weather is as shitty as it can get. We're presently hiding behind an island to stay out of the worst of it. The wind is still blowing more than seventy mph. Jimmie and I are going insane just sitting around. I can't possibly sleep anymore . . . We had a safety drill today. They showed us how to throw the life ring and where the emergency equipment is. Same old bullshit today when we set the anchor I was being blown around like a rag doll. The wind chill factor was minus-6 degrees. Really fucking cold. With all this maddening boredom sets in thoughts of home and all the things I miss, mostly you. I could write a list that would fill this pad . . . It's times like this that I wish I had some cod to kill. Total boredom does suck. Especially when there's no way of escaping it. I can't wait to have my coat back with my phone in it. Love, Jeff your despairing fisherman.

The same day, not far from where the *Arctic Rose* had taken shelter, the *Amber Dawn*, a trawler of similar size with a crew of five, flooded and sank. Three men were rescued. Two, Roman Telak and Doug Rowe, disappeared with the boat while trying to launch a life raft and were presumed dead. The crew of the ninety-one-foot *Amber Dawn* had been transferring fish to a larger ship, the factory processor *Katie Ann*, in the middle of the night when it began taking on water and listed heavily to one side. The men on the *Arctic Rose* heard about the sinking on the ship's radio.

As the weather relented, the *Arctic Rose* began to tow, although she stayed close to the protection of islands. Luckily, the cod they were targeting also stayed close to the islands. Despite the proximity of land, Eichelberger did not feel much safer. But the weather continued to improve, and soon the crew could see boats around them doing well, bringing up full nets. It made their meager results all the more frustrating.

Their equipment and boat limited them. They could not tow as quickly or for as many hours. Yet Rundall had found the right spot. The cod were there. The men of the *Arctic Rose* worked at their limit and in time made a few productive tows, enough that the processors in the factory fell behind. It was a troubling success: Rundall had to sit out a few tows to wait for the processing line to catch up, all the while losing valuable fishing time. This lag was another source of tension among the crew. The *Arctic Rose* was sometimes forced to jog with its net out of the water, while other boats towed around the clock, fish churning through their factories. Still, some fish was better than no fish. On March 9, Jeff wrote:

Hi Honey,

It's been a couple days so I thought I'd write. Things have been a cluster fuck lately. We hit the fish big time, but we've had nothing but issues with our machinery. Things are cooking up, I guess. Tomorrow we probably won't get any fish. Jimmie and I are getting fucked on the whole sleep thing. While everyone else does their regular shift, ours is staggered so that the freezers get broken to make room for the fish in the morning. I've lost all concept of a regular sleep pattern. Other than that things are okay. It was nice to get a full days work in again. There's an insane amount of giant cod on this boat. Our factory looks like a civil war blood field. Jimmie took pictures. He made today his random picture day. He used a whole camera and took pictures of pretty much nothing . . . Love, Jeff.

The *Arctic Rose* did not tow at night because it did not have enough workers to process any fish caught at night, especially with the losses of two men from the last trip. And even if the men could head and gut the fish fast enough, the boat's freezers could not freeze it fast enough. So a night tow was impractical. The little boat had all sorts of handicaps, small nets, small freezers, a slow line. The crew brought up no more than ten tons of fish at a time. Although her salary has nothing to do with how much fish is caught, even Eichelberger is happier when the fishing is good.

"If everyone else around me is miserable, it's no fun," she said. "If the crew is in a bad mood, your life stinks. I'm happy when the boat's doing well. My job is not that much harder when the boat catches a lot of fish."

Her workspace was a tiny corner of the factory, hard to get to and harder to get out of. She had to climb over or crawl under factory equipment to reach it. In an emergency, it would have been very difficult to get out quickly. She began sampling by opening a hatch on the truck. Fish flew at her, nearly hitting her in the face. She deflected them into her sampling baskets. Sometimes she pulled fish off the conveyor belt. Sometimes the haul was so small, she sampled the entire catch. She cataloged everything, the twelve cod, the dozens of small inconsequential fish, the urchins and starfish. A bad tow made for easier sampling. As a general rule, every ton of fish caught meant sampling a few hundred fish.

Her latest assignment, despite the coarse working conditions, was the kind of work she thought herself smart and lucky to have bargained for. For the most part, she enjoyed the company of this crew. She was in Alaska. She was at sea. And there, she was at peace.

It had been three years since Eichelberger signed her first contract with Alaskan Observers. Her first assignment in Alaska lasted eighteen days, aboard the trawler *Defender*. Her second boat was the *Christiana*, a long-liner. She worked one week, spending most of the days in transit from Dutch Harbor to Atka. There, the small boat was sidelined by a storm. She got seasick and had to endure the weather. While observers on trawlers generally work belowdecks, observers on long-liners work on deck. She wore a one-piece insulated suit called "a mustang suit." Instead of sorting fish by species, she tallied the number of fish brought aboard, since long-liners usually have clean catches—that is, they generally catch only the fish they are trying to catch. As a result, she wasn't required to move much and, standing still in the spray and wind, became very cold.

In Dutch Harbor, employees of Alaskan Observers are bunked in an apartment next to the Coast Guard station, close to the airport. Observers stay there while on standby for another assignment. Usually, an observer is on standby for a few days, no more than four or five, all the while drawing a salary. At the apartment, there is a rotating shelf of books and most of the comforts of home.

Eichelberger finished her first contract, which lasted ninety days, on a head-and-gut boat called the *Ocean Peace*. She shared one room with a crew of six. When she finished the assignment, she took a floatplane from the western end of Kodiak island back to the town of Kodiak. That summer of 1998 was invigorating, and she made good money, which allowed her to stay home in Colorado most of the fall without working much. She taught biology at a community college for some extra money. The experience sold her on the work. Before her first contract ended, she had already decided to ask for a second, this time during the winter.

In January 1999, she did her first assignment aboard a large pollock trawler, the *Arctic Fjord*. The job lasted seventy days. For a change, she was one of twelve women on board, most of whom worked as processors. She lived in relative comfort aboard the trawler. She shared one bedroom and a bathroom with another observer. The galley was large enough to have a salad bar. The vessel had an entertainment room with a big-screen TV and an extensive video library. It was her first easy assignment. The catch was clean, the hours predictable. She worked twelve hours and then had twelve hours off. She was in constant e-mail communication, by satellite, with the National Marine Fisheries Service. She had no impediments when transmitting her data. The captain and crew were at ease because by-catch—for pollock boats, salmon is by-catch—is generally not a concern. And they normally do not reach their limit of pollock.

"Everybody was laid-back and friendly in the wheelhouse," she said. "It felt comfortable, more like a bus. In general, people were more professional. There were more women, the environment was more civilized, more like a normal work environment."

After the winter aboard the *Arctic Fjord*, Eichelberger traveled in Great Britain, returning for yet another contract in June 1999. She spent the entire contract, ninety days, working aboard the *Unimak*, a relatively large head-and-gut boat required to keep an observer on board at all times. The *Unimak* fished for rockfish out of Seward and sole out of Dutch Harbor. It had a comfortable sampling station with a lighted table and running water.

That fall, she went home, this time to Columbus, Ohio. She and her boyfriend, Dennis, both took conventional jobs. She skipped the winter 2000 fishing season and had something of a normal life. In July 2000, she and Dennis moved again, to Prescott, Arizona. As the winter of 2001 approached, she had to make a decision. If she skipped the winter fishing season, she would be required to take remedial training as an observer. In the Alaskan fishery, if observers sit out more than eighteen consecutive months, they must be retrained. The agency has to spend extra money for the training, and with the demotion, the observer takes a pay cut. So Eichelberger returned to Dutch Harbor in January 2001 and reported to the Westward plant for what began as an easy assignment.

After almost two weeks at sea, Eichelberger had gotten used to the working conditions and the odd rhythms of fishing on the *Arctic Rose*. The boat caught fish sporadically. The hold was only half-full. Eichelberger usually sampled catches as the processors sorted them. It was nearly impossible to do it any other way because of the size of the boat. She identified, counted, and weighed the fish. She came up with a composition, by species, of the boat's typical catch. She also recorded the sex and length of the boat's target species of sole or cod, tedious and unexciting work made less comfortable in the small factory. Before sorting the day's final tow, the processors broke the freezers, slipping frozen sole into large paper sacks with the boat's name printed on them. This created room in the plate freezers for more gutted fish. While the crew did this, Eichelberger usually kept Egan company in the wheelhouse. When the crew was ready to sort again, she went back to the factory.

One night when Eichelberger was working late in the factory, she noticed that a conspicuous amount of water, more than the usual few inches, had collected on the factory floor. Jimmie Conrad and Jeff Meincke were sorting fish on the rear deck, where they could not see the water. The water was so deep, it lifted Eichelberger's sampling baskets off the floor. They began to float away. Concerned, she shouted to Jimmie and Jeff, "Guys, this is too much water." They found G. W. Kandris in the engine room. She wondered how the water had not started to trickle into the engine room. Apparently, someone had absentmindedly left the water running in the factory, the same water they used when heading and gutting fish. The pumps had been turned off. It was a potentially dangerous scenario. G.W. got the pumps running again, and the water receded.

At night, Kandris was concerned primarily with the engine and the oil pressure. He worried that it ran high. He was meticulous, good at diagnosing a problem. When the boat's winches broke down, he studied the winch manuals. Eventually, someone in Dutch Harbor had to work on them, but he at least understood the nature of the problem. His countenance belied his competence. He was missing his front teeth, a feature people noticed immediately and made presumptions about. Rightly or wrongly, people judged him for it. With Eichelberger, he talked fondly and with great pride about his son.

Eichelberger found Kandris rough around the edges, but likable. And from their conversations, she gathered he did not have a very good relationship with his mother.

"If you meet them when they're sober and working, they're smart, engaging, and fun guys," Eichelberger said. "But I wouldn't want to be around them at a party."

Sorting was the last thing Jimmie and Jeff did at night. They would go to sleep sometime in the early morning hours and get up around 10:00 a.m. or noon or when a new bag of fish was hauled up. Most bags were small, but occasionally the boat brought up a heavy bag, which was a concern in itself because it would have to be temporarily placed on top of the factory roof. A full net can weigh between ten to fifteen tons. On most boats, factory workers are not allowed on deck because they would only get in the way and become a danger to themselves. But on the *Arctic Rose*, when the bag came up, everyone came around for a look. They were bored and desperate for fish and wanted to see for themselves if their fortunes were changing.

"At least on a boat, time can go faster because you're working hard, you're so sleep-deprived, and delusional," Eichelberger said. "Time was slow on the *Arctic Rose*, because we were not catching fish."

On March 19, Jeff wrote:

Dear Jessica,

This has been the longest trip of the season. We're almost 3/4 full. It just keeps going and going. Our captain refuses to go back until we are full or out of fuel. This trip sucks ass. We basically slept for a week during this fiasco. I only have a month and a half left. It really hasn't seemed that long but damn it's been $2\frac{1}{2}$ months in a couple more days. I hope everything is alright in Washington. I'll be home soon. Good news about this trip is we started night towing again which means night shift is back into affect unfortunately. We just started night shift 2 days ago. Sorry about the handwriting, a little tired. We've been fucking busy lately. I've pulled two 20-plus hour shifts in the last week and a half. It sucked. The first one was okay because we caught a load of fish. The other one sucked because our net was fucked and the deck crew had to stay up and fix before the morning when we set again . . . It's just been really busy since the 13th. That was a

20-plus hour day. Well anyways I miss you and I'll be talking to you soon. Bye honey. Love, Jeff.

Eichelberger usually went to sleep between midnight and 2:00 a.m., after sorting the last batch of fish. She wouldn't have to get up until 10:00 a.m. when the next bag would be brought up, which meant she was keeping approximately the same hours as Jeff, Jimmie, and G.W. Because she did much of her work at night, Eichelberger got to know the night crew best. It was G.W. who first invited her to be the fourth player in a card game of spades. Until then, she had kept her distance, preferring to let the crew assume she was serious and reserved. She worked at keeping up the wall, even intimidating the crew as much as she could. As she was the only woman on board, it didn't hurt to appear aloof. Her interaction with the crew gradually grew comfortable. When fishing was slow, which was often, she played spades in the galley or chatted with Egan on the bridge at night when he took the helm. While captains and observers can have an adversarial relationship, the two also feel a natural gravity, as they are often the most educated people on the boat. The observer polices the captain; Captains assume observers are raving environmentalists and nickname them "Lefty" as a reference to their politics. But it is far more likely that captains and observers have much in common. Like Eichelberger, Kerry Egan plowed through books, reading one every two or three days. He brought grocery bags full of them aboard every trip. Although most boat captains are not college educated, they often come off as if they are. They are studied, curious, articulate, and philosophical. Their jobs give them time alone with their thoughts. To become certified as licensed captains, they must read and study as much as college students.

Since he steered the boat at night, Egan had many relatively uneventful hours to himself. The boat did not tow on his watch. He could read at the wheel, save for an occasional glance at the radar. His biggest worry was running out of books before the end of the trip. He, like Rundall, seemed to know a little bit about everything. He and Eichelberger spent hours talking on the bridge. Savvy on the subject of financial planning, he convinced her to start a retirement fund.

What seemed most important to him was his daughter and, at this particular time, her college education. He wanted her to have the means to be independent, he said.

By her third week, Eichelberger had finished reading all the books she had brought with her. Scavenging for something to read, she found a copy of *The Old Man and the Sea*. She got to the middle before she discovered there were thirty pages missing. She threw a fit in front of Jimmie, who in solidarity batted the book off the boat with a baseball bat, the same one the crew used to break ice off the boat's rigging. Jimmie sometimes batted sea urchins off the boat in the same manner, a release for the frustrations of the day. She also found time to play with the Rubik's Cube kept in the galley. She had learned the method of solving it long ago in grade school. While the crew slept, she aligned all the colors and left it on the galley table to the witness of no one. When Jimmie and Jeff found it, they could not believe someone had actually solved the puzzle. Convinced someone had taken it apart and reassembled it, they tried to dismantle the toy themselves. When they were unable to reconstruct the mess, they batted remnants of the cube off the boat. Like most things, amusement didn't come easy aboard the *Arctic Rose*. As much as she loathed the working conditions, Eichelberger liked the crew, especially Jimmie Conrad, who handled the frustrations of fishing well. He was funny when he was cynical and cynical when he was funny. He remembered lines from every movie. And he made breezy sense of things.

"I found him very engaging," she said. "His motor was always running."

He knew he had not made much of his time in school and was beginning to regret it. He didn't plan to stop drinking and partying entirely, but he was seriously considering what it would take to get his college degree, something no one in his family had done. The fishing money was supposed to help pay for a few more semesters at college. He talked about most of the things young men talk about, but with Jimmie it was a little different. His drinking stories were peppered with insight. He was an artful storyteller, a trait he'd likely picked up from his father.

Jeff Meincke, despite his numerous piercings—he had a bar under the skin of his neck—seemed like a nice boy out of his element. He was "one of those guys you meet and you hope he finishes school and doesn't get lured by a good fishing job," said Eichelberger. He told her and others he wanted to be a veterinarian and that he didn't plan to make a living fishing. He was planning to apply to Washington State University. At least that's what he said when the fishing was bad. At sea, his allergies didn't bother him. At home, there wasn't a tree he wasn't allergic to. His childhood was ruled by allergies and asthma, first diagnosed when he was eight. The steroids he ingested to reduce inflammation in his lungs stunted his growth. Colds turned into bronchitis. He was a hothouse flower, a small boy, vulnerable in a way other boys he knew weren't. He tried, almost literally, to outrun it. He played basketball, soccer, and baseball. His parents always kept an inhaler on the sidelines. He swam, wrestled, ran cross-country. His stride was slow, but he finished. He got good grades in school (he graduated high school with a 3.75 grade-point average), went to church, and grew up to be the kind of boy parents liked and the kind other kids called a nerd. Too religious, too smart, too polite. When he was a senior in high school, he fixed all of it, neglecting his school-work, drinking, smoking, trying drugs. His friends changed, too. They weren't Boy Scouts or Mormons anymore. They were urchins and dropouts, kids who hung out at the pool hall. But they accepted him and didn't think he was a nerd, and that was more important than anything. The winter he spent fishing aboard the *Arctic Rose* was supposed to have been his sophomore year at Chaminade University in Honolulu. He had dropped out after his first year. He received mediocre grades at first, although they had improved enough to get him on the dean's list by the end of his freshman year. But he was also homesick. He did not make good friends and felt like an outsider. He came back home and got a summer job working on a barge in southeast Alaska, processing salmon roe. The work was intoxicating and played to Jeff's romantic notions about manly labor and high adventure. But the work was seasonal, and when he returned to Olympia in the fall, he was forced to apply for jobs at restaurants, hardware stores, and a glass-cutting shop. He got turned down almost everywhere, so he filled newspaper boxes, grilled burgers at McDonald's, and loaded boxes for UPS. Then he met Jessica. And just when he thought the feeling was perfect, he was offered a job on the *Arctic Rose*.

It was obvious to Eichelberger that Rundall was the most skilled fisherman aboard. If a net got ripped, he was the only one who could really sew it back right. And on this small boat with too much bad luck to call it luck, Rundall was invaluable. He knew how to fix almost everything. Most captains rarely go out on deck, but Rundall did it often. Even the men who didn't like him trusted and respected his abilities on the boat. But he questioned the sacrifices the job required. In conversation, Rundall told Eichelberger he had tried driving barges between the Hawaiian islands so he could stop fishing altogether. Although she knew a lot of fishermen said such things, expressing empty sentiments about quitting, she believed Rundall. To her, he seemed stressed out and frustrated. The constant repairs to the net especially tested his nerves, because he had to do most of the work and did not have a spare net to use while he made repairs; the *Arctic Rose* was too small to carry an extra one. When the net was ripped, the boat didn't fish at all. Eichelberger remembered one night when Rundall stayed up to 3:00 a.m., five hours past his usual bedtime, fixing a net with Angel Mendez and Eddie Haynes. It was so badly torn, only Rundall could fix it properly.

During a spell of rough weather, Eichelberger said, the boat's net got stuck on the bottom and wouldn't come free. The resistance this created broke the winches. The net is attached to the winches by spools of thick steel cables. At the mouth end of the net is a footrope, a thick cable that forms the edge of the net opening. The footrope is guided by rollers, like automobile tires. If it gets caught on something, it can be slow to come free. Sometimes slowing down the boat and reeling the net up will free it from the bottom. Sometimes captains will open the throttle, accelerate quickly, and jerk the net free. The manuever is risky and could cause a boat to roll. Rundall was a conservative captain and did not take such risks. The net was stubborn to come free. The stern, from where the net was deployed, sank into the water and waves started to break over the deck. The situation lasted nearly five hours before the crew was able to free the net and restore the winches. They could only operate on half power. Rundall spent hours sending e-mails to a technician in Dutch Harbor, while G. W. Kandris and Mike Olney tried to fix the winch.

The constant repairs on deck might have been a reason Rundall was hard on Eddie Haynes, the inexperienced deckhand. Rundall thought he was slow on his feet and slow to make decisions. "Special Ed," he called him unkindly in exasperation. Haynes could also be sweet and gallant, the kind of guy who reminded the other men to behave when Eichelberger was around. He and Jim Mills were the most chivalrous when it came to Eichelberger. Mills, for example, always offered her a hand getting across the cluttered factory or asked if she needed the hose to clean up after sampling. Haynes scolded some of the men for blasting music containing vulgar language. It seemed to embarrass him. He reprimanded others for swearing. He also had a gift for exaggeration, about the land he owned or how he had saved the day by fixing a broken piece of equipment. Rundall was not sure if he was telling the truth or not. He suspected Haynes of intentionally breaking a piece of equipment so that he could fix it and take credit for the accomplishment. Few knew exactly what to make of Haynes. After Katurich left the boat, Haynes kept to himself, interacting mostly with Angel Mendez, and then only out of necessity.

But for the low morale, the mood aboard the ship in late March was fairly light. The crew got along well enough. The galley was far too small for everyone to eat together (the table seated only seven), but the situation resolved itself as the Mexican men made a habit of eating on the floor in the hall, their backs against the wall. To get to the bunks, you had to step over their legs. They seemed always in a good mood. The segregation occurred naturally. They spoke Spanish among themselves. The youngest, Alejandro Espino, twenty, the one they called David, was the most eager to learn English. He ventured out beyond his circle of Mexican friends and played video games with Jeff or G.W.

Shawn Bouchard and Jim Mills were the only ones who prayed before eating. Their ritual was conspicuous. It created a sometimes awkward void, around which the other men seemed at a loss for how to react. Bouchard alone voiced his objections to the presence of several *Playboy* magazines. He told the men that it was sinful and inappropriate to lust after naked women. But for the most part, Bouchard and Mills quietly read their Bibles and shared their views mostly with each other. They did not try to preach to the crew, and in turn the rest of the men did not begrudge them their religious convictions.

By the final month of the season, Kivlin seemed to have lost some of his motivation and enthusiasm to cook. It was just as likely that the galley's remaining ingredients limited him. He made French fries and thawed frozen vegetables. For breakfast, he made pancakes, waffles, bacon, sausage, and eggs cooked to order. He put out pastries and heated frozen pizza. He crafted pedestrian sandwiches and made an attempt at Mexican food a few times, all of it unremarkable and cafeteria grade to Eichelberger's memory. The men did not feast on salmon, halibut, and crab while Eichelberger was on the boat.

"My attitude is just don't do stuff like that when I'm around," Eichelberger said. "Sometimes they'll joke about it to test the waters. I let them know right away I would not react favorably. I want them to know I'm not one of those observers who is going to eat halibut with them."

Kivlin wore his long gray hair in a ponytail. Despite his obvious regret for taking the job, he had a reasonable attitude in the last weeks. He spoke with humor and warmth. He was good-natured, jovial. But by the end of the trip, Kivlin had managed to alienate some of the crew. He did not understand why the processors didn't work at night, and he let his views be known. He felt that the guys in the factory slacked off and that the boat would make more money if they worked more efficiently. The processors responded by telling him the factory was none of his business because he was just the cook. Their eating schedule was another source of tension. The crew did not eat at regular times. Sometimes a shift would go on longer than planned, and no one would tell Kivlin. The food would sit out untouched for hours and get cold, and the crew would then complain. Sometimes they would take an unplanned break, not tell Kivlin, walk into the galley, and grouse because he had not prepared a meal. It was a failure of communication on both sides, and it led to plenty of unnecessary grumbling.

The occasional yelling and bickering didn't tend to last. Despite his temper, Rundall did not dwell too long on his displeasure. The crew watched a lot of movies, the same ones, over and over, a predictable blend of horror and action. The men played cards and video games and slept often. They snacked on popcorn and potato chips. There weren't too many places to relax on the boat. Men sat in the galley or lay down in their bunks. The crew was generally discouraged from passing time in the wheelhouse. But there was no strict prohibition against visiting the wheelhouse as there might be on a bigger boat. Ken frequented the bridge. Because Aaron was factory foreman, he also spent more time on the bridge. Eichelberger and the men who worked nights spent more time than the others visiting the wheelhouse. At night, having company in the wheelhouse was sometimes a welcome distraction for Egan.

When Eichelberger disembarked, the *Arctic Rose*'s fish hold was barely half-full. Its winches were broken. Eichelberger made a quick, unsentimental departure. She didn't like good-byes and tended to avoid them, quickly slipping away to the observers' apartment. She shook hands with Rundall and Egan, thanked them for working with her. She was preoccupied with calling Dennis, checking her e-mail, finding out her next assignment. She soon learned that she was going back to Seattle for a debriefing. As bad as the fishing was, Eichelberger had found the crew to be full of humor. Because she liked the men, the trip had not been so terrible after all. She guessed she would not see any of the men again, but not for the reason she would be presented with days later in Arizona, when she received a phone call from the Coast Guard about a fishing boat called the *Arctic Rose* that sank with no survivors.

12

Solving the Mystery

Some nights he is on the bridge with the captain when the feeling beneath his feet changes and everything falls and the world swirls away from him. But most of the time he is belowdecks, in one of the staterooms, when the boat capsizes. It is dark. The men are the same men, but with no recognizable faces. They have no names, although he knows them all and understands their places in the order of things. Like him, they are very afraid. He is not hovering above them, watching with detached concern. He is with them. He is one of them. Water fills the space between them. It is cold, colder than anything he can imagine. And then there suddenly is light, a lot of it, more than there should be. He can see everything, the inside of the room, the horrified faces, the water moving higher and higher up his body. He is trying to get out. They all are. He feels the water as it rises. It reaches his face and begins to cover his mouth and nose, and he feels himself choking on the very thing he is trying to breathe. The boat sinks into the ocean of his subconscious. And that is when Lieutenant Jim Robertson wakes up from his dream.

It is the same dream, the one he has every few months. Each time it begins, he does not recognize it for what it is, just a dream. It is as if it is all happening for the first time, and it feels very real. The dream, he supposes, is the outlet for his feelings of guilt that no one could save them, guilt that no one could help them, guilt that even as he has dedicated the last two years of his working life to finding out why they died, he does not yet know the answer. So he gets up. He dresses. And he goes to work.

"The dream is extremely graphic," Robertson said. "I can feel all the emotions of being in the vessel. I am there."

The work and the unanswered questions and all of its frustrations had long ago crept into Robertson's sleeping hours. He developed the habit of keeping a notepad on his nightstand, ready for whatever thoughts followed him into his waking life. Sometimes his notes made sense hours later. Sometimes they did not.

At work, he told other inspectors about his dreams. They have had similar experiences, dreams about cases they became very involved in. So he is not alone. And that, he realized, is the only comfort those men had in their final moments, that they were not alone.

Like artists and renegades, the men of the *Arctic Rose* did not all function very well in life. They had vices they couldn't put away, illusions they wished to come true, a past they could not recover from, too much bad luck, or a sharp urge for something they had yet to find, that led them all somehow to a fishing dock in Seattle and to the runt of the fleet.

On March 21, 2001, the *Arctic Rose* entered Captain's Bay for the last time. Moored at the Offshore Systems dock, the boat took on 10,580 gallons of diesel fuel. Jennifer Eichelberger rolled her equipment off the boat, becoming the last person alive to leave the *Arctic Rose*. There are no living witnesses to the next few weeks aboard the boat. Meincke wrote a few letters in that time, about the only written record of what happened in the final days, days that were unremarkable by what few accounts exist. The fishing was disappointing, but it had been for most of the season. The crew left Dutch Harbor on March 23, with added fuel and water, expecting to return sometime in the middle of April. In his final letters, Meincke seemed spent of his curiosity for fishing. He longed for normal things like a bed and some privacy and looked forward to the basic amenities of adulthood, like having an apartment. His experience aboard the *Arctic Rose* left him ready to quit. The boat had a way of ending careers, like those of Jim Kelly, the former captain.

In the first few days out of port, the *Arctic Rose* battled the weather as she had throughout the season. Unable to fish much, the crew spent more time breaking ice off the deck than processing sole. Productivity was low, morale dipping. Because they could not work in rough seas, the fishermen stayed belowdecks and did their best to pass the time. Jeff wrote this letter to Jessica on March 25, one of several that week.

Dear Jessica,

We've stopped fishing because of the weather. I had to break ice when I woke up today. That sucked. It's been a long boring day of nothing. I guess we're headed north to target another kind of fish, yellowfin. Yellowfin sucks to process and isn't worth much but it's the only {fish} out there right now. I've been writing letters to everyone, my sister, parents, grandparents, you know. Not much to talk about today. I'm feeling a little better. I just wish I could be there now. One more trip after this one and I'll be home. Just over a month, that's not very long. I'm sorry I haven't sent any pictures but you'll get to see them all when I get home. You have to understand this really is the middle of nowhere. Dutch wouldn't exist without fishing . . . There really isn't anything that looks like woman out here. Not that it would matter because you are the only one for me. I miss your touch, your smart ass attitude that I've loved since the beginning. All the personal times we've had. Everything. I hate missing our anniversaries. I want to take you out and make you feel special and let you know that someone does care and that's me. Love, Jeff— freezing in the Bering Sea.

Two days later, the weather abated, allowing the boat to drag. The *Arctic Rose* fished the Slime Banks for yellowfin sole, the fish of least value to the crew. The men didn't catch much, but at least they had some work. Night fishing had ended. The trip was a late attempt to salvage what had been, at best, a very mediocre season. And so far that attempt was going poorly. Rundall considered moving to a new location. There were not too many places left to try. He decided to chase his luck north, plotting a course to St. Paul island so the boat could take on more fuel on its way to fishing grounds near the Zhemchug Canyon, at the edge of the Bering Sea shelf. The place required a long transit, about thirty-six hours, but once there, the *Arctic Rose* would not likely have to compete with many other boats. The crew hoped to start fishing April 1, the opening of the three-week B season, or secondary season, for flathead sole. The potential profits were worth the transit, as flathead sole contain roe in April and are worth more. Flathead spend the day feeding on the bottom, rising into the water column at night. So the most profitable trawling had to be done during the day. (Trawling at night increases the chance of capturing by-catch.) The boat arrived in St. Paul harbor the morning of March 30 for a quick layover, just enough time to fill the boat's fuel tanks and top off its water tanks. Records show the boat added 3,591 gallons of fuel.

What happened in the next few days and in the moments before the boat sank is what Coast Guard investigators spent years trying to find out. Well before the report was released, an idea of what caused the accident began to form in media reports, based on findings that were discussed and made public at the hearings. A fantastic event like an explosion or collision had been ruled out. So had a capsizing caused by the fishing net. Clearly the boat had flooded. The board was left to determine the triggering event. Suspicion had begun to fall on the boat's rear hatch, the weather-tight door from the factory out to the rear deck. A weather-tight door is impervious to water entering from the outside of the door and is different from a watertight door, which is waterproof from both sides. All but one of the *Arctic Rose*'s doors, the one to the engine room, were weather-tight doors.

The video from the second ROV mission showed that the boat's rear hatch was open when the *Arctic Rose* sank. The investigators thought it unlikely the crew had opened the door during an attempt to escape because it was on the starboard side of the boat, the side that first went into the water. Exiting that hatch would have meant exiting into water. Moreover, the rear hatch was not the preferred and practiced route of escape. It was much more likely that the hatch had been left open prior to the sinking. Operating on this presumption, investigators asked two stability experts to model a scenario in which water breached the rear hatch and found its way into the factory.

The task was given to Coast Guard naval architect Lieutenant George Borlase and to marine engineer Bruce Johnson, one of the nation's most respected stability experts and a professor at the U.S. Naval Academy. They used hydrostatics software to model a flooding scenario aboard the *Arctic Rose*. Constructing such a scenario with physical models would have been much more difficult, not to mention expensive. Ten years earlier, such software did not exist and the puzzle before them would have been exponentially more difficult. Borlase and Johnson based their calculations on the boat's dimensions and configuration and the size of the hatch opening. Hundreds of complex calculations took into account the volumes of water needed to sink the boat and how quickly the water could enter the boat based on the size of its openings. Their calculations also assumed the weather-tight door leading from the factory into the mudroom and galley was open, as former crew members had testified that it almost always was left that way. Arriving at the final calculation was a revelatory moment. What the software told them was shocking. Based on the variables and conditions Borlase and Johnson entered, the boat sank in a little more than four minutes.

"It was a big eye-opener," Robertson said. "It took our suspicions and really cemented that into a foundation of conviction."

In October 2003, close to the official end of the investigation, an article appeared in *Marine Technology*, a journal of the Society of Naval Architects and Marine Engineers, reporting Borlase and Johnson's findings and conclusions that the *Arctic Rose* probably sank because the rear hatch had been left open, triggering progressive flooding in all her compartments. It was one of nineteen flooding scenarios they modeled and the one the members of the Marine Board believe most likely happened.

On January 8, 2004, almost three years after the sinking, after numerous revisions, scores of interviews, and two trips to the wreck more than four hundred feet down at the Bering Sea bottom, the report was finally approved and released. The families of the crew were the first to read it. They all received telephone calls two weeks before the report was expected to be signed by Rear Admiral T. H. Gilmour, assistant commandant for marine safety, security and environmental protection, and released to the public. Just before the day arrived, a major ice storm hit the Pacific Northwest, freezing airplanes to the tarmac. Not all the families were able to travel to Seattle for the meeting with the board. David and Kathy Meincke attended. So did John Kivlin and the Rundalls. They were met at the Silver Cloud Inn, near the University of Washington, by Captain Morris, Commander Bingaman, Lieutenant Borlase, and Robertson, who had been promoted during the investigation from lieutenant to lieutenant commander. The families were told that the boat sank because it flooded and that while many factors contributed to the flooding, the misstep that could not be overcome was the open hatch. The boat, said investigators, probably lost all stability in a few minutes, and most of the men did not have enough time to get to the top deck and put on their survival suits. In its report, the board wrote, "The exact cause of this casualty is not known. However, casualties are very seldom caused by a single catastrophic event but rather are a series of events."

The *Arctic Rose* reached its final fishing ground on April 1, making two tows. The first net came up mostly empty. The second trawl was better, a full net, half of the fish flathead sole. The crew finished the second tow at about 8:30 p.m. Encouraged by his latest catch, Rundall planned to stay in the area and begin trawling again in the morning. He set the boat on a slow jog and relinquished control of the helm to Kerry Egan. After 10:00 p.m., Rundall spoke to John Nelson, first mate of the *Alaskan Rose*. Just before midnight, Nelson spotted the *Arctic Rose* on his radar, ten miles to the south and east. The *Arctic Rose* had about 7.5 tons of fish aboard, much of it sitting in pan freezers in the factory. That meant Jeff and Jimmie would be breaking the freezer and stuffing bags that night.

Colliding fronts created chaotic conditions that night. The *Arctic Rose*, meteorologists determined, got caught in the middle of a triple point, a phenomenon created when cold, warm, and occluded fronts intersect. Three distinct weather patterns crossed the path of the boat within a short period of time. Late that night, Egan contended with strong, localized storms and confused seas, with unpredictable wave heights and patterns. Winds reached forty-five knots, not the twenty knots previously reported. And the seas reached heights of twenty feet, instead of the heights of six to eight feet that meteorologists first guessed at. A short distance away, John Nelson noticed a substantial shift in wind direction between 8:00 p.m. and midnight. He reported that the weather "flared up a bit," then calmed down, symptoms of the triple point nearby.

Ten miles away, waves broke in the open sea, some over the small aft deck of the *Arctic Rose*. On a large deck, water from a breaking wave has room to move, spreading out harmlessly. But when waves break over a small deck, the water has nowhere to go and dissipates more slowly. The resulting amount of water is heavier and deeper and takes longer to drain through the scuppers. That night, some of the seawater hitting the back of the *Arctic Rose* entered the factory through the open hatch on the starboard side. The crew had left it tied open to ease exit and entry, to take breaks to smoke or urinate off the side of the boat. The factory already contained a small amount of water, left over from the day's work. Water is constantly used in the factory to clean fish, to freeze it. Grinder pumps, like giant garbage disposals, remove water and pieces of fish. But the floor was rarely completely dry, and the crew was accustomed to seeing a certain amount of water, an inch or two, on the factory floor.

Seawater from the rear deck continued to accumulate and breach the open hatch. The boat was trimmed forward seven degrees, causing any standing water on the boat to move forward. This helped water from the deck to enter the hatch. The building pool of water inside the factory mimicked the roll of the boat, exaggerating it in a phenomenon called "free surface effect." Even a relatively small amount of standing water in an enclosed compartment of a boat is very dangerous if it is not stationary and if the compartment is large. As the water moves from side to side, it creates sudden and destabilizing shifts in the distribution of weight on the boat. Aided by the forward trim of the boat, seawater from the factory moved toward the bow, entering the mudroom through another weather-tight door that was left open. From there, water entered the galley, separated from the mudroom by a regular household door. This door was also left open. The boat flooded quickly because all the doors were in alignment on starboard side. The water had a straight course, instead of a staggered course, to the boat's inner compartments. Once in the mudroom, water entered the engine room, where Kandris was posted. Jeff and Jimmie were probably done with most of their work for the night. They might have been deep in the boat's freezer hold. The sight and sound of accumulating water might have alarmed Kandris and the others. But by then, it was too late.

Since water entered the boat on the starboard side, most of the weight of the water was concentrated there. No less than one minute and forty seconds and no more than two minutes and forty seconds had elapsed since water first entered the rear hatch. Now, a dangerous amount had pooled on the boat's starboard side. The water's overwhelming weight caused the boat to heel sharply to starboard twenty-three degrees, allowing even more water to gush into the boat. The *Arctic Rose* was in the process of turning or was jogging downwind when she heeled. Another wave lifted the vessel's stern, planting the starboard side and bow deeper into the water. The list was so powerful, even the boat's heavy fishing gear was thrown. Startled by the violent and uncontrolled lean, Egan turned the rudder hard to port. It was his natural reaction. The boat, adjusting to the sudden rudder command, initially turned the opposite way. More water poured through the aft hatch and the starboard overboard chute, which had been left open. The boat was taking on water fast, leaning hard to starboard and unable to recover. Egan's first reaction was not to call for help, but to attempt to correct the list. By the time he realized he couldn't fix the problem, the cause was lost.

The sleeping men were violently wakened. They were confused and disoriented. They did not know it, but they had less than two minutes before the boat would sink. They tried to make their way out of their staterooms, taking the most rehearsed and practiced route, through the galley, into the mudroom, and out a door that led to the wheelhouse. But the passage, once easy and familiar, was now turned on its side, wet, dark, and treacherous. Water was now flooding into the boat at a rate of three tons per second. None of the men escaped from the lower berthing spaces. There was one other opening to the top deck, through a hatch in Mike Olney's stateroom, but the crew was not mindful of this obscure exit.

If they could reach the top deck, they could put on survival suits. Luckily, these were kept in a box on the port side of the deck, the side that was not underwater. But they never made it. Few men took another breath of fresh air again. Rundall, whose berth was located just behind the wheelhouse, jumped to his feet when he felt the sudden list. He kept his survival or immersion suit with him in his stateroom but did not immediately put it on. Instead, he scrambled up to the top deck, opened the storage box, and started removing the other suits, probably shouting the entire time. As the boat sank, stern first, into the water, Rundall yanked the lifesaving suits from their bags and threw them into the water with the hope that the other men could put them on. But doing so cost him precious time, time he could have used to put on his own suit. His last act as captain was both heroic and tragic. Instead of saving his own life by getting into an immersion suit, he tried to save the lives of others. In the end, the time he spent did no one any good. It was too late for the rest of the crew. And now it was too late for Rundall. The seawater caught up to him. Practically in the ocean, he fought to put on his own suit. While treading water, he struggled furiously to slip his legs and arms into the rubbery tangle of sleeves and openings. But he was already wet, soaked to the skin. The suit, now filled with water, provided him very little protection against the cold. Instead of affording him many hours, it afforded him just minutes.

He and the other men were drawn into darkness. The only light for miles was on their sinking boat. Gradually, as water smothered the craft, its lights grew dimmer and faded away. The vessel was underwater. Rundall, conscious for the moment, lived long enough to realize a captain's worst horror. He had lost his ship and all his men. Perhaps he wondered how long he would last and whether help would come in time.

Daybreak was some five hours away. By the time help arrived, Rundall was dead.

The board found that many factors, large and small, contributed to the death of the fifteen men—for instance, their own inexperience. They were not as conscientious as a veteran crew would have been about the safe operation of the boat. Unfamiliar with stability factors, they left water running in the factory, allowed sump pumps to clog with trash and debris, and failed to keep water and weather-tight doors closed and locked.

Some of the factors were beyond the control of the crew. For instance, the design of the factory was also flawed. Had just one of the weather-tight doors been located on the port side, the boat would have taken considerably longer to flood and sink, buying the crew valuable minutes to escape and get into their survival suits. The weather-tight door from the factory into the mudroom was originally an external door. After the factory was added, it became an interior door. Building the rear hatch on the starboard side of the factory was, simply, bad design. Why the decision was made to locate the door on that side is unknown. Perhaps there was no reason at all. Or perhaps the new hatch was located to mirror the position of the former hatch.

The Coast Guard also found some fault in its own procedures, specifically its dockside inspection program, which does not provide the regulations to allow its inspectors to assess a boat's structure, hull integrity, and mechanical and communications systems or to judge the competence of a crew.

The board also found the owner, David Olney, partially responsible because he failed to keep meticulous track of all the modifications made to the boat and the resulting changes in weight and because he failed to request another stability analysis from naval architects after those changes were made. As a result, the *Arctic Rose* was not in compliance with its official stability book at the time of the sinking. But, the board relented, such books, a standard in the industry, are complex and awkward, difficult for the typical mariner to understand and apply in the day-to-day operation of the boat. As a result, captains are inclined to operate the boat by feel, taking liberties with the hard numbers in the stability book.

"There are different schools of thought," Robertson said. "Some people believe it's an art and not a science. But I'm not one of those. There are a lot of nuances with stability, but we, as maritime safety officials, engineers, naval architects, have to provide fishermen with the best tools possible."

The board judged that communication between Olney and the naval architecture firm he hired was bad, that he did not allow his consultants to give him the best advice because he did not keep them fully informed of weight changes like added ballast, new plate freezers, or the relocation of a refrigeration system. Of particular concern was the 20,000 pounds of ballast, in the form of poured cement and boiler shot (round pieces of scrap steel), added to the bottom of the boat. When the boat's fuel tanks were full or nearly full, the stability book required the boat to be loaded with 25,000 pounds of cargo before it could fish safely. Those stability calculations, made in July 1999, took into account a 13,500-pound keel shoe, but not the 20,000 pounds of cement and steel that were added later. What investigators do not know is whether Rundall understood this or not, whether he realized he had most of the extra required weight already built into the boat. If he followed the guidelines set by the stability book, he might have thought he needed to add 25,000 pounds of cargo when he really needed to add only 5,000 pounds. And with such a lapse in information, the master of the boat might overload it by 20,000 pounds.

"What that would do," Robertson said, "is that it might improve stability, but it would also reduce the vessel's freeboard. We'll never know if that had a role in the sinking. If the master didn't know about it [the ballast], it may have had a role. We'll never know if Rundall knew."

From the testimony of former crew, investigators knew the boat had very little freeboard in the stern. This condition made it easier for seawater to wash up over the rear deck.

Olney operated the *Arctic Rose* as a head-and-gut boat, the likes of which are subject to fewer regulatory requirements. But because the fins and tails of fish were cut off, the *Arctic Rose* should have been classified as a processor. The key difference between the two classes of boat is that a processor must submit to a third-party survey and have a load line issued by a recognized authority, like Lloyds of London or the American Bureau of Shipping. The load line is critical to the safe operation of a boat. It is, literally, a line drawn through a circle on the hull of a boat. If the mark is above the waterline, the boat is loaded safely. If the mark is underwater, there is too much weight on the boat. The history of load lines goes back hundreds of years and was put into wide use by Lloyds of London on wooden cargo vessels carrying goods from the New World. Many of them sank because their operators, driven by greed, loaded them beyond their capabilities. To maintain a certified load line, vessels must be inspected every two years for watertight integrity and damage to the hull. All required bulkheads must be intact. (In the case of the *Arctic Rose*, only the forward collision and aft bulkheads would have been examined; the intermediate bulkheads would have been exempt.) All weather- and watertight doors must be sealed properly. And only then will a processor be granted a load line. What the investigators do not know for sure is whether having a load line would have prevented the *Arctic Rose* from sinking. Had it been properly classified as a processor, the *Arctic Rose* might in fact have passed an inspection and been given a load line. But being classified as a processor would have given the boat an extra layer of oversight.

"We can't say if it would have prevented the casualty or not," Robertson said. "But there's the possibility that [a load line] would have made it cost prohibitive to be in that kind of service, and the boat would have stayed tied up at the dock."

The board also found a flaw in the satellite communications system used by both the *Arctic Rose* and the *Alaskan Rose*. Had the Coast Guard been able to communicate immediately with the crew of the *Alaskan Rose*, Rundall's life and maybe the lives of others might have been saved. The board determined the satellite receiver aboard the *Alaskan Rose* had no way of distinguishing between priority messages and routine messages. Because the receiver did not have some kind of alarm or an automatic external printer, the Coast Guard's urgent messages went unread for hours, piling up in a queue along with junk messages. Because the boat's receiver was not set up to filter messages from other zones, it was cluttered with weather advisories from Russia. The receiver was also located out of view of the *Alaskan Rose*'s steering station. Nelson had no reason to check the messages on the receiver. He presumed the communication was inconsequential. And on just about any other night, it would have been.

Additionally, the board found, a bug in the software used by the Coast Guard communications station in Kodiak when it first reported the *Arctic Rose* missing caused the alert to be sent out, unknowingly, with the wrong priority. The message went out as a navigation warning instead of a safety alert.

The board, in its report, made thirty-one recommendations, many of which were procedural or bureaucratic in nature, but all intended to improve safety, seaworthiness, and communication for commercial fishing vessels. The board recommended that ships be required to install alarms that would go off when watertight doors were left open or when water in the fish factory reached a certain level. The board also wanted stricter stability requirements for boats the size of the *Arctic Rose*. But in the end, the board's recommendations were just that, mere suggestions. The board had no authority to change or adopt new regulations, nor did the assistant commandant who approved the report before it was released. To change existing regulations, the Coast Guard would have to lobby Congress for support in drafting new regulations. Once drafted, the approval process could take several years. The job of vetting the board's report belonged to Rear Admiral Gilmour. While he agreed, in principle, with all the board's recommendations, he softened the most substantial ones, saying such changes should not be mandatory and that the Coast Guard would recommend only voluntary compliance. Regulatory changes can take years and might not survive the expected political fight. But voluntary measures can be implemented immediately. So, the report concluded, fishing boats would be only encouraged, not required, to adhere to stricter stability requirements and install alarms on watertight doors and in fish factories, Gilmour stated. There is some history for voluntary guidelines to later become law.

Voluntary compliance also does not preclude the insurance industry from adopting the board's recommendations as "best practice," requiring the boats they insure to have devices like high-water alarms. Because fishing boats are required to carry expensive insurance policies, the insurance companies themselves become a de facto regulating body for the fishing industry. It was the insurance companies that first required vessels to carry stability books. While a Coast Guard regulation can take years, an insurance company can just write a rule into its policies.

Nonetheless, Gilmour agreed to act on the board's less drastic recommendations. For instance, he agreed to amend the regulatory definition of a fish-processing vessel so that it included head-and-gut vessels and to require fishing vessel captains to document all safety drills they hold. He also agreed to make stability books easier to understand, to encourage the design of fishing vessels that will not flood so quickly, to expand dockside inspections, to help fishing vessel owners track weight changes and alterations, to improve methods for collecting evidence at the scene of a sinking, and to develop workshops for fishermen on subjects like vessel safety, stability, and communications.

The board also recommended special recognition of the efforts of the crew of the *Alaskan Rose*, in particular John Nelson, during the search for survivors of the sinking. The board and the assistant commandant agreed on the final recommendation, that the investigation into the sinking of the *Arctic Rose* be closed.

"I can tell you from my standpoint that I'm very happy with the report and with the recommendations," Robertson said. "These recommendations are sound and would improve safety for all fishermen at sea. I don't have the power to make those changes. Other people have the big picture to worry about. My focus is this accident and how to prevent another accident like it from happening again."

After the sinking of the *Arctic Rose*, the cost of Arctic Sole Seafoods' insurance premiums rose from $130,000 a year to $500,000, leaving Olney unable to operate profitably. He was forced to hand over operation of the *Alaskan Rose* to a different company, which also changed her name to the *Tremont*, the name of the boat before Olney purchased and converted it. Although the *Tremont* was still the same boat with the same crew and owner, she was, for insurance purposes, a different boat run by a different company and was charged a lower premium.

By August 2002, all the families of the crew had settled lawsuits against Arctic Sole Seafoods, dividing about $9 million between them. The amounts of each settlement were not disclosed but were said to have ranged from about $200,000 to $1 million. The families of single men got less than families of men who left behind wives and children. Joan Branger, Shawn Bouchard's mother, wanted to pursue the matter at trial, she said, to expose the dangers of commercial fishing. A federal court ruled the families could try their cases in state court in Alaska, where award amounts are typically higher than in Washington State. But in the end, she decided to settle, becoming the last to do so. Jeff's parents received about $250,000 as settlement for their son's death. Ken Kivlin's son received about $360,000.

After giving her testimony in Seattle, Eichelberger flew to Anchorage and then to Seward on June 29 for an assignment aboard the catcher vessel *Ocean Hope*. It would be her last trip on the Bering. The *Ocean Hope* trawled for a little bit of everything, staying close to shore. She was bigger than the *Arctic Rose* but had a much smaller crew of four. Eichelberger got off the *Ocean Hope* July 18, the last day she worked in Alaska. She signed a one-year contract, beginning July 30, to work in California, out of the seaside village of Morro Bay, halfway between San Francisco and Los Angeles. She and her boyfriend, Dennis, rented a cottage near the marina. Eichelberger drove a car and ate in restaurants and slept every night in a real bed. Her assignments all lasted one day on small boats that fished close to shore.

In the year after the *Arctic Rose* sank, twenty-seven boats went down off Alaska. Nine fishermen died. Since September 11, 2001, the number of fishing boat inspections, both at the dock and at sea, have declined significantly because maintaining port security has consumed so much Coast Guard manpower. And fishing remains the most dangerous job in the United States, accounting for more deaths per capita than any other profession.

On the first Sunday in May 2003, David and Kathy Meincke attended the annual ceremony at Fishermen's Terminal to honor those lost at sea the previous season. They and David Olney were the only relatives of the *Arctic Rose* crew to attend that day. Kathy hoped she would see Olney there. They had talked to him only once before, two years earlier at the first memorial service for the crew of the *Arctic Rose*. As David and Kathy approached, Olney did not appear apprehensive, as he had the first time the three met. He wore his usual neutral expression, the face of self-control and stoicism and unshared pain.

The urge had been nibbling at Kathy for at least a month, maybe longer, the desire to talk to Olney just one more time. She wanted to forgive him. She had worked up the strength to do it. And one day it just left her, all the resentment and anger and hatred. She had forgiven him. Now she wanted badly to let him know. The feeling made her wonder if she was doing it more for her benefit or for his. Nonetheless, the feeling was very strong.

The Meinckes reintroduced themselves to Olney, making sure he knew who they were. David shook his hand. Kathy did not. She looked into his eyes. This time she saw something she had never seen in Olney before. It looked like true suffering.

"You had to see him," Kathy said. "That man is just haunted. He feels totally responsible. It was poor judgment on his part, and he knows it. This time, looking into his eyes, you can see that he's suffering something awful. I don't know if he'll ever come to grips with what happened."

They talked for about five minutes. Kathy asked how he was feeling, how his family was doing, how the business was doing. She asked about his other boat, the crew. It was just chitchat, polite and sincere, but not much more. Kathy never said, "I forgive you," or anything like that. It didn't make sense or seem appropriate to convey the feeling so directly. When they finished talking, David shook Olney's hand again. Kathy threw her arms around him and gave him a hug and held the embrace. A moment passed. As she backed away, she could see tears in his eyes. She said nothing more, and neither did Olney. She forgave him. And he knew it. She could see it in his face.

Acknowledgments

This book came from insurmountable pain. And that is what I have always tried to remember. The loss of the crew of the *Arctic Rose* caused suffering multiplied many times over by all those left behind, sons and mothers and girlfriends and fathers and brothers. This book is their pain translated into words and pages and in large part belongs to them.

Davey Rundall's parents, David and Lou Anne Rundall, and Jeff Meincke's parents, David and Kathy Meincke, always availed themselves and spent many days and hours talking with me if only because they wanted everyone to know what a great guy their son was. From the beginning, they gave me their trust, and for that I will always be grateful.

Other family members also gave freely of their time and their hearts: Ken Kivlin's son, John Kivlin, and his wife, Michelle Kivlin; Eddie Haynes's mother, Rose Workland, and his sister, Heidi Speidel; Jimmie Conrad's father, Bernie Conrad Sr.

Jessica Hermsen shared the letters Jeff wrote to her, and spoke eloquently of her grief at love's first unfurling.

Thanks to Benita Mendez for allowing a stranger to sit with her in her beautiful home in south Texas and to her neighbor Janey, who translated for me words that Benita must have found difficult to say.

Some chose to participate fully in the retelling of events and in the fleshing out of their loved ones. Some participated in the beginning and later excused themselves from the process. Some joined after overcoming their initial reluctance. Some simply wanted to be left alone and to move on. All made their choices with dignity. Everyone aboard the *Arctic Rose* deserved a rich description and accounting of their lives. My regret is that only some got them.

Thanks to Milosh Katurich for his honesty and his warmth, and for letting me share his roost in front of the coffee shop.

Jennifer Eichelberger provided me with the best description of life aboard the boat. Her astute observations, her equanimity, and her reasonable nature helped me draw a balanced portrait of the men who perished. She gave up a weekend for me in Morro Bay and allowed me to press her memory to its limit. The scenes and descriptions of the 2001 fishing season are constructed mostly from the memories of those who, like Eichelberger, either spent time on the *Arctic Rose* or on another Bering Sea vessel.

The names of most of the people interviewed for this book appear in it. Many do not. But their contributions were all valuable. Thanks to John Gauvin, Graham Redmayne, and Howard M. Johnson, who told me all I wanted to know about how seafood from Alaska is bought and consumed. Ken Gerken gave me a tour of the Marco Shipyard, and Charles Cannon explained the murkier points of vessel stability. From John Adams, I got a primer on the maritime insurance industry. Dave Burrage went over the life cycle of Gulf shrimp and the changing tides of the area fishermen. Thomas Wilderbuer, a NOAA biologist, explained the basics of a sole's life.

Paul Webb, now enjoying retirement in Juneau working for the Marine Exchange of Alaska, provided me with insight into life in Juneau and a ride from the airport. Don Graves gave me a tour of the UniSea fish processing plant in Dutch Harbor. Dave and Connie Stanton showed me life in Dutch Harbor from a local's point of view. Richard Knecht, director of the Museum of the Aleutians, filled me with fascinating facts about the Aleutian natives and their sad history.

From the stacks of the Brooklyn Public Library came a book in diary form, *The Whalers of Akutan*, by Knut B. Birkeland (Yale University Press, 1926), that I found to be an insightful glimpse into life on the Bering at the turn of the century. For physical and anatomical descriptions of various flatfish, I consulted the *Guide to*

Northeast Pacific Flatfishes, published by the Alaska Sea Grant College Program at the University of Alaska Fairbanks.

Court documents helped piece together the history of the *Arctic Rose* before she came into David Olney's hands, and provided a view of G. W. Kandris's difficult youth.

The Coast Guard was immensely helpful and cooperative, providing me with all the expertise and documents necessary to complete an accurate retelling of the search and rescue and the investigation into the cause of the sinking. The Marine Board of Captain Ronald Morris, Commander John Bingaman, and Lieutenant Commander Jim Robertson treated me not as a nuisance or impediment, but as a necessary participant in the process. Thanks, in particular, to Lieutenant Commander Todd Schmidt, who spent the better part of a sleep-deprived day going over details of the search and even fed me afterward, making me a turkey sandwich after all the restaurants on the base closed for the night. Thanks to Marsha Delaney for arranging my visit to the Coast Guard Air Station in Kodiak.

This story began as a three-day series in *Newsday*. It recounted the sinking, introduced the crew, and set up the exhaustive investigation that was to follow. The book grew out of a desire to follow the investigation to its end, to find out more about the people on board, and to understand all the circumstances, large and small, that surrounded and led to their deaths.

Thanks to former *Newsday* national editor Lonnie Isabel, now an assistant managing editor at the paper, for his thoughtful editing, and for seeing the relevance and value in a sad and incredible story about a fishing boat that sank off Alaska, four time zones away from New York. And thanks to other *Newsday* editors who supported the project and helped see all fifteen thousand words of it into the paper: former editor in chief Anthony Marro, former managing editors Charlotte Hall and Howard Schneider. Former news editor Ross Daly deftly handled the series' publication on three consecutive days in June 2001. After succeeding Lonnie Isabel as national editor, he also allowed me a generous amount of time away from the office to research the book.

Thanks always to my agent, Sally Wofford-Girand, for immediately recognizing the potential in this book and to my editor, Panio Gianopoulos, for helping me get the best out of the manuscript.

I also owe thanks to many friends and colleagues who gave me support in the form of empathy, commiseration, encouragement, inspiration, a constructive critique of the raw copy, and in one instance help with binding hundreds of manuscript pages. Thanks to Tina Susman, Joe Haberstroh, Mitra Kalita, Andrew Metz, Matthew McAllester, Stephanie McCrummen, Erin Garrett, Stephanie Schragger, Julie Kageler, Tom Farrey, Bill Radke, Holly Morris, Michael Rothfeld, and Tasha Blaine.

And thank you, Olivia, for putting up with your preoccupied father's extended absences.

A NOTE ON THE AUTHOR

Hugo Kugiya has worked as a journalist for seventeen years, most recently as a national correspondent for *Newsday*. He was also a reporter for the *Orlando Sentinel* and the *Seattle Times*. He was a finalist for the 2000 American Society of Newspaper Editors (ASNE) writing award. His 2001 series on the sinking of the *Arctic Rose* won *Newsday*'s Publisher's Award. He grew up primarily on the West Coast, has lived in Japan and South Korea, and now resides in Seattle with his daughter. This is his first book.

A NOTE ON THE TYPE

Linotype Garamond Three is based on seventeenth-century copies of Claude Garamond's types, cut by Jean Jannon. This version was designed for American Type Founders in 1917 by Morris Fuller Benton and Thomas Maitland Cleland, and adapted for mechanical composition by Linotype in 1936.